Library of
Davidson College

CORNELL STUDIES IN INDUSTRIAL AND LABOR RELATIONS
VOLUME XVIII

The Saul Wallen Papers

CORNELL STUDIES IN INDUSTRIAL AND LABOR RELATIONS

Cornell Studies in Industrial and Labor Relations and International Reports are research monographs developed by faculty and staff at the New York State School of Industrial and Labor Relations.

IN THIS SERIES

XVIII *The Saul Wallen Papers,* compiled and edited by Byron Yaffe. 232 pp. $4.00 cloth.

XVII *Competition and Collective Bargaining in the Needle Trades, 1910-1967,* by Jesse T. Carpenter. 936 pp. $17.50 cloth.

XVI *The Public Employment Service in Transition, 1933-1968: Evolution of a Placement Service into a Manpower Agency,* by Leonard P. Adams. 264 pp. $3.50 paper.

XV *Manufacturing Production Functions in the United States, 1957: An Interindustry and Interstate Comparison of Productivity,* by George H. Hildebrand and Ta-Chung Liu. 240 pp. Out of print.

XIV *Teaching Industrial Relations in High Schools: A Survey of Selected Practices in the United States,* by Robert E. Doherty. 108 pp. Out of print.

XIII *Fringe Benefits: Wages or Social Obligation?* by Donna Allen. 288 pp. $4.00 paper.

XII *Procedures and Policies of the New York State Labor Relations Board,* by Kurt L. Hanslowe. 224 pp. $4.00 cloth.

XI *Union Democracy: Practice and Ideal—An Analysis of Four Large Local Unions,* by Alice H. Cook. 256 pp. Out of print.

X *Conflict Within the AFL: A Study of Craft Versus Industrial Unionism, 1901-1938,* by James O. Morris. 336 pp. Out of print.

IX *Hawthorne Revisited:* MANAGEMENT AND THE WORKER, *Its Critics, and Developments in Human Relations in Industry,* by Henry A. Landsberger. 128 pp. $1.75 paper.

VIII *Workers and Industrial Change: A Case Study of Labor Mobility,* by Leonard P. Adams and Robert L. Aronson. 224 pp. Out of print.

VII *Empire in Wood: A History of the Carpenters' Union,* by Robert A. Christie. 376 pp. Out of print.

VI *The Industrial Mobility of Labor as a Probability Process,* by Isadore Blumen, Marvin Kogan, and Philip J. McCarthy. 176 pp. Out of print.

V *Nonferrous Metals Industry Unionism, 1932-1954: A Story of Leadership Controversy,* by Vernon H. Jensen. 344 pp. Out of print.

IV *The Labor Injunction in New York City, 1935-1950*, by Jacob Seidenberg. 192 pp. $1.00 paper.
III *Sources of Wage Information: Employer Associations*, by N. Arnold Tolles and Robert L. Raimon. 368 pp. Out of print.
II *AFL Attitudes toward Production: 1900-1932*, by Jean Trepp McKelvey. 160 pp. Out of print.
I *Wartime Manpower Mobilization: A Study of World War II Experience in the Buffalo-Niagara Area*, by Leonard P. Adams. 184 pp. Out of print.

CORNELL INTERNATIONAL INDUSTRIAL AND LABOR RELATIONS REPORTS

IN THIS SERIES

VIII *Industrial Wages in Chile*, by Peter Gregory. 128 pp. $5.50 cloth: $3.00 paper.
VII *Elites, Intellectuals, and Consensus: A Study of the Social Question and the Industrial Relations System in Chile*, by James O. Morris. 312 pp. $6.00 cloth.
VI *Poor Countries and Authoritarian Rule*, by Maurice F. Neufeld. 256 pp. $5.00 cloth.
V *Italy: School for Awakening Countries*, by Maurice F. Neufeld. 600 pp. $9.00 cloth. Out of print.
IV *Contemporary Collective Bargaining in Seven Countries*, Adolf Sturmthal, editor. 392 pp. Out of print.
III *Jobs and Workers in India*, by Oscar A. Ornati. 236 pp. Out of print.
II *American Labor and the International Labor Movement, 1940-1953*, by John P. Windmuller. 260 pp. Out of print.
I *Labor Unions and National Politics in Italian Industrial Plants*, by Maurice F. Neufeld. 160 pp. Out of print.

PUBLISHED AND DISTRIBUTED BY

THE NEW YORK STATE SCHOOL OF
INDUSTRIAL AND LABOR RELATIONS

A Statutory College of the State University

Cornell University, Ithaca, New York

SAUL WALLEN
June 29, 1910 – August 4, 1969

The Saul Wallen Papers:

A Neutral's Contribution to Industrial Peace

Compiled and
Edited by Byron Yaffe

New York State School of Industrial and Labor
Relations, A Statutory College of the State University at Cornell University, Ithaca, New York
1974

331.89
W197a

Copyright © 1974 by Cornell University
All rights reserved

Price: $4.00

ORDER FROM
Publications Division, New York State School
of Industrial and Labor Relations,
Cornell University, Ithaca, New York, 14850

Library of Congress Catalog Card Number: 74-620095
International Standard Book Number: 0-87546-056-9

76-3087

Composed by Dix Typesetting Company
Printed in the United States of America by
Hall Printing Company

Contents

Chronology — ix

Foreword — xi

CHAPTER I The Role of the Arbitrator and the Arbitration Process — 1

   1. *A Formula for New England Prosperity* — 2
   2. Untitled and Unpublished Speech — 5
   3. *Recent Supreme Court Decisions on Arbitration: An Arbitrator's View* — 8
   4. Book Review of *Labor Arbitration: A Dissenting View* — 20
   5. *Arbitrators and Judges—Dispelling the Hays Haze* — 26
   6. Factfinding and Arbitration Decisions — 38

CHAPTER II The Nature of the Agreement — 60

  A. Past Practice — 61
    1. *The Silent Contract vs. Express Provisions: The Arbitration of Local Working Conditions* — 61
    2. Arbitration Cases — 64
  B. Implicit Rights and Responsibilities — 70
    1. Arbitration Cases — 70
    2. *How Issues of Subcontracting and Plant Removal are Handled by Arbitrators* — 78
    3. Additional Cases — 82

Contents

CHAPTER III	Individual Rights and Obligations in a System of Industrial Discipline	86

    A. Purpose of Industrial Discipline   87
        1. In-plant Conduct   87
        2. Extraplant Conduct   90
    B. Employer and Employee Rights and Responsibilities   99
        1. Right to Fair Treatment   99
        2. Right to Representation   104
        3. Discrimination   105
        4. Individual *vs.* Concerted Rights   107
        5. Extenuating Extracontractual Considerations   109
        6. Rehabilitation of Handicapped Employees: Employer Rights and Responsibilities   122

CHAPTER IV	The Mediation Process	132

        1. *A Sparrow Who Got Caught In a Badminton Game: The Role of the Mediator in the Collective Bargaining Process*   133
        2. *The Board's Procedures*   138
        3. *Constraint and Variety in Arbitration Systems* by Charles C. Killingsworth and Saul Wallen   140

CHAPTER V	Industry and Society	142

        1. Arbitration Cases   143
        2. *National Emergency Disputes*   145
        3. *Industrial Relations Problems of Employing the Disadvantaged*   152
        4. *Urban Problems and the Private Sector*   159
        5. *Lessons from Arbitration in Dealing with Minority Problems*   167
        6. Report of October 4, 1950, Speech to United States Rubber Supervisory Employees   173
        7. Urban Coalition Letter   174

APPENDIX	Saul Wallen as Perceived by Others	177

        1. *Saul Wallen: A Lifetime Commitment to Problem Solving* by Marcia L. Greenbaum   177
        2. *Saul Wallen—Generous, Creative, and Concerned: How He Managed to Achieve So Much Is Suggested in This Affectionate Memoir* by Robert G. Spivack   196
        3. *For Saul Wallen* by James C. Hill   198

Subject Index   203

Chronology

Born, June 29, 1910
B.S., New York University School of Commerce, 1933
Labor Adjuster, The United Association of Dress Manufacturers, New York City, 1933-1935
Economist, New York State Department of Labor, U.S. Department of Labor, 1936-1942
Chairman, New England Regional War Labor Board, 1942-1945
Acting Chief, Division of Arbitration, U.S. Conciliation Service (temporary, 1945-1946)
Special Lecturer, Harvard University, 1946-1963
Labor Arbitrator and Mediator, 1945-1969
Umpire, General Motors Corporation—UAW(CIO), 1948-1949
President, National Academy of Arbitrators, 1954
Associate Umpire, Ford Motor Company—UAW, 1955-1959
Umpire, AFL-CIO Internal Disputes Plan, 1962-1969
Public Member, New York City Office of Collective Bargaining, 1967-1969
President, New York Urban Coalition, 1968-1969
Died, August 4, 1969

Foreword

SAUL WALLEN spent most of his professional life as a neutral in the resolution of industrial labor disputes. In this role he gained widespread respect in both the labor and management communities. He was trusted by both because of his fairness and understanding of the labor management relationship. He was able to find a common ground between disputing parties that often contributed to a constructive change in their relationship.

Wallen was a man of boundless energy with the courage to innovate; at the same time, he was a man of compassion and sensitivity. Perhaps most important, Wallen was a man with commitments: to legal, social, and economic justice; to the peaceful and constructive resolution of conflict; and to public service.

Wallen had the rare ability to reach the parties affected by his decisions: the men in the shop, the union representatives, and the supervisors. His decisions were written for them in a style that they understood and, more important, in a manner that conveyed his sensitivity and understanding of the nature of the labor-management relationship, his sense of fairness, and his compassion for humanity.

Because Wallen's work most effectively demonstrates why he was so successful as a neutral, this compilation of his opinions and papers was undertaken, not only to honor the memory of Saul Wallen, but also to provide insight into many of his views for those who are interested in the process of conflict resolution.

I feel privileged to have been given the opportunity to select and prepare for publication this collection of Wallen's opinions and papers. I have attempted in this collection to provide examples of Wallen's work which reflect his views on a broad spectrum of issues. Punctuation and spelling have been regularized and in some cases bibliographical material has been added.

Because Wallen's work expresses so many of his personal values in an understandable, and often very personal, way, I am persuaded that the reader, even if totally unfamiliar with Wallen's work, will readily understand why he was so widely trusted and respected by both parties in disputes.

This collection is divided into five general subject areas. The first chapter covers Wallen's views on the role of the arbitrator and the arbitration process. The second reveals his views regarding the nature of the collective bargaining agreement from which the arbitrator draws his authority, including the roles of past practice, implicit covenants, and inherent management rights in its interpretation. Chapter III examines Wallen's views on the purpose of a system of industrial discipline. Included in this chapter is a section on basic employee rights in such a system, including, for example, the right to procedural due process, the right to representation, and the right to equal treatment or non-discrimination in the workplace. The next chapter concerns Wallen's views on the mediation process not only in the resolution of interest disputes, but also as a tool available to the arbitrator in rights disputes. The last chapter contains decisions and speeches pertaining to the public's interest in labor-management relations and, conversely, industry's and labor's responsibility to the public as members of society. An appendix contains several tributes to Wallen made by colleagues and friends after his death.

I would like to express my appreciation to Brook Landis, my graduate research assistant, for his invaluable assistance in the selection and editing of these materials. I would also like to thank Mary Wallen and Pru Pemberton, Saul Wallen's secretary at the New York Urban Coalition, for their help in locating unpublished materials contained in this volume. Last, I would like to express my gratitude to the Ford Foundation for their support of its preparation and publication.

Byron Yaffe
Ithaca, New York

Chapter I

The Role of the Arbitrator and the Arbitration Process

SAUL WALLEN'S *involvement with the arbitration of labor disputes and grievances began well before he became a full-time arbitrator. As Director of the First Region (the New England Region) of the War Labor Board from 1942 to 1945, Wallen observed first hand the success of grievance arbitration on a large scale under the wartime "no strike-no lockout" pledges of labor and management.*

After the general success of grievance arbitration during the war, the dramatic upsurge of industrial strife that followed the Armistice led many authorities to advocate compulsory arbitration of all disputes under an existing agreement.[1] *Wallen's reaction to this drastic suggestion and his own prescriptions for industrial harmony are presented in the first two articles in this chapter. The first is an address delivered to the New England Council, a regional organization of industry, labor, and agriculture. The second is an untitled speech discovered in Saul Wallen's personal files after his death. It is not known where, or even if, this speech was delivered, but its content reveals many of his early attitudes regarding the desirability of arbitration as a necessary substitute for industrial strife. The speech also offers some insight into Wallen's motivation for choosing arbitration as a career and may explain in part why he was so eminently successful.*

---

[1] See Harold W. Davey, "Hazards in Labor Arbitration," *Industrial and Labor Relations Review* 1 (April 1948): 386 and 400, and Lloyd K. Garrison, "Proposals for a Labor-Management Board and a Charter of Fair Labor Practices," *University of Chicago Law Review* 14 (April 1947): 347 and 358.

The arbitration process again received significant attention in the famous 1960 Supreme Court Steelworkers Triology decisions.[2] Wallen basically agreed with the restrictions these decisions placed on judicial intervention in the arbitration process, but took exception to some of Justice William O. Douglas' "extravagant dicta which make arbitrators look nine feet tall."[3] Wallen made it very clear that he did not want to be placed above the parties and their contracts, and he respectfully declined the "degree of divination bordering on the oracular"[4] that the Court offered.

When the Trilogy decision and, in fact, the entire profession of labor arbitration were attacked broadside by Judge Paul Hays,[5] Wallen was one of the first, and certainly the most persuasive, of the defenders of his calling. Two of his replies, the first, a Harvard Law Review book review of one of Hays' works and the second a lecture at the Institute on Labor Law in Dallas, Texas, on October 29, 1965, are reproduced here.

The remainder of Chapter I is devoted to excerpts from numerous arbitration and factfinding opinions by Wallen that reveal some of his beliefs concerning the purpose of grievance handling and arbitration, the criteria to be used by arbitrators in the decision-making process, and the rights and responsibilities of management and union officers and representatives in the handling of disputes over contract interpretation and industrial self-government.

---

1. A Formula for New England Prosperity*

High wages plus maximum productivity equals mutual prosperity. This is the formula that New England management and labor must apply in order to solve the problem of stable employment and regional prosperity.

---

[2] USWA v. American Mfg. Co., 363 U.S. 564 (1960); USWA v. Warrior & Gulf Navigation Co., 363 U.S. 574 (1960); and USWA v. Enterprise Wheel & Car Corp., 363 U.S. 593 (1960).

[3] Saul Wallen, "Recent Supreme Court Decisions on Arbitration: An Arbitrator's View," *West Virginia Law Review* 63 (June 1961): 295, 305.

[4] *Ibid.*, p. 306.

[5] See Paul R. Hays, "The Future of Labor Arbitration," *Yale Law Journal* 74 (no. 6, May 1965): 1019-1038, and *Labor Arbitration: A Dissenting View* (New Haven: Yale University Press, 1966).

*The New England Council, *Toward Better Labor-Management Relations in New England*, 80th Quarterly Meeting, September 14, 1945 (Boston: New England Council, 1945).

The achievement of the goal of mutual prosperity depends in large measure upon the state of health of industrial relations in New England in the coming months and years. My purpose today is to suggest briefly some of the ways and means of maintaining the generally good relationship which has characterized the dealings between management and labor in New England during the war years.

Sound industrial relations must be grounded upon proper philosophical concepts. During this period of reconversion of plants and production, it would be well for industry and labor to reexamine their philosophies of a good industrial relations policy. The philosophy that dealing with organized workmen is as much a part of the economic process in a modern industrial society as dealing with customers, with raw material suppliers or with financial institutions is widely, but not universally, accepted by industry. Only if this philosophy is firmly rooted in the mind of management will the emotionalism that in the past has been detrimental to industrial relations be eliminated.

RESPECT FOR EACH OTHER'S RIGHTS

Similarly, labor must preach and live the philosophy that its dealings with management must be conducted so as not to deprive management of those functions and prerogatives in operating the enterprise that properly belong to it.

The application of these philosophies to specific cases will eliminate the arm's-length type of relationship between management and labor that is based upon fear and distrust. Labor will be freed from the fear that management's basic motive is to break the union. The psychology of combat, too often characteristic of the leadership of some labor organizations, will be allayed and the energies that might otherwise be devoted to conflict can be channelized so as to promote the welfare of the business organization and its employees. Management will be freed from the fear and distrust of the union's aims and purposes.

A way must be found to secure voluntary restrictions on the unlimited use of the weapons of economic force in labor conflicts. I am not one of those who believe that labor and management should enter into an unconditional no-strike, no-lockout pledge during peace time. The exigencies of the war emergency amply justified the giving of an unconditional no-strike, no-lockout pledge, but a complete ban on strikes or lockouts during peace time is in many ways incompatible with our heritage and traditions. On the other hand, widespread industrial conflict in the coming months will go far to wreck our reconversion effort and our drive for prosperity and full employment. Some way must be found to limit and confine the areas of industrial conflict and to resolve those issues peacefully which cannot be settled by direct agreement between the parties involved.

There are moral as well as practical reasons for the imposition of self-limitations on the use of economic force in the settlement of labor disputes. Very often strikes and lockouts bring about settlements of issues in dispute on the basis, not of justice, but of the relative strength of the contesting parties.

ECONOMIC FORCE IN LABOR DISPUTES

If it is conceded that the interests of our society are best served by the finding of just solutions to our economic problems, rather than solutions based primarily upon the superior strength of one of the contestants, then it must also be conceded that the picket line and the lockout are not always the best means of securing justice. A way must be found to insure that the answer to a particular problem is not based primarily on the brawn of the contestants.

Thus, practical and ethical considerations dictate the need for minimizing the use of economic force in labor disputes. Possibly that result could be achieved if labor and management agreed to refrain from work stoppages until such time as the issues in dispute between them, remaining after direct negotiations have proved futile, have been considered by a group of friends and neighbors of the disputants. Their judgment on the issues could be rendered in the form of a recommendation of the parties. A refusal by one of the parties to adopt the recommendation would free the other to take economic action.

The important distinction between the use of the lockout or strike weapon under such circumstances, in contrast with its use in the past, is that such action would then have the sanction of public opinion instead of occurring under the cloud of public disapproval. A lockout or a strike called to secure the acceptance of a recommendation which reasonable, informed men, after careful study, have found to be a fair disposition of a disputed issue, is quite a different matter in the eyes of the public from one which is called in order to force a unilateral solution of a joint problem.

The above remarks refer to areas of industrial conflict where in ordinary times the right to call a lockout or strike is conceded to exist. But there is another area of industrial conflict in which the use of these weapons is improper and unnecessary.

I refer to the day-to-day problems that arise in many industrial plants, involving the application or interpretation of the collective agreement. We must avoid at all cost stoppages of work over plant grievances and encourage, with all of our efforts, the use of the grievance procedures, and recourse to final and binding arbitration for the settlement of all grievances arising under the terms of a collective agreement between a company and a union.

With the passing of the War Labor Board, the reliance on the grievance machinery of labor agreements and upon arbitration as a final step in the grievance mechanism will increase greatly. The principle of arbitration in this sphere has been widely accepted during the war years. Many in industry, formerly opposed to this practice, have become convinced that it provides a sound means for achieving fair and equitable settlements of day-to-day problems which cannot be resolved by the parties themselves.

ARBITRATION AND COLLECTIVE BARGAINING

I am not proposing arbitration of grievances as a substitute for genuine collective bargaining during each step of the grievance procedure. Arbitration should not be so easily available as to make it feasible for the parties to by-pass the negotiation steps in the grievance procedure. However, it should be used for the final settlement of all grievances in which all efforts for settlement through negotiations have proved futile. In my opinion, the acceptance of this principle by the forthcoming Labor-Management Conference to be called by President Truman will mark a long step toward stable industrial relations in the future.

* * *

2. Untitled and Unpublished Speech*

On one point the discordant voices of labor and management have blended in harmony. They both stoutly proclaim their opposition to the compulsory arbitration of labor disputes. Both see in it the stultification of collective bargaining and the extension of governmental control of the economic process. That same note, although in a minor key, is sustained when alternatives that will maintain both freedom and a modicum of industrial peace are discussed. Both profess to place reliance on direct negotiations, with the aid of government confined to capable, impartial mediation, and, failing agreement, on voluntary arbitration as a means of averting strikes.

---

*Located in Wallen's personal files, not dated.

Even if compulsory arbitration were desirable on other grounds, (and I do not believe that it is), its imposition on these reluctant, not to say unwilling, groups makes dubious the chances that it will live up to the hopes of its sincere proponents. So the search for the key to industrial peace continues. It is therefore timely to ask if voluntary arbitration is the answer to labor disputes. Can it replace the work stoppage in a significant proportion of labor disputes? Both management and labor have learned something of the cost of strikes. Why have they not in greater numbers used arbitration in the place of obdurate standpattism or aggressive picket lines?

Arbitration of labor disputes in the past has been glorified uncritically, like home and mother, or damned unrelievedly, like sin. More recently its virtues and limitations have been appraised more dispassionately, and it has made important, though largely unadvertised, strides toward creating harmony in place of strife. In one major field of labor relations, the settlement of disputes arising out of the application and interpretation of existing collective agreements, arbitration has pretty nearly come of age. In the other major field, the settlement of disputes over the terms of a new collective agreement, arbitration (except in a few industries) is still a boy trying to do a man's job. And it is likely to keep on wearing knee pants, unless labor and management consciously take affirmative steps to mold it into an effective substitute for the plant shutdown.

The collective agreement is the basic law of the plant in the matter of wages, hours, and working conditions. It is developed by negotiation and compromise between the employer and his organized workmen, but as with any body of law it is often susceptible of varying interpretations when applied to concrete cases. Sometimes its meaning must be construed to apply to circumstances that the parties had never envisioned when the agreement was drawn.

These questions of the relation of the basic law of the plant to specific problems of worker-management relations are usually raised through grievances, usually entered by workers and occasionally by the employer. Most labor agreements spell out a procedure whereby such grievances are discussed first between the union steward and the foreman and then by successively higher representatives of the parties in their respective organizations, in an effort to dispose of the grievance by agreement. If, after a discussion of the grievance at the highest level called for in the contract, no agreement is reached on the disposition of the problem, it is provided in many agreements that the question may be submitted to a neutral person for hearing and determination.

Only a few years ago this sensible way of disposing of conflicts of opinion was strenuously opposed—sometimes by the few labor unions who had the strength to impose a unilateral interpretation of the rules, but mainly by employers who maintained that the surrender of the right to have the final word on the disposition of such grievances was a fatal impairment of the right of management to manage. Arbitration of grievances, the argument ran, substitutes in the last analysis, the judgment of a man outside of the company (called an arbitrator) for the judgment of those who have been delegated the responsibility for managing the business of the company. I recall one case argued before the Regional War Labor Board, of which I was a public member, in which the point was made by a company that "A complicated manufacturing business cannot be run by disinterested (or noninterested) third parties. It must be managed by vitally interested, responsible men carefully selected because of their many years of experience in industrial management and their broad ability and broad-mindedness. . . . When an arbitrator's judgment is substituted for that of management, management control is undermined." This company (reflecting a not uncommon management viewpoint) saw ". . . a continual urge on the part of arbitrators to stray from their jurisdictional field of activity as specified in the collective bargaining agreement, and to enter the field of management policy-making. . . . There seems to be an irrepressible desire by arbitrators to become benevolent policy-making autocrats in the field of management control as applied to employee relations."

Such an attitude is not only arrogantly self-righteous, but it also ignores realities of human character. Managements and unions are composed of human beings, subject like all of us to opposing pressures from the desire to be fair and the desire to protect or advance one's self and from all those urges that produce conflict between justice and self-interest. The company executive caught between a cost-conscious top management and a costly though reasonable grievance of the men frequently, but not always, rules on the side of justice. The union leader caught between a militant rank and file clamoring for results and an inner knowledge that their position is unfair frequently, but not always, has the courage to tell his own people the truth. The attitude illustrated by the quotations in the preceding paragraph presupposes, of course, complete management infallibility in resulting conflicts between justice and self-interest—in a world where self-interest pays off in cash.

It is undoubtedly true that the failure of contracts to provide for arbitration of grievances was the cause of a substantial number of strikes, and the growth in the use of arbitration of grievances arising under contracts has largely replaced the strike as a means of redress against arbitrary management decisions.

Today the arbitration of grievances is well established in American industrial relations. There is essential fairness to the proposition that differences between organized workers and managers over the application and interpretation of collective bargaining agreements should be submitted to a referee who has no partisan interest in the outcome. The proposition has been demonstrated by enough actual experience to assure arbitration a fixed place in industrial relations. Nor is there any questioning of the fact that a fair disposition of grievances contributes to the good will that is basic to sustained labor peace.

* * *

The arbitration of grievances arising under contracts has gained wide acceptance in a large measure because the arbitrator's discretion is not unfettered. He has to interpret and apply the agreement to a specific set of facts. The agreement is the basic law of the plant, but it was legislated by labor and management themselves through collective bargaining and not by a third party. The agreement is the touchstone of the arbitrator's decision. While an arbitrator often has considerable leeway in squaring the agreement with a given set of facts, he cannot depart too far from the rules that the parties themselves have formulated by collective bargaining. Thus the risks involved in grievance arbitration are not great. Bound as he is to the rules that labor and management themselves have agreed on, the arbitrator cannot substitute his own view as to proper union or management conduct for the view of the parties directly involved. The charge that arbitrators tend to become "benevolent policy-making autocrats in the field of management control as applied to employee relations" is a general indictment which has no validity. A reading of arbitration decisions will show that in the vast majority of cases their disposition is governed by the terms of the agreement.

---

3. Recent Supreme Court Decisions on Arbitration: An Arbitrator's View*

With an estimated ninty-five per cent of the 125,000 collective agreements reported to be in force in this country containing clauses calling for the arbitration of grievances, one is impelled to ask why this method

---

West Virginia Law Review 63 (no. 4, June 1961): 295-308 This paper was originally delivered at the 11th Annual Labor-Management Conference, West Virginia University, April 20, 1961. Footnotes were added by the editor of the *West Virginia Law Review*.

of settling disputes arising during a contract's term has grown so tremendously in the last two decades.

For, after all, these grievances arise under contracts and involve their interpretation or application. And contract interpretation is grist for the mill of the courts. Parties to collective bargaining agreements were free to say to one another "We have made a contract. If one of us believes the other has broken it, he is free to bring an action at law. The courts are the proper forum for a determination of rights and obligations under contracts, including those between management and labor." Yet American management and labor have chosen not to do this. Why?

One part of the answer lies in those characteristics of a labor agreement that set it off from the ordinary commercial contract. A labor agreement, while assuredly a contract and enforceable at law, has certain unique characteristics. In the ordinary transaction between buyer and seller the parties are free to disagree and make a deal elsewhere. In the labor agreement the parties are under heavy pressure to come to an agreement. They cannot go elsewhere. They must in the end come to terms. The alternatives, the strike or the lockout, may be too costly. Professor (now Solicitor General) [Archibald] Cox states that this partially explains the gaps and deliberate ambiguities in collective bargaining agreements which create distinctive problems of interpretation. We all know of cases where the parties, faced with a deadline and stuck on a knotty problem, agree on the wording of a clause each knowing that the other places a different meaning on it. At the moment it is more important to secure a strike-averting agreement than it is to secure a firm understanding on the sticky point. That can come later, if they are lucky, by not having to face the issue during the agreement's life; if they are not so lucky, by a gamble on an arbitrator's ruling. It was a problem such as this which once prompted Dean Harry Shulman, in a decision he rendered as umpire under the Ford Motor Company-UAW contract, to write . . . as follows:

> Each side states that the other's negotiators knew the true intent of the clause but that it assented to the language employed to save the other side's face. The parties are not in agreement on whose face is to be saved but they apparently do agree that the umpire's face is expendable.

The second unique feature of collective bargaining agreements is that the pressure to have some agreement rather than none, with all that implies in terms of economic conflict, means that the decider or the arbitrator can rarely say that the parties' minds did not meet on the question put to him and that as a consequence there was no contract. The parties have a continuing relationship which they thought they stabilized. They do not relish having to do the job again.

These characteristics of labor agreements that set them off from commercial contracts account in part for the development of arbitration as the chief means of settling disputes as to the meaning and application of contracts between managements and unions. The arbitration process, to the extent that it has developed a corps of men familiar with industrial relations problems and with some feel for the actual operating problems of a plant and a local union, is more conducive to realistic interpretation of vague or ambiguous labor agreements than are the courts. This is not said in derogation of the talents of judges; it is just that their experience has for the most part been in a different sphere.

But there are a number of other reasons that account for the development of arbitration under collective agreements. Parties may choose arbitration to avoid the cumbersomeness and formality of the law. They may choose it in order to have the dispute decided promptly, finally and near its locus. They may wish to have it decided by one familiar with industrial relations problems so that the resolution of ambiguities in their contract can be realistically related to actual conditions of the plant and of the local union. They may wish to have a hand in the selection of the decider. They may wish the dispute decided informally and quickly without making a "federal case" of it with all that that implies in terms of exacerbated feelings and diversion from the actual goal of production. They may recognize that the language of their contract, conceived in the crisis atmosphere of an imminent or actual strike, expresses inelegantly or imperfectly their intent and they do not conceive of the established judicial tribunals as having the orientation or interest necessary to properly establish their intent. Or, as is sometimes the case, one party may accede to arbitration of grievances not because it is convinced of the efficacy of this method of settling disputes at all, but because the alternative is a strike and an agreement is not possible without yielding on this point.

To say the foregoing is not to say that the law and the courts have no interest and carry on no activity in grievance and contract administration. Prior to the passage of the Labor-Management Relations Act of 1947, the laws of nearly half the states gave arbitration a statutory base which made promises to arbitrate enforceable by the courts and placed the judicial system behind the enforcement of compliance with awards.

But when one party goes to court to compel arbitration, the other has the right to claim that the problem involved is not covered by the promise to arbitrate. And when one party goes to court to compel compliance with an award, the other may properly raise the defense that the arbitrator has exceeded his powers. The arbitrator can decide on the scope of his powers only if specifically authorized by the parties to do so. If not so authorized, the courts have generally held that an agreement to arbitrate is based on the contract and that it is for the court to decide whether the contract contains a promise to arbitrate the dispute tendered.

With this thesis one could scarcely quarrel. Both management and labor should be free, unless they plainly otherwise contract, to have the existence of a contractual obligation to arbitrate passed upon. If they did not in fact agree to arbitrate a particular kind of dispute—i.e., one not involving the application or interpretation of the agreement—they should not be compelled to submit to that forum. And unless they had agreed in advance to have the arbitrator decide the scope of his own powers the court remains the proper forum for such determination.

One of the interesting but scarcely noted features of industrial relations is that a number of the largest corporations and unions have contracted to keep wholly away from the courts when it comes to handling disputes arising under their labor agreements. Thus, as an example, the contract between Ford Motor Company and the UAW, and also the one between General Motors and the same union, contain the following provisions:

> It shall be the function of the umpire, and he shall be empowered . . . . to make a decision in cases of *alleged* violations of the terms of this Agreement . . . . of *alleged* improper classification of employees, of *alleged* violations of negotiated rates and upon the scope of his powers. [Emphasis added.]
>
> There shall be no appeal from an umpire's decision. It shall be final and binding on the union, its members, the employee or employees involved and the Company. The Union will discourage any attempts of its members and will not encourage or cooperate with any of its members in any appeal to any court or labor board from a decision of the umpire.

Also contained in these agreements are specific limitations on the powers of the umpire. He is denied power to add to or subtract from, or modify any of the terms of the agreement. He may not establish wage scales, rates on new jobs or change any wage except as specifically empowered in the agreement. He has no power to rule on cases arising under the articles dealing with either health and safety or production standards. On the other hand, the no-strike clause is specifically *not* applicable to disputes over production standards, health and safety grievances, or rates on new jobs and, after having followed certain specified procedures, employees may legally strike over such matters during the life of the contract.

The Aluminum Company of America contracts contain similar provisions.

The parties to these agreements—the giants of American industry and labor—have made their own delimitations between the areas subject to arbitral review and the areas where they prefer to rely solely on their own devices. Disputes over whether a subject falls within either area or within one or the other of them they have empowered their umpire to decide.

Provisions such as these, however, are the exception and not the rule. Most agreements do not empower the arbitrator to rule on his own jurisdiction. Nor do they pledge the parties not to challenge his jurisdictional holdings in the courts. And most contain an unconditional no-strike clause.

Despite that fact, however, the percentage of arbitration awards challenged in the courts were relatively small, perhaps a few hundred per year of the scores of thousands of issues submitted to arbitration. But in a significant number of the cases litigated, the courts have shown a propensity, under the guise of determining whether an agreement to arbitrate the particular dispute had indeed been made, to hold for arbitrability or (more often) for nonarbitrability because of the judge's views on the merits. Where this occurred, the courts assumed the very function which the parties by contract had agreed to have performed by an arbitrator.

With the passage of the Labor-Management Relations Act and its interpretation by the Supreme Court in 1957 in *Lincoln Mills*,[1] agreements to arbitrate were deemed enforceable under federal law. *Lincoln Mills* charged the federal courts with the duty to develop a body of labor law from federal labor policy and judge-made law in the state courts. In three landmark decisions the Supreme Court did just that in the matter of the enforceability of agreements to arbitrate. These decisions not only limited the role of the courts in passing on arbitrability but also set forth the court's views as to the nature and character of collective agreements and the obligations of arbitrators thereunder that have set the industrial relations fraternity a'buzzing.

United Steelworkers v. *American Manufacturing Company*[2] is the first of the three. In this case the union brought a suit to compel the company to arbitrate the grievance of one Sparks, filed when the company refused to reinstate him following an industrial injury as a result of which he had received a compensation rating of 25 percent permanent partial disability. The company pleaded to the court that it was not obligated to arbitrate because (1) Sparks is estopped from claiming reinstatement by virtue of his settlement of the workmen's compensation claim on the basis of a permanent partial disability, (2) Sparks is not physically able to do the work, (3) this type of dispute is not arbitrable under the agreement.

---

[1] Textile Workers Union v. Lincoln Mills, 353 U.S. 448 (1957).
[2] 363 U.S. 564 (1960).

The agreement contained the standard form of arbitration clause and the usual no-strike, no-lockout clause. The lower court refused to compel arbitration on the basis that the grievance is "A frivolous, patently baseless one, not subject to arbitration under the collective bargaining agreement." This conclusion was arrived at on the basis of a review of the evidence as to Sparks' disability and an evaluation of the employer's claim that no opening was available for one so disabled.

The Supreme Court reversed the lower court and ordered arbitration. This is a result with which one can scarcely disagree, for it is obvious that the lower court's reasoning was not that it was frivolous to claim that the agreement called for an arbitrator to decide whether or not the claim for reinstatement lacked merit, but that it was frivolous to press the claim itself. Hence the court, not an arbitrator, decided the merits of the claim contrary to long-established principles obliging the courts to enforce agreements to arbitrate and to refrain from themselves passing on the merits.

The second case involved *United Steelworkers* v. *Warrior and Gulf Navigation Co.*[3] This company transports steel by barge. At its terminal it performs maintenance and repair work on its barges, those doing that work constituting the bargaining unit represented by the Steelworkers. Between 1956 and 1958 the company laid off employees, reducing the unit from forty-two to twenty-three men. This reduction was due in part to the fact that the company contracted out the maintenance work previously done by its people to neighboring contracting companies. These companies used Warrior and Gulf's supervisors to lay out the work and hired some of Warrior and Gulf's laid-off employees at reduced wages. In fact some of those hired were assigned to work on Warrior and Gulf's barges.

The result was a grievance "protesting the Company's actions of arbitrarily and unreasonably contracting out work . . . . that previously has been performed by Company employees . . . . the Company is in violation of the contract by inducing a partial lockout of the number of employees who would otherwise be working were it not for this unfair practice."

The contract had a no-strike, no-lockout clause and a grievance procedure reading in part as follows:

> Issues . . . which are strictly a function of management shall not be subject to arbitration. . . .
>
> Should differences arise . . . as to the meaning and application of the provisions of this Agreement, or should any local trouble of any kind arise, . . . the matter shall be handled in a five-step grievance procedure the last step of which is referral to an umpire whose decision is final.[4]

---

[3]363 U.S. 574 (1960).
[4]*Id.* at 576.

The company refused to arbitrate the grievance and the union sued to compel it. The district court dismissed the suit "after hearing evidence much of which went to the merits of the grievance." That court said that the agreement did not "confide in an arbitrator the right to review the defendant's business judgment in contracting out work"; that "the contracting out of repair and maintenance work, as well as construction work, is strictly a function of management not limited in any respect by the labor agreement involved here." The court of appeals affirmed by a divided vote, the majority holding that the agreement had withdrawn from the grievance procedure "matters which are strictly a function of management" and that contracting out was embraced by this withdrawal.

The Supreme Court, holding that because federal policy is to promote collective bargaining agreements and because a provision for grievance arbitration in agreements is a major factor in achieving industrial peace any doubt about the scope of an arbitration clause should be resolved in favor of coverage, said that:

> The grievance alleged that the contracting out was a violation of the collective bargaining agreement. There was therefore a dispute as to the meaning and application of the provisions of this Agreement which the parties had agreed would be determined by arbitration.[5]

Mr. Justice [Charles E.] Whittaker in a strong dissent pointed out that the employer had contracted out for nineteen years, and that the absence of union demurrer was acquiescence in the principle that it was "strictly a function of management." He also stressed that the union had tried unsuccessfully to get a clause banning subcontracting into the agreement. He pointed to a line of judicial decisions which say that arbitration will not be compelled by the courts unless the writing manifests a clear intent to submit the particular class of question. He found that in this case the parties' conduct over the years was an acquiescence in the proposition that contracting out of work was strictly a function of management and, by the terms of the arbitration clause, not subject to arbitration.

Although this case is assuredly a closer one than *American Manufacturing*, I can find little to criticize in its result. The issue before the court was not did the subcontracting violate the agreement, but does the agreement require arbitration of that question. These parties signed a very broad arbitration clause. They agreed to arbitrate not only differences "as to the meaning and application of the provisions of this Agreement" but also "any local trouble of any kind." True, they also said "matters which are strictly a function of management shall not be subject to arbitration."

---

[5]*Id.* at 585.

To say that the question whether a claim that the subcontracting here complained of violated the agreement is not arbitrable, one would have to decide that it was strictly a function of management.

But there is subcontracting and subcontracting. Some kinds of subcontracting may well have been regarded over the years by these parties as "strictly a function of management." If in the past the company had subcontracted only its surplus work or only work requiring specialized skills its people didn't possess or work requiring access to equipment the contractor had and the company did not have, and if now it is contracting out the *very* work the bargaining unit people used to do, at lower rates of pay while they are on layoff in massive numbers, a viable question is created whether the agreement *as a whole* is not violated thereby. And where there is an apparent conflict between the exercise by management of its functions and the meaning and application of the agreement, an arbitrable question surely exists.

For all agreements rest upon an implied covenant of good faith and fair dealing. Subcontracting in the ordinary course of business—"make or buy" decisions based on considerations dealing with the need for flexibility in business operations, or on the need for gaining access to items or techniques not available in the plant or on the need to meet time schedules and the like—may assuredly be a function or reserved right of management under a contract which does not plainly bar it. But **subcontracting undertaken** to evade the very wage standards the collective agreement was drawn to defend may well raise a lively question about the integrity of that agreement. Professor Archibald Cox has expressed this thought better than I can:

> The notion that ordinary commercial contracts spell out their obligations is a silly canard. Every contract, whether a typical commercial contract or a labor agreement contains "an implied convenant of good faith and fair dealing." One who sells a retail milk business impliedly promises that he will not solicit former customers. A lease of coal lands in exchange for a schedule of royalties implies an obligation to mine the coal diligently. Under the Coca-Cola-type contract there should be no hesitation in setting aside a discharge aimed at circumventing seniority or defeating a grievance even though the contract says nothing about discharges because such a discharge destroys the right of the employees to have the fruits of their bargain. Upon this familiar principle of contracts one might fairly conclude in the absence of other evidence that the provisions of a collective bargaining agreement establishing wages and labor standards imply an obligation not to seek a substitute labor supply at lower wages or inferior standards. The implied promise would prohibit subcontracting for this purpose. But there are limitations to the covenant of honesty and fair dealing. A manufacturer who sells goods when the price is high is not precluded from doubling his output because this would impair the value of the buyer's purchase. A collective bargaining agreement does not

imply a promise that the employer will not deprive the union and the employees of its benefits by closing an obsolete plant or dropping an unprofitable line of business. Similarly, the implied covenant of good faith and fair dealing can hardly be supposed to reach subcontracting which is based upon business considerations other than the cost of acquiring labor under the collective agreement. In such a case either management is free to act or some limitation must be found in the very nature of a collective bargaining agreement.[6]

I do not mean to infer that the union necessarily has a good case on the merits in *Warrior and Gulf.* All subcontracting cases are uphill fights for unions. Where the agreement does not limit contracting, the presumptions strongly favor management. I mean to say only that it presents a legitimate question whether the particular contracting was a substantial nullification of the agreement. That kind of question is arbitrable.

The third case, *United Steelworkers* v. *Enterprise Wheel and Car Corp.*,[7] dealt with the enforcement of an award. An arbitrator reinstated with back pay certain employees discharged for participation in a walkout. After the walkout but before the award the contract expired and was not renewed. The back pay award did not stop at the expiration date; it covered the period thereafter. The company refused to comply, saying the arbitrator, by causing his award to be effective for a period beyond the contract's expiration, exceeded his powers.

The Court held that the arbitrator premised his award on his construction of the contract and that it was not the Court's function to interpret the contract differently. It ordered enforcement.

With this holding I find myself in sharp disagreement, as I suspect most arbitrators are. Most of us have proceeded on the basis that our powers are coextensive with the agreement and lapse therewith. In this case, once the agreement lapsed the reinstated men were employees at will. Their right to back pay flowed from the agreement and ended with it. In my opinion the Court had ample grounds for saying that the arbitrator exceeded his authority in causing back pay to run beyond the date rights continued to accrue to the employee. I should add that I distinguish this case from one where, for example, vacation pay is earned *under* an agreement but does not fall due until *after* its expiration. In that case the arbitrator would be called upon to rule on a claim for the enforcement of a right accruing under the agreement though payable at a later date.

Thus we see that the *results* of the three Supreme Court decisions are in themselves not startling. The *American* decision is in the orthodox

---

[6]See Cox, "Reflections upon Labor Arbitration," *Harvard Law Review* 72 (1959): 1482, 1496.
[7]363 U.S. 593 (1960).

tradition. The *Warrior & Gulf* finding, while more controversial, has a broad body of opinion to back it. Only *Enterprise* is not easy to digest. What is there about these cases then, that has caused such a furor in legal and industrial relations circles, especially among lawyers specializing in industrial relations law for management?

Two things. First, in its desire to limit judicial intervention in arbitration, the Supreme Court has said that a claim is arbitrable so long as it *alleges* a violation of some agreement provision. Thus many functions of management believed by industry to be beyond arbitral review may now be subjected to arbitral scrutiny for signs of conflict with the agreement's provisions. This has caused deep concern in the ranks of management although it is worthy of note that the giants of industry had by contract long ago empowered their arbitrators to rule on *alleged* violations of the agreement and to pass on their own jurisdiction within plainly delimited areas.

Second, the decisions by their tone, may raise expectations that arbitrators should or will broaden the scope of their powers beyond the limits envisioned by the parties when they drew their agreement.

For the Court appears to have engaged in extravagant dicta which make arbitrators look nine feet tall. Thus in the *American* case the Court said:

> Arbitration is a stabilizing influence only as it serves as a vehicle for handling *every* and *all* disputes that arise under the agreement....
> The processing of even frivolous claims may have therapeutic values which those who are not a part of the plant environment are not aware of. [Emphasis added.][8]

And in *Warrior*:

> Apart from matters that the parties specifically exclude, *all* of the questions on which the parties disagree must therefore come within the scope of the grievance and arbitration provisions of the collective agreement....
> The parties expect that his [the arbitrator's] judgment of a particular grievance will reflect not only what the contract says but, insofar as the collective bargaining agreement permits, such factors as the effect on productivity of particular result, its consequence to the morale of the shop, his judgment whether tensions will be heightened or diminished. [Emphasis added.][9]

This last quote, when literally applied by an arbitrator, nearly always brings on him the wrath of one of the parties and often both. It has been my experience that American labor relations have achieved that state of maturity in which the parties want me or my colleagues to decide only what the contract says or to give them a fair construction of what it says

---
[8] 363 U.S. at 567, 568.
[9] 363 U.S. at 581.

unclearly or implicitly. They most emphatically do not seek my views on what will raise productivity. Nor do they ask me to make that decision which will be best for morale. Whose morale? Some of our decisions cause worker morale to soar, while acting as a terrific depressant on the morale of managers, and vice versa. Some of our decisions cause not only tensions but hypertension in bargaining unit ranks while they at the same time lower management's blood pressure to near normal, at least for a while.

The decisions have imputed to arbitration and to arbitrators a mystique, a degree of divination bordering on the oracular and a responsibility for shaping the parties' destinies that few arbitrators relish and fewer possess or exercise. Their general tenor seems to put arbitrators *above* the parties and *above* their contract.

Most of us conceive our role as confined within the four walls of the contract. We strive to apply its terms where they are clear, to interpret them when they are imperfectly expressed, to construe them to cover cases falling in the gaps between the stated terms, and to refuse to venture outside those walls which represent the limits of our jurisdiction. Of course we consider past practice (the Court calls it the common law of the shop). We form judgments as to the parties' probable intent, where it is unclear, on the basis of reason and logic in the light of the parties' joint objectives. We sometimes look to practice in the industry or area. But we strive to apply these concepts within the limits of the logic imposed by that which the parties themselves negotiated.

The tone of the Court's decisions implies an opposite course for arbitrators. The Court's philosophical approach appears to be based on an extreme exposition of a philosophy which was useful in an earlier day in certain specific types of industrial relations situations but which is not generally in accord with today's labor relations scene.

It is true that there is other language in the decisions which conceive of the arbitrator as playing a more traditional and conservative role in industrial relations. Thus in *Enterprise* the opinion states:

> Nevertheless an arbitrator is confined to interpretation and application of the Agreement; he does not sit to dispense his own brand of industrial justice. He may, of course, look for guidance from many sources, yet his award is legitimate only so long as it draws its essence from the collective bargaining agreement. When the arbitrator's words manifest an infidelity to this obligation, courts have no choice but to refuse enforcement of the award.[10]

But the above does not strike the dominant note in these cases.

What are the practical implications of the Supreme Court's decisions

---

[10] 363 U.S. at 597, 598.

for collective bargaining? Those in management who panic may rush in to insist on tightening the so-called standard arbitration clauses to sharply delimit arbitration. They are bound to meet with sharp resistance from union negotiators especially when they get into the supremely sensitive areas such as subcontracting and the like.

And if managements push for limitations on the scope of the arbitration clause the unions will undoubtedly counter with proposals for limitations on the no-strike clause. It might be said that this would be a fair deal—restrict the scope of arbitration but preserve the right to strike or lock out over those matters outside the scope of arbitral review.

This formula is all right for the large companies and large unions who meet more or less on equal terms and whose multiplant facilities permit them to weather these crises without crushing losses. But what about the smaller single-plant employer who just can't afford a strike during the contract's life? Or what about the weak union unable to mount strikes between contract terminations? The balance of forces between the giants encourages settlements without arbitration and without strikes. The imbalance to be found in the smaller enterprises may lead to more strikes than the parties or the economy can afford.

It seems to me that strong campaigns undertaken to secure drastic revisions of arbitration clauses would be ill advised at this time. I suspect that a rash of strikes over this issue is likely. It must be remembered that of the scores of thousands of grievances arbitrated each year, only a few hundred ever get into courts. And a fair number of these involve a few companies or unions who never did have confidence in the arbitration process, in contrast to the overwhelming majority of American companies and unions among whom arbitration, at first tried with reluctance, has won an enduring place.

In my view, it would be well for contract negotiators to do little for the time being about this subject, to let the dust settle.

I doubt that these decisions will prompt arbitrators to arrogate to themselves powers they have not hitherto exercised. Nor do I believe that the unions will urge them to do so. For the full implications of these decisions could be as restrictive of union prerogatives as of management prerogatives. If I am wrong, and self-restraint is not shown, there will be time to draw tighter arbitration clauses.

Observers may differ about the efficacy of the institution of collective bargaining as a wage-setting device, as a distributor of power, as an influence on prices and on the economic process. But few disagree over the proposition that arbitration of disputes arising under agreements has proved its worth in stabilizing shop relations, in minimizing work stoppages, and in imparting to worker and manager alike a new sense of dignity in their relationship. It is now up to management and labor to distill from these Supreme Court decisions those positive values which will serve to protect and strengthen the arbitration process.

4. Book Review*

Labor Arbitration: A Dissenting View. Paul R. Hays.[1] New Haven: Yale University Press. 1966. Pp. vii, 125. $4.50.

Judge Paul Hays, who was for many years a teacher of law at Columbia and an arbitrator of labor disputes and who in 1961 was appointed a judge of the Court of Appeals for the Second Circuit, thinks little of the law, and less of the practice, of labor arbitration. He would drastically reshape its future either by casting it adrift from the law or by bringing it more firmly under the control of the courts.

This, in capsule, is Judge Hays's thesis in *Labor Arbitration: A Dissenting View*, a slim volume based on the Storrs Lectures on Jurisprudence he delivered at the Yale Law School in 1964. To the men in the field whom he so severely criticizes, his analysis is superficial, his appraisals are undocumented, his criticisms are unfair, and his solutions are unworkable. Those who are tempted to conclude that this is a reaction to be expected from a member of a group so roundly criticized should also be aware that management and labor representatives, whom Judge Hays portrays as the victims of the misdeeds of the arbitration process, have declined to join him in his denunciation of private arbitration as currently practiced. On the contrary, without foregoing their right to criticize particular arbitrators or particular decisions, they tend to reject both Hays's generalizations and his solutions. In his dissent, Hays appears to be a minority of one.

In his discussion of the law of labor arbitration, Hays's chief bête noire seems to be the Supreme Court's dicta in *United Steelworkers* v. *Warrior and Gulf Navigation Company*[2] and its companion cases, the so-called Trilogy. The Court, in an opinion he describes as extravagantly favorable to the arbitration process, "comes to the conclusion that the silence of the collective agreement does not mean that the matter on which the agreement is silent is to be left to management's discretion," Hays asserts. He criticizes the Court for stating that when a no-strike clause is included in a labor

---
*Harvard Law Review 81 (1967): 507-511.
[1] Judge, United States Court of Appeals for the Second Circuit.
[2] 363 U.S. 574 (1960).

agreement "in a very real sense everything that management does is subject to the agreement, for either management is prohibited or limited in the action it takes, or if not, it is protected from interference by strikes."[3]

Many arbitrators agree that some of the language of the Supreme Court's decisions in the Trilogy cases can be read to magnify an arbitrator's powers in interpreting contracts and that by their tone these decisions confer on arbitrators an aura of power they neither possess nor aspire to. At the same time, it should not be overlooked that elsewhere in these opinions the Court confines arbitrators to making decisions that draw their essence from the agreement rather than from their own notions of industrial justice.

But if the Court erred in its emphasis, it did not err in the essence of its holdings. Arbitration of disputes arising during the life of collective agreements *is* imbedded in the national labor policy. It was approved by labor and management at President Truman's Labor-Management Conference in 1946. It was endorsed by the Congress in the Taft-Hartley Act in 1947. It enjoys the support not only of the leadership of the unions but of companies, large and small, thoughout American industry. Initially thrust on generally reluctant managements by the War Labor Board, arbitration has won a firm place in industrial relations.

The essence of the Supreme Court's decisions in the Trilogy is that arbitrators need not buy the "reserved rights of management" theory lock, stock, and barrel. Since, in the absence of a collective agreement, management has the right to order and dispose in its relations with its employees as it sees fit (provided it stays within the bounds of the National Labor Relations Act and other applicable statutes), the "reserved rights" theory argues that when management signs a labor agreement it fetters its discretion only as the agreement explicitly provides.

If experience is the foundation of the law, then the law must meet the real needs of those whose lives it governs. The reserved rights doctrine, if applied with the emphasis Judge Hays seems to favor, does not meet that test and the Supreme Court recognized that fact. It does not meet that test because the labor agreement itself is not posited on that doctrine. It is posited on a recognition that the agreement regulates the main terms of an ongoing way of in-plant life, but that it can neither spell out all those terms nor relegate to one of the parties sole discretion over unforeseen problems arising from its administration.

An example may be helpful. A labor agreement spells out the basic work week as forty hours and provides for payment at time and one-half for hours worked in excess of forty. It is silent, however, on whether

---

[3]363 U.S. at 583.

overtime work is voluntary or compulsory. The long-standing practice in the plant and in the industry has been to treat overtime as voluntary. Can it reasonably be said that with the signing of the agreement there was an intent to change that practice and to permit management now to compel overtime against the desires of the employees?

The reserved rights of management advocates would so interpret the contract because its silence leaves the matter unregulated and hence subject to management's sole dominion. The Supreme Court, in the Trilogy, impliedly disagreed, reasoning that the agreement was negotiated against a background of ongoing practices and traditions born of the consent inherent in custom and to be changed consensually, not unilaterally. It upheld the right of arbitrators to interpret a labor agreement against the background of the particular plant's or industry's practices and to apply these ongoing rules of the parties' own conduct to the omissions or ambiguities in their written instruments. And it held that arbitrators, not the courts, should do the interpreting and the applying unless the parties' contrary intention is plainly stated.

Judge Hays finds this distasteful, if not downright shocking. The examples he cites in his book are mainly in terms of the restraints imposed by the courts and arbitrators on management's freedom to act unilaterally. But experience as an arbitrator must have revealed to him, as it has to most of his ex-colleagues, that unions as well as management are shackled by the customary ways, by in-plant practices not mentioned in the agreement.

For instance, the agreement specifies that the first shift begin at 12:01 A.M. on Monday. It does not provide for what has been the custom from time immemorial—that a limited number of first shift workers must report one hour early on Sunday night to "light up," or prepare machinery for use by the full shift after the weekend shutdown. A rebellious group of employees—or the union in their behalf—now claims that their starting time is 12:01 A.M. Monday, not 11:00 P.M. Sunday; that the contract plainly so states; and that appearance for "light up" may not be compelled. Would Judge Hays side with them on the ground that the agreement is clear? If he did he'd be hooted off the premises, probably by both parties, for the alternative to the early report for the few is a late start on the first shift for the many, with a consequent loss of production to the company and of pay to the men. Or would he posit a ruling for management on the argument that it is management's reserved right to require people to report early? If he did, why could not management order them in two or three hours early? Yet, how could such a holding be reconciled with the agreement's clear terms?

Judge Hays criticizes the preferred position the Court has accorded to arbitration based upon the superior skill of labor arbitrators. The skill is more securely grounded in Justice [William O.] Douglas's rhetoric, Judge Hays holds, than in actual fact. In Hays's view the average man who arbitrates ad hoc is an odd hack. "There are only a handful of arbitrators," writes Hays "who . . . have the knowledge, training, skill, and character to make them good judges and therefore good arbitrators. In literally thousands of cases every year, decisions are made by arbitrators who are wholly unfitted for their jobs—who do not have the requisite knowledge, training, skill, intelligence, and character" (p. 112).

The documentation for these sweeping charges is nonexistent. Hays admits as much in his book when he deplores the lack of objective studies of the arbitration process. But the charges are really beside the point because the test must be comparative rather than absolute. The real question is whether labor arbitrators in their specialized field perform less creditably than do ordinary judges in that field. No one can answer it with assurance, but empirical observation does seem to bear out the special competence of the arbitrators. While it is true that there are novices in this relatively new field, the majority are men who have had experience in the field, who know something of the specialized area of labor relations, collective agreements, personnel administration, job evaluation plans, incentive systems, multilevel relationships in managements and unions and, most important, the sensitive atmosphere that surrounds union-management relationships.

Judge Hays maintains that arbitration is neither more nor less than contract interpretation, that labor contract interpretation is ordinary grist for the judicial mill, that judges and judges alone are expert at interpreting contracts, and that others are interlopers who prevent the process. This is a fallacy.

Labor arbitration is more than the interpretation of contracts. It involves their interpretation in the context of an ongoing relationship in which the rights and the wrongs are weighed against the parties' needs and aspirations which may transcend the immediate cause. It requires of the decider a sensitivity to the parties' whole relationship precedent and antecedent to the case at hand. This is not to say that such considerations dominate arbitral decisions. It is to say only that they may temper them in cases where other factors are in balance.

Judges in disputes over ordinary contracts seldom face the same choices. Their concern is with the instrument and with little or nothing beyond it. Their underlying assumption is that the contracting parties are free to part and to contract with others regardless of the consequences of the current dispute. In the case of labor disputes this is not so. The contestants are bound to a relationship in which divorce is not allowed and that fact gives a unique cast to the process of decision.

Are judges as qualified for this task as arbitators? The answer is that they can be if they specialize in the field of labor relations, but the specialist judge is a rarity in our legal system. Labor relations *is* a speciality, with its own terminology, its own basic assumptions, its own structure, and, most significantly, its own flavor. In the short period of two decades, arbitration has become a specialty not because it was forced on reluctant managements by aggressive unions but because it has fulfilled a need which no other institution was equipped to fulfill. It may well be that not all its practitioners are as well trained or qualified for their tasks as the judges who grace the bench of the Second Circuit are for theirs, but that is not the true test. The test is comparative performance generally in producing satisfactory results. The practitioners in the field are in the best position to provide an answer. This reviewer's experience is that most lawyers on both sides would rather take a chance with an arbitrator in a labor case than they would with a judge.

Judge Hays excoriates arbitrators for issuing what he calls "rigged" awards. These are awards where there is no genuine dispute between the parties about the interpretations of the agreement, but where one party is unable to convince a constituency and wishes to utilize the directory power of the arbitrator to impose his view. That such awards are a perversion of the arbitration process cannot be gainsaid. But there is no evidence that they constitute more than a microscopic segment of awards. Judge Hays suggests no legitimate basis for the inference that they characterize the arbitration process as a whole.

Hays accuses arbitrators of writing awards calculated not to dispose of the issue bluntly but to please one of the parties (impliedly the unions) in order that they may be chosen for future arbitration cases. How arbitrators accomplish this feat, he does not explain. Arbitrators nearly always are the mutual choice of the parties. No matter how much an arbitrator pleases the winner, the irate loser can veto him for the future. And if he writes a decision that has a little bit in it for each party but not enough for either to accomplish justice, his cowardice becomes immediately apparent to both, and he courts the likelihood that both will axe him.

Hays states he has been "forced" to the conclusion, based on his own long observation of the process "and upon the hints I pick up in the literature here and there, that labor arbitration has fatal shortcomings as a system for the judicial administration of contract violations" (p. 111). He holds that a "system of adjudication in which the judge depends for his livelihood, or for a substantial part of his livelihood or even for substantial supplements to his regular income, on whether he pleases those who hire him to judge is per se a thoroughly undesirable system" (p. 112). Hays thus views arbitrators as cravens interested only in their survival in the field and little or not at all in their own integrity or self-respect. But the pressures on arbitrators are not primarily from the parties; they are from within. With each decision, an arbitrator lays his integrity on the line. Few have failed to meet the challenge. The external pressures are countervailing. The need for living with himself is inexorable. If some arbitrators fail the test, they do not long survive. And those who do survive have met a test judges are not called upon to meet—the test of acceptability in an area where two contestants freely make him their mutual choice.

The solutions offered by Judge Hays have little to commend them. He proposes that the courts "not lend themselves at all to the arbitration process" (p. 113). Significantly, he says nothing about whether, were the courts to withdraw from the enforcement of agreements to arbitrate or from enforcement of awards, the party desiring compliance should be free to strike or lock out. If his answer is that it should be free in this respect, that solution would change the national labor policy in a profound and significant way. The strike problem in American industrial relations is vexing enough today. It should not be compounded. If his answer is that there should be no enforcement of promises to arbitrate or of arbitration awards and that at the same time strikes to enforce those terms should be barred, it flies in the face of experience. In the great majority of contracts barring certain subjects from arbitration, the right to strike or lock out in disputes involving those subjects is retained. It is scarcely likely to be otherwise if parties are left free to pick and choose which cases they will arbitrate and which they will not.

Hays suggests that if the use of the courts for the purpose of enforcing arbitration were withdrawn, it would leave the courts available for the enforcement of collective bargaining agreements through their regular procedures. In the alternative he speaks of the possibility of setting up labor courts after the European model. What these proposals overlook is the fact that labor and management purposely chose private arbitration to avoid precisely these alternatives. They chose to forgo use of the courts in the interest of determination of day-to-day disputes in the plant or near it, in full view of the rank-and-file worker, lower union official, and line supervisor, with these people having a role in the process. The remoteness and austerity of the judicial route they purposely eschewed, in order to avoid the dehydration and hardening of their relationship likely to stem from recourse to what they regard as alien procedures. In his desire to impose the judicial model, Judge Hays neglects the values inherent in the arbitration process that contribute to the kind of labor relations most collective bargainers aspire to and many achieve.

5. Arbitrators and Judges—
Dispelling the Hays Haze*

To say that arbitration today is an established part of American industrial relations is to utter a commonplace. While its origins are ancient, its widespread acceptance in this country dates only from World War II. Forced by the War Labor Board on generally reluctant managements, it has become standard equipment in collective agreements in relationships where power is about equally distributed between the parties or where the stronger party forbears from the full exercise of his power.

ARBITRATION AN ESTABLISHED INSTITUTION

In only a handful of collective bargaining relationships have proposals for the curtailment of the scope of arbitration or proposals for its abolition been given serious consideration. Thus the national Teamster agreement, concluded in early 1964, eliminated grievance arbitration except for discharge cases.[1] The General Electric and Westinghouse settlements of late 1963 curtailed arbitration substantially.[2] In both cases one party—the union in the Teamster case and the companies in the G.E. and Westinghouse cases—had the will and the strength to impose such a curtailment of the arbitration process on the other.

However, there is no evidence that these were the precursors of a trend away from arbitration. I mentioned that orginally management was the reluctant party when arbitration was imposed extensively by War Labor Board fiat. The test of the efficacy of the process for the achievement of the kind of stability both companies and unions need during the term of their agreements is demonstrated by the fact that when sporadic rank-and-file demands for the abolition of the arbitration clause are raised in such major industries as automobiles, steel, or aluminum management and the union leaderships quickly close ranks to stave off this eventuality.

---

*Southwestern Legal Foundation, *Labor Law Developments, Proceedings of the 12th Annual Institute on Labor Law* (Washington: BNA, 1966): 159-172.

[1]William E. Simkin, "Danger Signs for Labor Arbitration," in *Labor Arbitration—Perspectives and Problems, Proceedings of the 17th Annual Meeting, National Academy of Arbitrators* (Washington: BNA, 1964): 209-210.

[2]*Ibid.*

There is even a trend in the opposite direction. The percentage of contracts with arbitration clauses to govern disputes arising during their term is popularly estimated at 90 to 95 percent, and still rising. Furthermore, a few nonunionized companies with advanced personnel policies have introduced arbitration into their personnel relations systems and actually give aggrieved employees the right to third party review of grievances not satisfactorily settled by discussion.[3]

The Rule of Law at the Workplace

The wide acceptance of arbitration as the handmaiden of collective bargaining in this extraordinarily short period of time is significant. Archibald Cox, then Solicitor General, noted that

> It is hard to think of any institution that has accomplished so much in the short span of 25 or 30 years, and this is true whether one measures accomplishment by the static standard of industrial peace or the more important criterion of accomplishment in meeting the needs of men.
> Take first the simply stated but vital goal of establishing a rule of law in the mine, mill and factory—the substitution of a rule of law for the arbitrary and capricious power of the boss. Men have few greater concerns than this kind of justice. What equal example is there of extending a rule of law—both substantive rights and duties and also the machinery to administer them—into so large an area of human life affecting so many people within so short a time. Nothing less has been done by collective bargaining through the rules it brings into the shop and the industrial jurisprudence being made and administered through grievance procedures and arbitration.[4]

Cox here touches not only on arbitration's utility as a keeper of the peace during a contract's life—what he calls "the static standard of industrial peace"—but also on the "more important criterion of accomplishment in meeting the needs of men"—that of establishing a rule of law rather than arbitrary power at the workplace. In a too-little noted but highly significant book, *Democratic Values and the Rights of Mangement*, Professor Eli Ginzberg, director of the Conservation of Human Resources Project at Columbia University and chairman of the National Manpower Advisory Committee, and his associates uncover the wellsprings from which this great impulse toward a rule of law at the workplace flows in the following passages:

> During his formative years, the [American] . . . . worker is indoctrinated

---

[3]For example, see personnel manual of Northrop Nortronics, *Working with Northrup*, pp. III-22 to III-30.

[4]Archibald Cox, "Procedure and Creativity," in *Labor Arbitration—Perspectives and Problems, Proceedings of the 17th Annual Meeting, National Academy of Arbitrators* (Washington: BNA, 1964), pp. 253-254.

with ideas of equality and freedom—with the belief that every man is as good as every other man. . . .

Nurtured on this heady drink of freedom and equality, of liberty and justice, he cannot fail to become restive, disturbed, antagonistic by what he finds in the employment situation. From the moment the starting whistle blows, his freedom is in suspense; justice is in jeopardy; one man is clearly the superior of another; power and authority permeate the work place. . . .

The average man . . . . sees his life as a whole. He cannot live without tension by one set of values in the hours during which he works and live by an entirely different set of values during the hours when he is off of the job.

But, in the arena of work itself where he spends so much of life and energy, his is mocked. Small wonder, therefore, that it is here that he is seeking to realize the democratic values which he holds dear.

FEATURES OF PRIVATE ARBITRATION

The process which has aided in the democratization of this area of American life has been the system of private arbitration as it has developed in this country. The chief features of that system are (a) the privity of the relationship—the arbitrator interprets and applies the parties' own contract in the context of their own relationship and circumstances; (b) the arbitrator is selected by and serves at the pleasure of both parties; (c) the arbitrator is paid for his services by the parties; (d) the arbitrator is responsible and answerable only to the parties within the framework of existing law; and (e) the courts will enforce the promise to arbitrate and the award itself, reserving for judicial review the question of the existence of such a promise and determination of allegations of procedural irregularities.

In response to the need, there has developed in this country a corps of men who are available for the specialized work of labor arbitration and who devote themselves to it in varying degrees. A relatively small number are full-time practitioners. This work is their career and from it they draw their livelihood. A larger number combine arbitration with other careers—the law, teaching, or other pursuits—which permit them to devote a considerable, but less than full, time to arbitration work. There is still a larger number who are called upon for only an occasional case and whose main locus of interest lies elsewhere.

There have been stinging criticisms of *arbitrators* but little of *arbitration* as a process. Some management spokesmen have attacked arbitrators as innovators and meddlers who stray from the function of strict construction. Some labor spokesmen have attacked them for their conservative outlook and their inhibitions about breaking new ground. But few that I know of have seriously advanced the proposition that the *system* is inherently faulty and that it should be basically changed or replaced.

From those of you who are thinking that up to now I have been engaged in painfully elaborating the obvious, I ask indulgence. I have set forth the foregoing merely as a backdrop for the main thrust of this paper. It is to inquire into whether there are in fact basic defects in the process and whether, therefore, it should be drastically overhauled or discarded. More specifically, it is to examine the validity of a judgment advanced recently by a distinguished source that the system of private arbitration as we know it today is a thoroughly undesirable system.

THE HAYS INDICTMENT OF ARBITRATION

This judgment was pronounced recently by Judge Paul Hays, United States Court of Appeals for the Second Circuit. In the third of his Storrs Lectures delivered at the Yale Law School in November 1964, published in the *Yale Law Journal*,[5] Judge Hays delivered himself of a condemnation of the process so sweeping and so undocumented as to call for answer, if only because of the place of distinction he held as a teacher of law and now holds as a jurist. He said:

> Pending scholarly studies and evaluations, I am forced to the conclusion based upon observation during twenty-three years of very active practice in the area of arbitration and as an arbitrator, and from suggestions in the more intelligent literature in the field, that labor arbitration has fatal shortcomings as a system for the judicial administration of contract violations. . . . An arbitrator is a third party called in to determine a controversy over whether one of the parties to a collective agreement has violated that agreement. He is not a wise counsellor and statesman to whom the management and the union look for advice on how to run their affairs or how to increase production or lessen tensions. He is merely an ad hoc judge to whom is submitted the question of whether the collective bargaining agreement has been violated. The chances are very good that, in all but a tiny percentage of arbitrations, this is the first time he has had anything to do with the plant, and that he knows nothing of the background of the dispute or of the "common law" of the industry. In fact there is a considerable possibility that this is his first arbitration case. He does not in fact have any expertise in these matters and is not actually expected to have any, since it is expected that he will listen to the evidence presented by the two parties and decide on the basis of the evidence whether the charge of contract violation is or is not sustained. For this task he requires exactly the same expertise which judges have and use every day. He must be expert in analyzing issues, in weighing evidence, and in contract interpretation.
>
> There are only a handful of arbitrators who, like Shulman and Cox, have the knowledge, training, skill and character which would make them good judges and therefore make them good arbitrators. In literally thousands of

---

[5] Paul R. Hays, "The Future of Labor Arbitration," *Yale Law Journal* 74 (no. 6, May 1965): 1019-1038.

cases every year decisions are made by arbitrators who are wholly unfitted for their jobs, who do not have the requisite knowledge, training, skill, intelligence and character. In fact, a proportion of arbitration awards, no one knows how large a proportion, is decided not on the basis of the evidence or of the contract or other proper considerations, but in a way calculated to encourage the arbitrator's being hired for other arbitration cases. It makes no difference whether or not a large majority of cases is decided this way. A system of adjudication in which the judge depends for his livelihood, or for a substantial part of his livelihood or even for substantial supplements to his regular income on pleasing those who hire him to judge is per se a thoroughly undesirable system. In no proper system of justice should a judge be submitted to such pressures; on the contrary, a judge should be carefully insulated from any pressure of this type.[6]

Now, Judge Hays was for many years a scholarly and erudite member of the arbitrators' ranks who in recent years donned the robes of a judge. Coming from a less distinguished source, his undocumented critical speculations might well have been dismissed with casual notice. But his credentials cannot lightly be disregarded. Can it be that he is right and that the great bulk of observers among students, management representatives, labor leaders, and the judiciary are wrong? If so, we must take that fact into account in shaping our institutions. If not, his misplaced criticisms must be answered, lest they tarnish a valuable social tool. A consideration of his criticisms is the task I propose to undertake today.

I think we may safely assume that when Judge Hays described the typical arbitrator as an itinerant, uninformed ad hoc judge, a sort of barefoot boy with Bible, knowing little of labor relations, nothing of the plant in which he serves or of the relationship between the parties or of the "common law" of the industry, he was not being autobiographical. For in point of fact he was highly regarded as an arbitrator, called back to serve repeatedly by the same parties, and he perforce learned a great deal about them and their "common law." And as his service increased, his value to the parties grew. This is not a matter on which I am speculating, by the way. Judge Hays followed me as arbitrator in numerous relationships, and I him, so I know firsthand whereof I speak.

We may also safely assume that he was not being autobiographical when he wrote that "a proportion of arbitration awards . . . is decided not on the basis of the evidence or of the contract or other proper considerations, but in a way calculated to encourage the arbitrator's being hired for other arbitration cases." I have read many of his decisions, cited to me by the parties, and in none have I found a trace of such calculation.

Finally, we may safely assume that Judge Hays was not being autobiographical when he spoke of pressures generated by the fact that

---
[6]*Ibid.*, p. 1034.

as an arbitrator, he was among those who depended for his livelihood or part of it on "pleasing those who hired him to judge." He is rugged, independent, and pressure-proof—of this there is no doubt.

It is therefore plain that Judge Hays was not speaking either of himself or of the "handful of arbitrators who, like Shulman and Cox, have the knowledge, training, skill and character which would make them good judges and therefore make them good arbitrators." He was speaking only of the vast majority of arbitrators, who apparently do not have the knowledge, training, skill, and character which would make them good judges and who presumably are the ones who are wholly unfitted for their jobs.

Do the facts square with Judge Hays's theories? I submit they do not. His first point, it appears, is that there is nothing more to arbitrating than to judging, that it calls for no other kind of expertise, and that only those few qualified to be judges are qualified to be arbitrators.

First, I submit that labor arbitration is in fact a distinct specialty and that the generality of arbitrators who are experienced do have a knowledge of industrial relations, an understanding of the problems of the interrelationship of levels of authority in multilayered organizations such as companies and unions, some knowledge of the problems of trade union administration, some feeling for the problems of production and of the roadblocks and obstacles to smooth in-plant administration, a considerable knowledge of the processes of industry, and a wide acquaintanceship with the techniques of wage incentives, job evaluation, and other features of wage administration that are basically simple but, until mastered, are gibberish to the uninformed. Furthermore, they need this knowledge intelligently to analyze and decide many, though by no means all, of the cases that come before them.

This point may have escaped Judge Hays but it has not escaped other distinguished scholars knowledgeable both in jurisprudence and in labor arbitration. I refer specifically to Professor Lon L. Fuller, Carter Professor of General Jurisprudence, Harvard Law School, who wrote:

> In the nature of things few judges can have had any very extensive experience in the field of industrial relations. Arbitrators, on the other hand, are compelled to acquire a knowledge of industrial processes, modes of compensation, complex incentive plans, job classifications, shift arrangements, and procedures for layoff and recall.
> Naturally not all arbitrators stand on a parity with respect to this knowledge. But there are open to the arbitrator, even the novice, quick methods of education not available to the courts. . . .[7]

---

[7] Lon L. Fuller, "Collective Bargaining and the Arbitrator," in *Collective Bargaining and the Arbitrator's Role, Proceedings of the 15th Annual Meeting, National Academy of Arbitrators*, (Washington: BNA, 1962): 17.

THE ARBITRATOR'S "EXPERTISE"

In this sense, the experienced arbitrator does have the kind of "expertise" to which the Supreme Court referred in the Trilogy. In many cases he has served before with the same parties, has learned something of the particular plant and industry, and is already familiar with the pattern of their relationships and the peculiarities of their special terminology. In a significant number of relationships he is their permanent umpire, serving for the contract's term and continually renewed as successive contracts are negotiated. But even where the particular plant and the parties are new to him, his background enables him quickly to grasp and comprehend what often would be obscure to someone not previously exposed.

Of course he is not "the wise counsellor and statesman to whom management and the union look for advice on how to run their affairs or how to increase production or lessen tensions." The language of the Supreme Court in the Trilogy cases from which Judge Hays drew this quotation in his lecture was extravagant and implies a role few arbitrators play and fewer desire to preempt. But a good arbitrator is more than an "ad hoc judge . . . . expert in analyzing issues, in weighing evidence, and in contract interpretation." He must do that in the specialized context of labor relations, in the special community of an industrial plant and a local union. To be meaningful and convincing to the parties, his decisions should impart an understanding and comprehension of that atmosphere and should convey to them the conviction that their controversy is being decided not with reference to abstractions remote from their ken but with reference to the realities which govern their day-to-day in-plant lives.

I do not mean to imply that this is an expertise judges cannot quickly acquire if they made labor cases a field of concentration. But I believe it is also true that the "expertise which judges have and use every day . . . ," that of "analyzing issues, . . . weighing evidence, and . . . contract interpretation" is only part of the expertise an arbitrator employs, because the judge does not ordinarily employ them in the same specialized atmosphere as does the arbitrator.

Arbitrators Meet the Test of the Marketplace

For these reasons I find somewhat cavalier Judge Hays's dismissal of the average arbitrator as wholly unfitted for his job, as lacking the requisite knowledge, training, skill, intelligence, and character. His criticism does not square with the fact that, once established, arbitrators appear to have a high survivability rate, are chosen again and again by people who do not deem them unfitted for their jobs, who appear to show some regard for their skill and intelligence and even some admiration for their character. I cannot, of course, speak about all arbitrators. There are undoubtedly some who lack the requisite knowledge, skill, intelligence, and character. But I think it safe to say that the arbitrators who decide the majority of cases presented to arbitration in this country, the ones who, whether they practice full time, part time, or occasionally, are called back time and again to serve have met a test no judge is ever called upon to meet—the test of the marketplace, the judgment of those in a position freely to contract for their services.

THE ARBITRATOR'S MOTIVES

I turn next to Judge Hays's second sweeping generalization—"In fact, a proportion of arbitration awards, no one knows how large a proportion, is decided not on the basis of the evidence or of the contract or other proper considerations, but in a way calculated to encourage the arbitrator's being hired for other arbitration cases." This, I submit, is arrant nonsense. The surest way for an arbitrator *not* to be hired for other arbitration cases by at least one of the same parties is to render a decision without regard to the evidence or the contract. Surely Judge Hays could not have had this type of case in mind.

Possibly he meant that there are arbitrators who decided a dispute between Company A and Union B without regard to the evidence or the contract in order to encourage Union C and Company D to agree upon him for their cases. This presupposes a naivete on the part of the parties that does not in fact exist. As this audience undoubtedly knows, arbitrators are not chosen by caprice. They are checked upon, cross-referenced, and indexed by trade associations, union research departments, law firms, individual industrial relations directors, and union business agents. There are even several firms which make a specialty of providing information about individual arbitrators and their performance as reported by companies that have used them before—a sort of private FBI whose dossiers are available for a fee. Opinions about their intelligence, performance, character, and adherence to evidence and contract terms are solicited from many sources before they become the selection of both parties, at least in any case of significance to the parties. The statement that arbitration opinions which ignore the evidence or the contract are written so as to encourage either the same or other parties to hire the writer for other arbitration cases is, on analysis, incomprehensible.

CAN PAID ARBITRATORS BE HONEST JUDGES?

I turn next to the third count in Judge Hays' indictment of arbitration. He charges that "A system of adjudication in which the judge depends for his livelihood, or for a substantial part of his livelihood or even for substantial supplement to his regular income, on pleasing those who hire him to judge is per se a thoroughly undesirable system."

Apparently, Judge Hays views the majority of arbitrators as craven, cringing creatures who write their decisions in mortal fear of the displeasure of the losing party and who therefore let that fear temper their judgments in some way he does not explain. Or he may be implying that because the arbitrator fears the displeasure of the loser, which displeasure may have the tangible effect of a loss of future income, he contrives to write his decisions in such a way that there will be no loser.

Counteracting Pressures in Arbitration

His statement misconceives the nature of the impact of arbitral decisions. It ignores the fact that if an arbitrator makes a dishonest decision in order to please one party, he thereby automatically alienates another who holds a veto power over his future services. In arbitration one man's pleasure is his opponent's pain and the pressures on the arbitrator, to the extent they exist at all, are countervailing.

The Reactions of the Losers

More than that, this charge does no credit to the parties in arbitration cases. It implies that losers in arbitration cases are automatically indignant, that they possess no sense of the worth of their case; that they are incapable of admitting that there may have been another side to the question at issue, and that they are automatically moved to economic retaliation against the decider. The facts are quite to the contrary. In the vast majority of arbitration cases the loser takes his licking gracefully; from time to time he is even convinced by the decision; more often than not, he knew he had a losing case when he entered or when he left the hearing room; and he is not at all impelled to work out his displeasure by blacklisting the arbitrator.

It must be conceded, however, that an arbitrator from time to time displeases some parties to a degree that they are impelled to apply economic sanctions against him. Does the fear that this may happen becloud his ability to make a fair decision? The answer is no, for two reasons. The first is that a career arbitrator who gets past his first case quickly learns, if he did not already know, that he would do well to avoid becoming dependent solely on one set of parties and to so spread his activities that a loss of the business of one set of parties does not seriously curtail his income. If, on the other hand, he has chosen to put all his eggs in one basket, his work is under such close scrutiny that he can do no less than decide cases according to the merits if he expects to have his services continued beyond its current term, or even beyond the current case.

THE JUDICIAL TEMPERAMENT: ARBITRATORS AND JUDGES

The second reason is more fundamental. Judge Hays's charge denigrates arbitrators unfairly and exalts the judiciary unduly. It presupposes that arbitrators are without character, professional responsibility, or pride in their calling and that they are responsive only to the tug of money. At the same time it assumes that judges, freed from money concerns by virtue of civil service status, are per se freed from pressures which may affect their decisions.

The first presupposition is a gratuitous attack on the character and accomplishments of the many hundreds of men who have served honorably and efficiently as arbitrators in many thousands of disputes over the years. It may surprise Judge Hays to learn that there are some men in this world who think that to meet the challenge to act honorably and decide fairly is more important than the possible loss of future income, and that not all such men are judges. To impute to arbitrators as a class the sort of cravenness embodied in Judge Hays' third charge is unjust in the extreme.

The second assumption is equally groundless. The judiciary is made up of men—mortals like us all—who may have been insulated from the pressures of concern for money but who may be prey to other more subtle pressures that could conceivably affect their decisions—the elected judge concerned about reelection, the appointed judge sensitive to the possibility of pressure from his political mentor, the subtle biases of birth or class with their influence on unconscious behavior. The great Cardozo stated it aptly:

> The spirit of the age, as it is revealed to each of us, is too often only the spirit of the group in which the accidents of birth or education or occupation or fellowship have given us a place. No effort or revolution of the mind will overthrow utterly and at all times the empires of these subconscious loyalties.[8]

The essence of the judicial temperament does not lie in an absolute freedom from biases, predilections, or even temptations. Even the saints never achieved that state of grace. It lies in the possession and exercise of those traits of character and moral strength that enable a man to recognize and exorcise these human weaknesses.

What magic is there in the judicial robe that ensures that judges will

---

[8]Benjamin Cardozo, *The Nature of the Judicial Process* (New Haven: Yale University Press, 1921): 174-175.

not yield to the pressures which surround them that is not also present in the business suit donned by the arbitrator? Who is to say that the sum total of the pressures on judges is the less or the greater than on arbitrators? Judge Hays appears to feel confident that he can render these Olympian judgments on arbitrators as a class with scarcely a nod to arbitrators as individuals.

The plain and simple fact of the matter is that all but a tiny minority of the judiciary possess judicial temperament in the sense that I have used the term and discharge their responsibilities in a manner that is a credit to their noble calling. Judge Hays has not supported either with fact or with logic his charge that the vast majority of arbitrators have done less. And I can think of no more fitting group than this Institute, with participants who have practiced before both, on which to test the hypothesis that arbitrators have performed as honorably and as competently in their sphere as judges have in theirs.

FLAWS IN JUDGE HAYS'S SOLUTION

A few more thoughts, and I shall have done. In his Storrs lecture Judge Hays posed optional solutions for the sad state of arbitration. In my opinion, they are as faulty as his diagnosis of the problem.

His first solution is "that the law get out of arbitration and leave the procedure exclusively to the parties." He would withdraw the courts from the enforcement of the promise to arbitrate and from the enforcement of awards, permitting those who think arbitration praiseworthy to indulge in it and relieving those who, like him, think it is usually undesirable from having to witness the spectacle of our courts rubber stamping the questionable results which the arbitrators have reached.

This solution overlooks the basic fact that grievance handling in American industrial relations is based very largely on the unconditional or slightly limited no-strike, no-lockout clause. Does he propose that, with arbitration wholly voluntary, such clauses be repealed and that the strike or lockout weapon be freely employed as the enforcer of engagements to arbitrate or as the persuader in grievance settlements? Or, on the other hand, does he propose the continuance of such clauses and the installation of voluntarism only on arbitration as the means of finally disposing of grievances?

His alternative solution is equally impractical. He states:

> For those who believe, for example, that a special expertise in labor problems is desirable for those who pass upon violations of collective bargaining agreements, there is the suggestion that we set up in this country a

system of labor courts after the model which has been so successful in countries like Germany, Sweden and Denmark.[9]

This suggestion overlooks a number of crucial matters. One is that trade agreements in these countries are relatively short, simple documents, covering only the broadest terms of employment and leaving either to legislative regulation or managerial discretion a whole host of other terms and conditions of employment.[10] The volume and detail of the collective agreements found in American industrial relations are unique. As a consequence those subjects susceptible of arbitration in the industrial courts of these countries are limited. By contrast, the variety and complexity of the issues that are arbitrated in the United States are many times greater, and the task of the industrial courts would thus be many times compounded.

In Sweden, there is a labor court for all of industry and a special arbitration board for piecework disputes in the building industry. One observer reports that the latter board hears about 300 disputes a year which is nearly twice as many as the National Labor Court hears for all the rest of Swedish industry.[11]

In Denmark the Permanent Board of Arbitration established by law is empowered to settle disputes about the interpretation of agreements, if requested by the parties. In practice, however, this type of case would be handled by an industry's own arbitration board headed by a privately selected arbitrator.[12]

But more than that, the industrial courts in the nations Judge Hays mentions hear grievances arising out of much smaller, much less diverse, much more compact economies. The chances of successfully implanting such a system on the diversity we have here are problematical at best.

I do not wish to be misunderstood. I do not intend, in refuting Judge Hays's charges, to present arbitration as we know it today as a model of perfection or the men who practice it as paragons of virtue. Arbitration needs much constructive criticism, and occasionally it gets it. But it deserves better than Judge Hays' broadside.

---

[9]Hays, *op. cit.*, p. 1037.
[10]William H. McPherson, "Grievance Settlement Procedures in Western Europe," *Industrial Relations Research Association, Proceedings of the 15th Annual Meeting, December 27-28, 1962* (Pittsburgh: IRRA, 1963): 26, 27, 33.
[11]Paul H. Norgren, *The Swedish Collective Bargaining System* (Cambridge: Harvard University Press, 1941):222.
[12]U.S. Bureau of Labor Statistics, *Labor Management Relations in Scandinavia*, Bulletin no. 1038 (Washington: U.S. Dept. of Labor, 1951).

6. Factfinding and Arbitration Decisions

In the following factfinding report Wallen answered a recalcitrant school board that feared grievance adjudication in much the same manner that private employers did before the War Labor Board. Wallen's decision explains the necessity for a mechanism to determine grievances and further explains the advantages of arbitration as the final stage of any such mechanism, as opposed to either the employer retaining the final say or the courts adjudicating the merits of individual grievances.

Decision of Factfinder in re *Lowell School Committee (Lowell, Mass.) and Lowell Teachers Organization*, May 19, 1967 (48 LA 1044)

* * *

GRIEVANCE PROCEDURE AND ARBITRATION

There was substantial agreement on the structure of a grievance procedure as set forth in Article II A 1 to 5 of Appendix A attached thereto. The conflict on this issue centers on the organization's proposal that grievances not settled in the lower steps of the grievance procedure be submitted to final and binding arbitration vis-a-vis the school committee's proposal that its decisions on such grievances be deemed final, the organization having the right to file a breach of contract action at law.

The need for a grievance procedure is apparent. Employees who feel that they are being treated in violation of their rights are entitled as a matter of good administration and elementary justice to be heard and to be represented. Unresolved grievances, whether real or fancied, depress morale, breed discontent, and reduce efficiency. Hence a mechanism for resolving grievances is essential.

But where grievances are heard and the parties hold opposing views on the justice of the matter, a mechanism for breaking the deadlock is also essential. When two parties meet as equals and draw up an agreement, one party cannot in good conscience insist that if there is a dispute over what it means, his decision will be determinative. It is elementary that there must be a referee or an umpire to judge disputes over the application of the rules of the game.

For the school committee to insist, as it has so far, that it shall be the last word on grievances is tantamount to the home team insisting on the right of its manager to call balls and strikes.

The well-nigh universal method of determining disputes over the meaning or application or collective agreements in American industry is final and binding arbitration by an arbitrator or board of the parties' mutual choice. This results in an impartial review of the merits of the case in the light of the commitments both parties made in their contract, in a speedy disposition of the case after a full and fair hearing and in a resolution on the merits without the interposition of technicalities and delays often involved in court proceedings.

If a party enters into an engagement in good faith, he does not fear third-party review of allegations that he has not fulfilled his commitment. On the contrary he favors it in the interest of clearing the air and ending the disgruntlement of the party who believes himself aggrieved.

Arbitration of grievances is the rule not only in labor agreements; its use is widespread in disputes arising out of commercial contracts. With the growth of collective bargaining in the public service, it is widely employed to resolve grievances in public agencies of all kinds....

* * *

The Lowell School Committee's opposition to this means of resolving grievances not settled by negotiations has never been satisfactorily explained. It appears to have stemmed initially from a misunderstanding by the school committee of the meaning of the term. In order to dispel any lingering misimpressions, it seems worthwhile to spell out what arbitration of grievances does not involve as well as what it does involve.

Arbitration of grievances does *not* involve a determination of the terms of new contracts. These are to be negotiated by the parties, with or without the aid of a mediator and factfinder. They are not to be imposed by a third party, including an arbitrator.

Arbitration of grievances can occur only after the parties have made a contract but have a disagreement over what it means or how it shall be applied. The arbitrator is barred from changing the parties' agreement; he may only interpret or apply it.

Arbitration of grievances may *not* be invoked as a means of making policy determinations for the administration of the school system. This is a function of the school committee that an arbitrator is not permitted to invade.

Arbitration may be invoked to determine if an act of a school administrator contravenes the commitments the school committee undertook in its contract with the Lowell Teachers' Organization.

If arbitration becomes necessary, the parties may select an arbiter of their mutual choice or they may ask a disinterested agency such as the American Arbitration Association or the State Board of Conciliation and Arbitration to appoint one if they fail to agree.

The school committee argues that whenever a grievance of a teacher remains unresolved, the teacher or the organization is free to file a suit at law. If seriously advanced as a reasonable alternative for arbitration as a means of speedily resolving unsettled grievances, it is a spurious alternative.

In the first place, lawsuits are usually time-consuming, expensive affairs involving pleadings, service of papers, lawyers, briefs, lengthy hearings, and appeals at great cost to the parties. Most of the grievances likely to arise in the day-to-day administration of a school system are simply not of a nature that lend themselves to this sort of procedure. The result is that the aggrieved teacher or the organization is likely to do nothing about such grievances.

If the school committee is aware of this possibility but nonetheless offers suits at law as a serious alternative to arbitration, it in effect says that it does not wish to have grievances of teachers decided on their merits for it proposes a means of determining the merits that it knows can seldom be employed.

If the school committee does, in fact, not wish to have grievances decided on their merits, it does the school system a great disservice. Disgruntled teachers who believe they are being handled unfairly and without a full hearing before a neutral body can scarcely be counted on to provide the community with the quality of education it expects.

In the second place, in a suit at law over a grievance alleging a breach of contract, the remedy the courts will usually afford is money damages. But most grievances arising under employment contracts involve insignificant claims for money damages. Nonetheless they may involve important rights and responsibilities of value to the parties but not measurable in money terms. The school committee cannot be aware of this fact and still persist in offering a suit at law as a viable means of settling grievances.

Third, Chapter 149 of the General Laws in Section 178K establishing collective bargaining for municipal employees sanctions "arbitration of disputes over the interpretation or application of the terms of a written agreement." Hence the inclusion of an arbitration clause in the contract with the Lowell Teachers Organization would not require the Lowell School Committee to break new ground or enter an area not within the contemplation of the legislators.

I am convinced that an arbitration clause for the disposition of unresolved grievances belongs in the grievance procedure....

The Arbitrator and the Arbitration Process 41

* * *

In the next decision, Wallen comments on the appropriate role of the arbitrator under a permanent umpire system, as well as the duties of the parties, before he gives his first grievance arbitration decision under their contract.

Arbitration decision in *General Tire and Rubber Company, Waco Plant and United Rubber, Cork, Linoleum and Plastic Workers of America, CIO, Local 312*, Jan. 24, 1949

This is the first decision by the umpire under the currently effective agreement between the General Tire and Rubber Company and Local No. 312 of the United Rubber, Cork, Linoleum and Plastic Workers of America, CIO. It is therefore in order to make some general observations as to the nature of the umpire function.

The basic terms of the relationship between these parties have been established by collective bargaining. The term "collective bargaining" sometimes means an amicable exploration of joint problems resulting in friendly agreement; sometimes it means a difficult, suspicious, unfriendly relationship out of which a meeting of the minds occurs only after pressure, threats of economic conflict, or strikes or lockouts. No matter what meaning the term has had in the relations between these parties in the past, the time has now come for them to develop a relationship based on a friendly desire to make a common undertaking work well. It is time for the parties to accept each other in good faith, to learn and understand each other's problems, and, without neglecting their own basic interests, to find mutually acceptable solutions to those problems. Only in this way will both parties reap the benefits of collective bargaining in the form of security, production, employment, and good conditions. This requires, however, that the leadership of both sides lay aside the mistrusts and suspicions created by conflicts now past and turn their attention constructively to the future.

The acceptance by the parties of the principle of the umpire system indicates that they are prepared to take this step forward. It is an indication of a desire to substitute reason and logic for force and passion in their day-to-day dealings. The umpire hopes to administer his trust with justice to the legitimate claims of both parties when judged in the light of the agreement they negotiated and thus to improve the character and quality of their collective bargaining relationship.

It will be the task of the umpire not only to provide answers in specific cases but also to develop principles and approaches to guide the parties when they discuss future grievances and make their friendly settlement easier. It is to be hoped that the parties will regard his decisions not alone in terms of the specific case, but also in terms of their broader principles to be applied for the duration of their contract.

* * *

In this case Wallen was asked to determine whether or not a previous award by another arbitrator had been complied with. Wallen made it clear to the parties that it was not his function to rehear the previous grievance or pass on the adequacy of the remedy, but merely to determine if the previous award had been complied with fully; he further elaborated on the usefulness of an abbreviated form of stare decisis or at least a conscientious respect for previous arbitral determinations.

Arbitration decision in *B.F. Goodrich Company and United Rubber, Cork, Linoleum and Plastic Workers of America, Local 43,* August 21, 1961

* * *

It is true that a *principle* embodied in a decision could conceivably be discarded in a future case if the arbitrator was so convinced that he or his predecessor erred that he could not in good conscience apply that principle in a subsequent case. And even a reversal of a principle established in an earlier case is likely to be the rare and unusual occurrence, for a conscientious arbitrator must weigh very carefully the virtue of continuing stability in the administration of the agreement as against any doubts he may have about the wisdom of a prior decision, his own or someone else's. He should reverse an established principle only on a showing of drastically altered circumstances or on a conviction of error so deep and profound as to overcome all other considerations.

* * *

Wallen here discusses the remedy powers available to the arbitrator to correct contract violations. In this case not only was the contract silent with respect to the arbitrator's powers to grant monetary relief, except for unjustified suspension or discharge, but such enabling language was specifically rejected by the company when it was proposed during contract negotiations.

Arbitration decision in *Firestone Tire and Rubber Co. and United Rubber, Cork, Linoleum and Plastic Workers of America, CIO, Local 261,* July 19, 1954

* * *

It is true that in the 1948 negotiations the union proposed and the company rejected language which would have required the company to pay employees for the time lost in the event they were improperly laid off. This language, if adopted, would have made back pay in such cases mandatory and the board of arbitration would have been without discretion to vary the requirement for such payment with the circumstances of each case. The rejection of this language, however, did not deprive the board of arbitration of the power to award back pay in such cases if in its discretion such was justified by the circumstances of the case and constituted a necessary and appropiate remedy for the right of which the employees affected were deprived....

The company argues that in the absence of specific authority, spelled out in the agreement, to make employees whole in such cases the board of arbitration is without power to make employees whole for the loss of earnings resulting from the company's maladministration of the seniority or equalization of hours provisions. This argument flies in the face of reason and of well-nigh universal labor relations practice. The agreement conferred upon the employees certain rights to jobs as spelled out in the seniority provisions. The administration of these provisions and, consequently, effective control over these rights, resides in the company subject to protest by the union through the grievance procedure. It is axiomatic that when one party is deprived by another of a right, clearly defined in the agreement, and he is thereby caused to suffer a monetary loss he is entitled not only to a reinstatement of that right but to recovery of the loss the wrongful action of the other party imposed upon him. To hold otherwise would be to give one party license to violate the agreement, whether intentionally or otherwise, on repeated occasions without any responsibility for the losses inflicted on the other party.

The power conferred upon the board of arbitration to apply the terms of the agreement carries with it the implied power to prescribe appropriate remedies for its misapplication. Had the language the union sought in 1948 been incorporated in the agreement the nature and extent of the remedy would have been fixed, leaving the board with no discretion in these matters. In the absence of such language, the board retains the power to temper the nature and extent of the remedy to the facts and circumstances of each case. If it awards back pay, that action is not punitive, as the company contends; it is remedial. Punitive damages are those awarded over and above the amount granted to make the damaged person whole. A back pay award to an employee because he lost employment by virtue of the failure of management to administer properly the seniority provisions is not granted to punish the company; it is granted to make up the loss inflicted on the employee. Similarly in the matter of equalization of hours.

* * *

Briefly, the following two decisions demonstrate the overriding respect Wallen gave clear and precise language, even if the results did not square with his own notions of fairness and reasonableness. They also shed some light as to the weight Wallen gave to reason and equity as factors to be considered in his decision-making process, particularly when he was considering the past practice of the parties.

Raytheon Manufacturing Company and International Brotherhood of Electrical Workers, AFL-CIO, Local 1505, July 1, 1957 (establishment of job classification)

* * *

... if ... terms are clear and explicit on their face then they must be taken to reflect the parties' intent. Only if they are ambiguous or unclear, would I have the right to interpret them in a manner which leads to a result that squares with *my own notions of fairness or reasonableness.* It is not the arbitrator's function to interpret language in such a manner as to yield a result he may deem more reasonable if to do so he must set aside the plain meaning of the words agreed upon by the parties. Where the parties set forth clearly their intent, he must assume that they did so advisedly, after canvassing carefully their respective interests. [Emphasis added.]

* * *

Brown Company and United Mine Workers of America District 50, Local 12175, April 1, 1948 (payment of overtime)

* * *

In determining the intent of parties to a contract, the meaning attached to the disputed language by the parties themselves in the past as shown by their actions is an important but not controlling factor. It may be qualified by a consideration of the circumstances under which these actions were taken. And it must be considered in the light of the reasonableness and equitableness of the results flowing from a given construction. An interpretation that would have an unreasonable or inequitable result is justified only where the evidence is overwhelming that the parties intended such a result.

In this unique case Wallen was unable to determine any common intent or meeting of the minds concerning the application of the agreement to a piece-rate dispute. Rather than construct an interpretation, and in light of the impending agreement expiration and the absence of a no-strike clause in the agreement, Wallen issued a finding of "no agreement."

Arbitration decision in *Merrow Machine Company and International Union of Electrical Workers, Local 249,* November 8, 1961

* * *

DISCUSSION

On their faces, the memorandum and Section F-7, both part of the new agreement, are antagonistic. The former recognizes the company's right "to put into effect . . . . a new system of time study for incentive payments. . . . " It does not say how or under what conditions the new system is to be put into effect. The latter guarantees existing piecework rates against reduction except on the occurrences of contingencies not present here. There cannot be *both* a right to replace established piece rates with new incentives and a guarantee of existing piece rates. Once a piece rate is replaced by a new incentive standard, which yields the same earnings for greater efficiency or lower earnings for the same efficiency, the existing piece rate is effectively reduced.

The basic question involved is whether the parties intended the memorandum to be subordinate to Section F-7 or whether they intended Section F-7 to be subordinate to the memorandum. It is plain that there was no meeting of the minds on this point. Neither party expressed his intent to the other for they did not meet face to face during this crucial stage of the negotiations.

Each party claims to have conveyed his intent to the mediator but there is no evidence that he conveyed that intent to the other party. Indeed, if he had, there would likely have been no agreement for it is plain that agreement was reached here precisely because each party relied on his own understanding of the relationship between Section F-7 and the memorandum. The parties authorized me to ask the mediator whether in his separate conversations with the parties, a common interpretation of the relationship between the disputed clauses was expressed. This I did, only to be informed that the rules of his agency forbid disclosure of conversations in mediation sessions.

Inasmuch as the history of negotiations sheds no light on the intent of the *parties* one is compelled to search for the intent of the *instrument*. Which is the more reasonable construction of the conflicting clauses? One possible test might be what parties similarly situated normally do when they agree on the installation of a new incentive system. But that test furnishes no useful guides here. When negotiators in collective bargaining agree on the installation of a new incentive system they usually agree on specific methods to be followed in its installation. And those methods are by no means uniform. In some cases they agree on the free replacement of existing, unchanged rates by new incentive standards. In others they agree on a gradual replacement of old standards by new ones as jobs are changed. In still others they agree on the immediate installation of the new standards combined with the transfer of excess earnings to the base rates. And there are other combinations. Each agreement is hand tailored; there is no prevailing pattern which can be said to constitute the intent implicit in this instrument.

The intent of a writing is sometimes established by adopting that construction which is the more logical under all the surrounding circumstances. But this too is of no help in this case. It was fully consonant with logic for the company to press for language enabling it to immediately replace existing piece rates with new incentive standards and it places no strain on one's imagination to interpret the two clauses in this manner. It was equally logical for the union to press for protection of existing piece rates even while agreeing to the use of a new system in setting rates on new or changed operations and it does not stretch one's credulity to read the agreement as so providing.

I find, therefore, that this is a case where the parties' minds never met and where the intent of the instrument is not established by recourse to the usual rules of contract construction. While such a finding may not be uncommon in judicial review of commercial contracts, it is rare in arbitral review of labor contracts. That is because the labor agreement usually represents a binding engagement for a protracted period in which the parties' relationship cannot be abruptly broken by a finding of no-contract without dire consequences to both. The labor agreement, written to assure continuity of production, usually binds the parties to bar strikes or lockouts during its life. A finding that the parties did not agree serves either to rupture their agreement entirely thus placing their continuing relationship in peril or, if their agreement survives in all other respects, to deprive them of the strike or lockout weapons which constitute the underlying incentive for coming to terms on the issue still open.

* * *

But, as said earlier, the agreement in this case is very nearly unique for these times. It does not contain a no-strike, no-lockout clause. It does not contain an arbitration clause. And it is within a few weeks of its expiration. These parties specifically contemplated the possibility of settling their differences over the meaning of their agreement by use of the strike or the lockout. An arbitral decision on this point at issue, absent convincing evidence of intent one way or the other, can only prejudice the current negotiations for a new contract in which the point here involved will be very much in issue regardless of any ruling in this case.

The following cases demonstrate Wallen's views regarding the parties' responsibility to each other and to employees in processing grievances. As will be seen, Wallen frequently applied the concepts of good faith, fair dealing, and neglect or undue delay in remedying meritorious grievances.

In the first one, Wallen outlines the circumstances under which retroactive awards are appropriate.

William Whitman Company, Arlington Mills Division, and United Textile Workers of America, Local 113, AFL, July 15, 1947

* * *

ARBITRATOR'S ANALYSIS

Good industrial relations practice recognizes the worth of the general principle that grievances over adjustments in wage rates are made retroactive to the date of the grievance. If undue delays in adjusting such grievances are avoided, then the employee is assured of fair treatment as of the day the inequity involved became a live issue. It is also a spur for the prompt disposition of misunderstandings between the parties. The worth of this principle has been recognized by the inclusion of specific language in contracts, and, in the absence of such provisions, in arbitration awards and by the War Labor Board during the war years.

But like all general principles, this one is valid in the absence of special circumstances which would make another rule appropriate to the particular case. Among the special circumstances that might call for the modification of this principle in a given case are the following:

    a. Undue delay in pressing or prosecuting the grievance on the part of the union. A union should not be permitted to neglect a grievance solely because it feels certain of a retroactive adjustment. This encourages delays in grievance handling and beclouds the employer's cost picture.

b. The development of new circumstances during the course of a dispute that affects its outcome. The development of such new circumstances may alter the retroactive date.

c. The existence of a period of time during which the employer was unable to settle the case due to circumstances beyond his control.

In short, the presumption is in favor of making grievance adjustments retroactive to the date of filing in the absence of contract provision to the contrary; but this presumption can be rebutted by facts that would establish its inappropriateness in a given case.

* * *

While Wallen favored the prompt disposition of grievances, as the previous case demonstrated, he also required that fair dealing be demonstrated. In this case, the company demanded that a grievance be held nonarbitrable because it was not processed promptly by the union and exceeded the allowable time limit for filling. Wallen dismissed the company's demand because the parties' past history was characterized by loose handling of deadlines.

Firestone Tire and Rubber Company and United Rubber, Cork, Linoleum and Plastic Workers of America, Local 336, May 18, 1959

---

* * *

I am impelled to reject the company's claim of untimeliness in the appeal of this grievance on several grounds.

The first is that grievance handling between these parties has been characterized by looseness in the matter of time limits for some years. The company may pull the pin if it wishes and tighten up on this practice, but having condoned loose handling it is not fair to permit it to do so on a particular grievance ex post facto. Rather it should be permitted to do so only after having given proper notice of an intention to revert to the basic provisions of the agreement.

* * *

In the two following cases, Wallen criticizes the disciplinary tactic of setting a trap for an employee suspected of wrongdoing and instead suggests a more constructive course of action, including consultation with the union and warnings to employees.

N.H. Poore Company and International Fur and Leather Workers Union, CIO, Local 21, April 16, 1947

* * *

To begin with, the arbitrator must observe that the setting of a trap instead of warning an employee and the union following an instance where the employee is strongly suspected of engaging in a practice that violates shop rules, is a questionable device if the aim of the parties is to maintain good industrial relations and a wholesome atmosphere in the department. The wiser course would have been to question the employee regarding the March twentieth incident in the presence of the steward and either to discharge her if the evidence was conclusive or to warn her if the circumstances were suspicious but guilt was not conclusively proven. This course is especially appropriate when it involves a worker of fourteen years' service whose job performance was acknowledged to be good and whose prior conduct in no way gave rise to suspicions as to her honesty.

The second observation is that if the company chose not to follow such a course of action, but decided instead to set a trap, it was under an obligation to set one that would work, and that would yield evidence of guilt beyond a reasonable doubt. The plan followed by the company to establish guilt has not proved beyond a reasonable doubt that Mrs. M_____ is guilty as charged. And in a case of this nature, where the charge is not an infraction of routine shop discipline, but is instead tantamount to a charge that the employee was stealing, proof beyond a reasonable doubt is required. This principle must be applied to cases of this kind, for they involve the good name of the individual involved, and that good name would be no less jeopardized by the finding of an arbitrator than it would be by the decision of a court.

* * *

Woonsocket Rayon, Inc., and Industrial Trades Union of America, Sept. 30, 1947

* * *

There is, however, one important aspect of the case which, while not altering its outcome, nevertheless deserves comment, for it is at the basis of the union's attitude toward the facts of the case. That is the fact that the company, instead of informing the union of its suspicions of H_____'s wrongdoing and enlisting its cooperation in eliminating it, chose instead to set a trap for the man and to confront him and the union with an accomplished fact. The union stated it had no desire to condone a practice of its members that endangers several hundred other union members, but it believed that trap-setting is destructive of the improved relationship that has developed between these parties over a period of years. The more moderate approach of informing the union committee of its suspicions so that both might cooperate in straightening out the individual involved would have been more in keeping with a relationship in which both parties are intent on fostering cooperation and good will.

The arbitrator is constrained to agree that the act of setting a trap for workers suspected of wrongdoing is not conducive to an atmosphere favorable to the continued development of good industrial relations. Were the feeling to become general that such an action is characteristic of the basic approach to discipline, it would tend to create a feeling of hostility toward management and an atmosphere of suspicion among workers. I am certain that the company has a more enlightened approach to such problems. I am equally certain that the union realizes that fact. I am of the belief, on the other hand, that the use of this technique in this case must be considered a step backward rather than a step in the direction of better industrial relations and should be avoided in the future. This is not to say that a company must always consult a union before gathering evidence and imposing discipline. But in cases where there is only a suspicion of a first offense it would be wiser to pursue the more moderate course of warning and notice and to leave the technique employed here for use in cases where warnings had been given.

On the other hand, howevermuch I may disagree with the course pursued by the company, I do not believe it mitigates the seriousness of the offense of which H_____ was guilty. His failure to test water endangered the health of many persons. It remains a serious offense warranting severe discipline even though it was discovered by use of a device which I feel is not the best way to conduct a relationship with a union.

Under the circumstances it must be ruled that H_____ was discharged for just cause. One certainly cannot blame the company for not wishing to trust this man with the job of testing water any longer. As an arbitrator, I would be remiss in my duty if I were to compel the company to reinstate H_____ under these conditions. On the other hand, I am cognizant of his fourteen years of service and of his otherwise reasonably satisfactory performance on his job. If a place could be found for him in some other department, the loss of his present job and the loss of pay for the past several months would constitute a reasonably severe punishment and would in all likelihood assure his being a model employee. It must be stressed, however, that this is a matter for the company's judgment and, while it constitutes my sincere recommendation as a course of action, it is not to be considered in the nature of an award.

The following six cases set forth Wallen's views regarding the rights and responsibilities of employees and union representatives in dealing with grievances and illegal work stoppages arising from unresolved grievances.

Trailways of New England, Inc., and Division 1318, Amalgamated Transit Union, AFL-CIO, December 22, 1965

* * *

1. The question before this board with respect to each grievant is whether or not he was discharged for cause within the meaning of that term as used in the parties' agreement dated April 23, 1961. The existence of cause involves a determination whether each grievant was in fact a participant, instigator, or leader of the illegal work stoppage; the circumstances, degree, or extent of his involvement; and if involved, whether that action considered in the light of the relevant aspects of his record of employment with the company justified the penalty meted out.

* * *

Before considering each individual case, a few general statements about the stoppage itself are in order.

The importance of this case to the parties lies as much in the need for the division to realize the nature of its obligations under its agreement with this management as it does in the justice of the penalties levied in the individual cases.

This division had a contract with the company that embodied many favorable terms and conditions of employment. These benefits did not spring full-blown from nowhere. They were made possible by the organizing efforts and the sacrifices of generations of trade unionists and by the ingenuity and energy of an alert management. Like most of the American labor movement, the Amalgamated had to struggle for the foothold which made it possible to achieve what the current generation of unionists too often take for granted.

Labor unions went through numerous strikes and conflicts to achieve written agreements with employers reluctant to recognize them. The collective agreement becomes the bedrock on which the whole structure of benefits—wages, union security, vacations, and protections against arbitrary treatment was built. This structure was created step by step and stone by stone.

The success of a union's efforts is made possible by the continued growth and prosperity of the employer. The growth of the service and the enhancement of efficiency are the sources of the gains in wages and benefits for the men. The collective agreement guarantees those benefits and at the same time protects the worker against arbitrary treatment.

In return for the concessions made to the union in collective bargaining, the employer secures one concession that is basic to his security as well as to the security of the men in his employ. That is a pledge that during the term of the agreement when a dispute arises it will be disposed of by processing through the grievance procedure. Implicit in the pledge to use the grievance procedure to settle such disputes is an understanding that work will be continued without interruption by either strikes or lockouts so that the company may continue to offer its services to the public and the men will continue to earn wages to their mutual benefit.

Whoever on the union's side subverts this commitment by instigating, leading, condoning, or participating in a wildcat strike attacks the fundamental basis of collective bargaining. He defiles that which the union has set out to achieve—a fair agreement to cover the terms of employment. He dishonors the pledged word of his union leadership and despoils the efforts of those who preceded him in erecting the structure of industrial relations which has replaced the jungle warfare of an earlier day.

Because he strikes so devastating a blow at the basic aims of both the management and his own union, such a person merits a severe measure of discipline. While the penalty should be graded to the degree of involvement and intensity of participation, it should properly be severe enough to impress on the leaders and on others that the leaders of and participants in a wildcat strike basically engage in an antiunion as well as an antimanagement act.

Protection against arbitrary treatment at the hands of management resides in the agreement's grievance and arbitration procedures. There are those who feel that these procedures are too time consuming and that in the end they do no more than to return to the employee that which he should not have been deprived of in the first place. The grievance procedure is indeed time consuming and arbitration does involve delay. But that is highly preferable to the alternative—lost wages on the part of many, interrupted service and losses to management, and the risk of loss of future business and employment.

The union leadership has a special responsibility to honor the pledged word of the union to abide by the agreement's constraints in exchange for garnering its benefits. The leaders of any organization, in return for the satisfactions of leadership—the sense of power, the rewards of personal satisfaction, and the perquisites of the office—must accept the responsibilities as well. At the very least, these include the obligation to refrain from promoting, encouraging, or condoning an illegal walkout.

This is the lesson which must be learned from the case at hand—that illegal work stoppages serve all involved ill; that they are antiunion as well as antimanagement in nature; and that they undo that which the long history of collective bargaining as we know it in this country has striven to create.

Having stressed the union's obligation to abide by the agreement's terms and procedures rather than to engage in wildcat strikes, we must stress as well the employer's obligation to abide by the terms of the agreement in dealing with violations of its provisions. It may not arbitrarily hand out the discharge penalty and expect it to be upheld where an employee was clearly absent from work for reasons disassociated with the stoppage. Nor may it mete out the same penalty to all where the classes of acts engaged in with respect to participation and/or leadership were different. The case of each employee involved in the illegal stoppage must be considered on its own merits.

. . . . The case of the instigator, of the active leader, or of the overt participant is not the same as that of the participant who did not favor the stoppage and would rather not have engaged in it but who lacked the strength or the will to act counter to the pressures of his peer group. Only the individual of rare courage and unusual strength of character will undertake a defiance of the will of his fellows even when he knows that their actions are wrong. The ordinary person reluctantly strings along with the group in such circumstances, lacking the fortitude to act in defiance of the group's position and in accordance with his own convictions. This is not a phenomenon confined to workers or trade unions. It characterizes human behavior in all walks of life that must be taken into account in dealing with human problems of all kinds.

We do not imply that such weakness is to be condoned and that such persons are to be relieved of culpability for their acts. But we do believe that any fair and realistic assessment of penalties for violations of the group's contractual commitments in such circumstances should take into account the nature, quality, and degree of the individual's involvement.

* * *

Against this background, we now turn to an examination of the evidence addressed to each grievant's involvement in the work stoppage.

I. This first category is comprised of former employees in a position of union leadership during the period of the stoppage. Each union official whether president, president-elect, vice-president, secretary-treasurer, or member of the executive board had an obligation of responsibility to both the union members and the company. As the executors and administrators of the agreement they had an obligation to do all in their power to see that the terms and conditions of the agreement were abided by the employees. It was one of their duties and functions concomitant with their leadership positions to raise their voices, even if convinced they would fall on deaf ears, to proclaim that a work stoppage is not the way to settle a dispute between the company and the union, that the parties have negotiated grievance and arbitration procedures to cover just such situations, and that to refuse to work before having even followed the existing procedures was a breach of the agreement likely to subject those engaging in that course to significant penalties.

* * *

Borden Chemical Company and International Chemical Workers Union, Local 553, December 9, 1959

* * *

The lesson to be drawn from this unfortunate case is that grievances real or fancied, must be handled through the orderly procedures of the contract and not by "hitting the bricks." Not only management but union members are entitled to rely on the contract negotiated for the parties' joint benefit as an instrument that promotes stability and order. That is its purpose. The grievance procedure may appear to take longer than it should but its end result is justice through reason.

* * *

Aluminum Company of America and Aluminum Workers International Union, Local 104, December 19, 1963

* * *

In any social group, including a union or a company, someone must act to accomplish the aims of the group. Where there is a measure of democracy, these acts are reviewable. In a unionized plant the agreement is the constitution by which the propriety of such acts are judged and the grievance procedure is the means by which such review is initiated and achieved. Just as a local union could not function if no business could be conducted pending a determination in the courts of the propriety of every action the officers or the majority propose to undertake, so a plant could not function if employees were free to refuse to perform a work assignment pending a determination in the grievance procedure that the order is or is not sanctioned by the agreement. Thus employees, including union officers, are obligated to obey such orders and perform such assignments even if wholly convinced of their impropriety. They may do so under protest and simultaneously file a grievance. They may not refuse such an assignment on the plea that it is in contravention of the agreement.

If, after having processed the grievance, it is established that the order did violate the agreement and a monetary or other loss for which the employee could be made whole was caused him, there is a basis in contract and equity for the employee to be made whole. If, on the other hand, the action taken was one not susceptible to such a remedy, the company will be adjured to desist from repeating the order. If, despite such a ruling, the company persists in making the same kind of assignment, a remedy designed to bar repeated agreement violations would have to be developed.

* * *

Aluminum Company of America and Aluminum Workers International Union, Local 104, December 18, 1963

* * *

The union leadership has a special responsibility to honor the pledged word of the union to abide by the agreement's constraints in exchange for garnering its benefits. . . . The responsibilities of leadership include the taking of positive, firm, and decisive steps to make it plain to their followers that a violation of the no-strike pledge is forbidden. If a wildcat strike is threatened, they have the responsibility to make clear the union's position that it is illegal and improper. By their conduct, the union leaders must not only refrain from condoning the strike but also make plain their repudiation of it and make manifest their attempts to end it. They should be held responsible for maintaining a firm position against a violation of the no-strike pledge, not only in their own councils but in a public way so that the rank and file will know, by means of all media of communication, that such a stoppage is destructive of the agreement and of the rights and interests of all concerned.

* * *

B.F. Goodrich Company and United Rubber, Cork, Linoleum and Plastic Workers of America, CIO, November 15, 1951

* * *

Article IV gives the company the responsibility to direct the working force. An employee who refuses to accept such direction is subject to discipline. Furthermore, an employee who instigates or incites fellow employees to refuse such direction also violates the agreement and is likewise subject to discipline. This principle is essential to enable the enterprise to function and to prevent the state of anarchy that would result if employees could make their own decisions as to which orders they will accept and which they will refuse.

* * *

.... If full-time union representatives [on the company payroll] are irresponsible, they must be curbed or displaced not by company action but by action growing out of the sense of responsibility of their organization. After all, their opposite numbers on management's side may take actions of equally drastic import. They are held responsible only to their own organization—the company—and not to the union. We see no justice in holding the full-time union representative responsible not only to his union and its members but to the company as well.

* * *

Nor should the foregoing be construed to mean that a committeeman or other union officer working in the plant may with impunity advise or direct fellow employees to refuse to obey orders of supervision. Such persons are primarily employees and act only secondarily as union representatives. They have a lesser degree of responsibility for authoritative decision making than do full-time union representatives. Their opportunity to check with higher levels on the propriety of a possible course of action is greater. They are responsible to management as employees as well as to their constituents and their organization as union representatives.

* * *

Boston Edison Company and Utility Workers Union of America, CIO, Local 369, May 19, 1953

* * *

.... A shop steward occupies the dual position of employee and spokesman for other employees. He has every right, and even the obligation, to be as vigorous in his defense of the union's and the workers' rights as he can be, but he is bound to exercise that vigor within the limits of normal conduct. If F_____ had struck S_____, it certainly could not be argued that his shop steward status protects him from the consequence. The verbal assault which occurred in the instant case may present a difference in degree but not in kind. While normal conduct at the L Street Station may well encompass the use of profanity for emphasis in speech, we do not believe it embraces the directing of personal insults of the type involved here at representatives of the other side. A shop steward has no license to ignore the rules of decent relations with fellow human beings, be they from the management or the union side. F____'s defense that he was talking to S____, the foreman, but not to S____, the individual, is a distinction we fail to fathom.

* * *

The next two cases deal with the job rights of union representatives who are also employees and whose job performance is interfered with by grievance representation duties. Wallen discusses the necessity for accommodation of business efficiency with the effective administration of the contract.

The Fafnir Bearing Company and United Automobile Workers of America, Local 133, September 15, 1960

* * *

Was the refusal to assign D____ to the four-machine job under these circumstances a violation of Section 2.3? That provision bars discrimination against "any Union officer or member by reason of his proper union activities."

D____'s "proper union activities" kept him away from his job a good part of the time. He was refused the opportunity to be put on a job considered superior to the one he was on solely because of the effect of those activities. This refusal, bottomed solely on the consequences of his proper union activities, violated Section 2.3.

The company's refusal to assign D____ was based on the assertion that his limited availability would have made such an assignment inefficient. Such inefficiency as may be involved is the inevitable price of administration of a collective bargaining agreement.

All business management is a compromise between the *most* efficient method and the one that is practical under current circumstances. Maximum efficiency in production might dictate the purchase of a multimillion-dollar machine; but management prudently forgoes this goal during the useful life of its current equipment because it balances the costs against the savings. Maximum efficiency might (theoretically) dictate the forced retirement of executives at 55. But to do so might so shake executive morale as to make it impractical. Maximum efficiency might dictate that a plant should be moved from a long-established location to a new one. But a company's sense of responsibility to the community causes it to forgo such an advantage in favor of modernization of the present location. Thus in business life maximum efficiency is forgone in favor of optimum efficiency.

So is it with the problem at hand. Maximum efficiency might dictate the manning of each job in the plant by men who will work it eight hours a day. But collective bargaining and written agreements are public policy. And the desirability of a grievance procedure, staffed by intelligent management and union representatives, is not only of the essence of collective bargaining but is recognized as sound personnel administration as well. An important unit of that procedure is the steward-foreman level. To make the procedure work, so that the obligations of the law and the contract are met and the benefits of a well-functioning grievance procedure can be realized, it is necessary to sacrifice the efficiency inherent in having jobs filled by stewards manned a full eight-hour day.

To say that an employee who is also a committeeman must suffer a handicap in his work career solely because he is engaged in activities sanctioned by the agreement is to impose on him liabilities arising solely out of his union activities. The imposition of such a handicap was intended to be barred by Section 2.3.

* * *

Curtiss-Wright Corporation and United Automobile Workers of America, AFL-CIO, Local 669, April 6, 1956

* * *

Is there any sanction in the agreement for holding that a chief steward who handles grievances in his area as required and who also is excused for union business because he is a part-time union official is ineligible for a promotion for which he otherwise qualified in terms of seniority and ability?

I find there is not. Such a man is, and properly should be, eligible for a promotion as are all other employees. The fact that part of his time may be taken in performing his duties as a steward or other union official is not a proper reason for passing him over. In his status as chief steward and elections committee member, D_____ is required to work when not handling grievances or properly excused for committee duties. The demands on his time are the same in his present job as they would be in the one to which he seeks promotion. If he is eligible to hold his present job, despite his record of absences due to union or union-company affairs, he is in all logic equally eligible to hold the job he seeks for which he is concededly otherwise qualified. So long as he is required to and does work his merit and ability on the job are subject to determination and recognition in accordance with the rules prescribed in the agreement. The fact that he is away from his job part of the time does not detract from either his seniority or his ability, the two promotion criteria set forth in the agreement.

* * *

Chapter II

The Nature of the Agreement

CLOSELY RELATED to Wallen's perception of the role of an arbitrator and the function of the arbitration process were his views regarding the nature of the collective bargaining agreement from which the arbitrator draws his authority. Wallen characterized the arbitrator's responsibility as that of rendering intelligent decisions "within the limits of the logic imposed by that which the parties themselves negotiated."[1] This chapter will attempt to examine Wallen's views regarding the nature of the negotiated collective bargaining agreement, which both limits and is the source of the arbitrator's authority.

There is virtually universal agreement among arbitrators that the collective bargaining agreement is in many ways different from the ordinary legal contract. The agreement is often characterized as an instrument of self-government.[2] This contractual function has frequently affected arbitrators' perceptions and rulings on the rights and obligations under such agreements. Frequently arbitrators are influenced by the past practice of the parties which often affects the parties' intent and expectations. In addition implicit agreements, such as informal grievance settlements and oral agreements made during both the negotiation and administration of the agreement, are generally accepted as a necessary part of the system of industrial government and must be so considered by the arbitrator.

---

[1] Saul Wallen, "Recent Supreme Court Decisions on Arbitration: An Arbitrator's View," *West Virginia Law Review* 63 (no. 4, June 1961): 295-308 at 306.
[2] Archibald Cox, "Reflections Upon Labor Arbitration," *Harvard Law Review* 72 (1959): 1492.

Wallen, in his lengthy career as an arbitrator, had many opportunities to expound his views regarding the nature of the agreement he was called upon to interpret, including the role that past practice, implicit covenants, and inherent management rights play in its interpretation. The following exerpts attempt to reveal Wallen's values in this regard.

Several of the decisions and opinions included in this chapter are among Wallen's most controversial, being both praised and damned by the parties and disinterested commentators. Particularly controversial was the Coca Cola Bottling Company *decision, where Wallen found an implied requirement of just cause for discharge in an agreement containing no explicit provision to that effect.*

Wallen's subcontracting decisions generated significant disagreement because of his rejection both of the unions' position that the recognition clause and seniority clauses constitute absolute bars to the contracting out of bargaining unit work and of managements' position that subcontracting is an inherent reserved right of management. Wallen's rejection of both of these positions, needless to say, generated significant opposition in both camps.

Wallen's arbitration decision in New Britain Machine Company *has been described by James C. Hill as arbitral heresy, but "heresy cut from the same cloth as some of the great dissenting opinions of Justice Holmes, Brandeis, and Cardoza, which have become the cornerstones of accepted Constitutional law today."*[3]

A. Past Practice

1. *The Silent Contract vs. Express Provisions: The Arbitration of Local Working Conditions**

In this article Wallen discussed and compared arbitration cases involving disputes over the discontinuance of local work practices and conditions under

---

[3]James C. Hill, "Remarks at Memorial Service for Saul Wallen," August 6, 1969.

Collective Bargaining and the Arbitrator's Role, Proceedings of the 15th Annual National Academy of Arbitrators, Mark L. Kahn, ed. (Washington: BNA, 1962).

contracts with and without specific clauses guaranteeing past practices and local working conditions. The excerpts reflect some of Wallen's general views concerning the role of past practice in arbitral decision making.

Not long ago I met a friend whose outlook on life has much to commend it to industrial relations practitioners. After an exchange of greetings, I asked him "How's your wife?" His reply was, "Compared to what?"

Implicit in his query was the recognition that the degree of toleration of one's present state can be measured only in relation to realistic alternatives and not in relation to unattainable panaceas.

Undoubtedly this concept was implicit in the thoughts of the framers of this program when they asked me to make comparisons of arbitration awards under contracts without a clause guaranteeing past practices or local working conditions with awards under contracts containing such a clause and when, in a giddy moment, I accepted.

I was asked to compare the restrictions imposed upon management under present practices subsumed or implied as part of a contract guaranteeing the continuation of existing work practices with those prevailing under contracts silent on the subject in such a specific area as crew sizes, contracting out of work, paid lunchtime, washup-time privileges, spell or relief arrangements, and the like. Put in language more likely to be encountered at the collective bargaining table, the problem for investigation may be stated thus: does it make a lot of difference whether or not an express provision dealing with the maintenance of past practices or local working conditions is inserted in a contract?

In the heat of battle, a conflict over the inclusion or elimination of a clause guaranteeing existing work practices is likely to be made into an all-or-none proposition. The impression given by management is that the excision or noninclusion of such a guarantee will create a managerial Valhalla in which industry planners will be free to pursue the goal of efficiency without the inhibitions of the past. Of course, the vow is made that in so doing, the best interests of the stockholders, the employees, the management, and the public will be considered with instantaneous justice for all. The possibility that the weight of the past may still be borne by parties under a contract silent on the subject of work practices scarcely enters the calculations.

The other side of the shield reflects the impression created by unions that noninclusion or reformation of clauses guaranteeing work practices are designed to eliminate any past practice, custom, or even local agreement and that the past, with its benefits and burdens, will no longer stand between the shivering employee and the rampaging employer.

The hard facts of life reveal, however, that under the silent contract the past nonetheless imposes restrictions on managerial prerogative and that under the contract with the express provision there remains a considerable latitude for change where change is due. It is true that this is not uniform in all areas of contract administration and that, overall, the express provision places greater restraints on managerial prerogative than does the silent contract. But the picture is not nearly as black or white as it has been portrayed.

* * *

The uses of past practice in the interpretation and application of contracts containing no specific past practice clause are well known. Richard Mittenthal in his excellent contribution to the analysis of this subject presented at these meetings a year ago summarized the function of past practice in contract administration and interpretation as follows:

> Past practice can help the arbitrator in a variety of ways in interpreting the agreement. It may be used to clarify what is ambiguous, to give substance to what is general, and perhaps even to modify or amend what is seemingly unambiguous. It may also, apart from any basis in the agreement, be used to establish a separate enforceable condition of employment.[2]

The use of past practice to clarify what is ambiguous and to give substance to a contract's generalities is too commonplace to require discussion. The norms of conduct laid down by the parties themselves are employed to establish their intent under contract language that can be read several ways or that is vague or unclear because it is broadly written. The presence or absence of a past practice clause would scarcely serve to alter the use of past practice for this purpose.

The proposition that past practice can be used "to modify or amend what is seemingly unambiguous" rests on a more dubious foundation. Those who argue that it is often permissible, when an arbitrator is confronted with a conflict between an established practice and a seemingly clear and unambiguous contract provision, to regard the practice as an amendment to the agreement[3] rest their argument on the legal theory of reformation.[4] They maintain that the parties' day-to-day actions, when they run counter to the plain meaning of the contract's words, evidence an intent to substitute that which they actually do for that which they

---

[2] Richard Mittenthal, "Past Practice and The Administration of Collective Bargaining Agreements," *Arbitration and Public Policy* (Washington: BNA, 1961): 30-31.

[3] As did Mittenthal; also Benjamin Aaron, "The Uses of the Past in Arbitration," *Arbitration Today* (Washington: BNA, 1955): 1-12.

[4] See, for example, General Controls Co. (Jones), 31 LA 240.

said in writing they would do. Williston is usually quoted in support of this "reformation" doctrine.

But this approach, it seems to me, is in derogation of an important function of the collective bargaining agreement. The labor agreement, while sharing some of the characteristics of a commercial contract, is something more. Harry Shulman saw the collective agreement as "in part . . . a dictated statement of rules, particularized and clear; in part . . . a constitution for future governance requiring all the capacity for adaptation to future needs that a constitution for governance implies; . . ."[5]

To these attributes I would add one that is, I think, frequently overlooked. The collective agreement is also a tool of in-plant administration, an instrument of control, employed both by management and union administrators. In a fair-sized enterprise the men who drafted the agreement are usually far from the scene of its day-to-day administration. The gap between making and execution of policy is often wide and may lead to far different results at the bench than was intended at the bargaining table.

Where this happens, there is much to be said for the idea that the collective agreement's clear language should be considered as the lodestar that enables the top management of the company or the union to correct the deviations from course introduced by subordinates during their day-to-day operations. If the deviations are regarded as evidence of an intent to modify the clear terms of the agreement, the agreement's value as an instrument of control is thereby diminished. At best, this reformation theory must be approached warily and, if invoked at all, applied only where the course of conduct that runs counter to the language was known to and approved by those with the power to contract.

* * *

2. Arbitration Cases

The following rather interesting "trilogy" of cases demonstrates how Wallen applied some of the views expressed in the previous article.

General Tire and Rubber Company and United Rubber, Cork, Linoleum and Plastic Workers of America, Local 9, December 9, 1966

---

[5]Harry Shulman, "The Role of Arbitration in the Collective Bargaining Process," in *Collective Bargaining and Arbitration* (Berkeley: Institute of Industrial Relations, University of California, 1949).

The Nature of the Agreement

In this case Wallen required mutual intent for the establishment of a binding past practice. Precedent established by pressure or force contrary to the wishes of one of the parties was deemed insufficient to establish a binding past practice.

* * *

These grievances rest on no claimed contractual violation. No contract provision states that management must replace all absentees with overtime. On the contrary, the management clause Article V, reserves to the company the right to direct the work force and this includes the right to determine whether or not work shall be done. The rest of the agreement determines who shall do the work in line with seniority, overtime distribution rules, etc., if the company decides to do the work.

However, the union's claim rests on an alleged practice to man all absentees' jobs with overtime in these tire departments if any are manned. A practice is an *agreed-upon, jointly accepted* way of doing things. While it may develop out of custom, that custom reflects a tacit understanding that the practice is the product of a meeting of the minds.

What we have here at best is a way of replacing absentees which has grown, not out of a meeting of the minds that it is proper, but out of the company's need to overcome the refusal of any of the affected builders to accept overtime if all were not offered it. When the company yields to this tactic, a practice enforceable as a right under the agreement is not created thereby because the underlying mutuality is absent. The men's pressure tactics may have consistently induced management to yield but they did not create an enforceable *right* to have the company yield. If it chooses to stand its ground on its clear right to man a job or not, management may do so and the fact that it yielded to the men's refusal to work overtime in the past does not mean it must yield in the future.

This still leaves the men free to refuse proffered overtime if they choose. But nothing in the agreement or elsewhere compels management to replace any or all absentees by overtime.

* * *

General Tire and Rubber Company and United Rubber, Cork, Linoleum and Plastic Workers of America, Local 9, April 8, 1959

In this case, acquiescence over time was considered by Wallen as evidence of mutuality of intent and hence the basis for a valid claim of a binding practice.

* * *

This case brings to mind the story of the chambermaid in a summer hotel who, on her first day on the job, entered Room 604 where she was promptly raped. Later, in describing her experience she said, "After that, it was rape, rape, rape all summer long!"

We may safely conclude that in this case there was, after a bit, acquiescence. The same is true of the case at hand. Whether or not a foreman told the man to use the No. 1 rate originally, they did it for over ten years with the full knowledge of supervision and the company's timekeeping department. The application of the No. 1 rate to the No. 3 calendar was not outlandish or illogical. Nor was this a case of overpayment due to some manual or clerical error. The long continuance of the use of the No. 1 rate on the No. 3 calendar without demurrer must be deemed evidence of at least a tacit understanding that it was appropriate.

* * *

Sylvania Electric Products, Inc., and International Union of Electrical, Radio, and Machine Workers and its Affiliated Local 352, January 10, 1962

In this case there was also evidence of past management acquiescence when a union time study engineer had been allowed unlimited plant access without contractual right and clearly contrary to contractual procedures. Wallen here limited the liability created by the past practice and allowed management to exercise its clear contractual rights, even if it entailed altering past policies.

* * *

I have a full appreciation of past practice's role in the administration of labor agreements. I recognize the validity of its use to clarify ambiguities, to give substance to generalities, perhaps to create obligations to continue conditions of employment not covered by an agreement. But I draw the line at using past practice to modify or amend what is unambiguous in an agreement. A labor agreement is an amalgam of the interests of many parties. On the union's side there are the international, the local union, and the members. On the company's side there are the corporation, the division, the plant officials, and the foreman. It does not lie in the hands of any single pair of these to compromise the interests of the others by regarding actions of theirs which are counter to the agreement's terms as a manifestation of power to change those terms where they are clear.

A moment's reflection will confirm the validity of this thesis. Suppose in the years past a strong plant manager had adamantly refused to let the local union send any time study man into the plant. Suppose a weak union leadership had accepted this refusal. Suppose further, the same contract language as we have here. Would a more vigorous union leadership now be barred from asserting its right to use a time study man on the theory that the parties prior conduct had in effect negated that right?

* * *

In the following two cases Wallen limited the effect of past practices acquiesced to by management where the practice violated clear and reasonable work rules and contractual obligations.

The Fafnir Bearing Company and United Automobile Workers of America, Local 133, January 22, 1962

* * *

It is first essential to pin down exactly what the claimed practice was. It was for the men to remove the last billet from the furnace at about 2:30, forge it, reload the furnace, stow tools, and then go to wash up. When the men drifted into taking out the last billet earlier and doing all the postliminary tasks in order to be finished by 2:30 so they could leave at that hour to wash up, they violated the rule. And while supervision had trouble policing the rule, there is no evidence that they acquiesced in its violation to the point of assenting to a new practice.

Hence the most the union can now press for is the restoration of the rule as it previously existed. To the extent that the men finished their last billet earlier and left the forge shop at 2:30, they violated the rule.

Management apparently sought to curb the violation by insisting that the men not leave to wash up until 2:42 P.M. Thus if the last billet was forged at 2:30 the men would have about twelve minutes to reload the furnace, clean up around the workplace, and stow tools and would still have eighteen minutes to clean up.

This is about what the men were supposed to do originally and did for many years. It would scarcely seem to matter if the rule is stated in terms of working until 2:30 or leaving for the shower room at 2:42. The result is the same. Forging ends at 2:30 in either case and washup follows reloading tool storage.

A long-standing past practice like washup time may not be unilaterally altered unless a change in conditions occurs making the practice obsolete. If this does not happen, the union may properly insist on enforcement of the practice. But it may not insist upon a right to have the men's unilateral violations of the prior rule enforced as a practice. And that is what is being asked here. The union wants the right to leave the forge shop at 2:30. That was not the original practice. It was a perversion thereof. What the men are entitled to, and all they are entitled to, is a restoration of the old practice before it was perverted. That is that the men are to continue forging until 2:30, then reload, clean up the work area and stow tools, and then go to the shower room. If this can be done in less than twelve minutes, well and good. If it takes until 2:42 there is still ample time, in the present state of use of the available shower facilities, for the men to shower and check out by 3:00 P.M.

* * *

Firestone Tire and Rubber Company and United Rubber, Cork, Linoleum, and Plastic Workers of America, Local 336, December 8, 1960

* * *

.... Employees may not ignore specifications, boost earnings thereby, and use the earnings thus illegitimately achieved as a basis for the establishment of revised piece rates when a job is revised. The employee has an affirmative obligation to adhere to specifications. He earns no vested right to ignore them merely because supervision is not omnipresent and constantly reminding him to follow them. Unless departure from specifications is in fact authorized, the employees may not claim a right to a continuation of their benefits solely because management failed to enforce them in the past.

* * *

.... An employee has no vested right in the fruits of improper conduct even if he is not punished for it. If [he is] not disciplined, that which occurred in the past is overlooked but no future rights are thereby created. Supervisors have a right to expect employees to adhere to specifications and, where deviated from, to require such adherence from any given point on.

* * *

In the next two cases Wallen did not find that the past practice of the parties created a binding precedent, and management was accordingly given the opportunity to alter its methods and rules. In both cases, the first one dealing with the invocation of new rules and the second dealing with the reinstatement of rules allowed to lapse, Wallen required management to give clear notice of the change and an explanation before enforcing the changed rules and policies through disciplinary action.

The Crescent Company, Inc., and United Steelworkers of America, AFL-CIO, December 3, 1959

* * *

.... When a past practice is discontinued an obligation is created to announce and explain the new rule in clear and unequivocal terms. An essential of sound personnel administration is the issuance of clear-cut orders and, where these involved a break with prior procedures, they should be accompanied by an explanation.

* * *

Goodall-Sanford, Inc., and United Textile Workers of America, AFL, Local 1802, August 29, 1952

* * *

.... This arbitrator has stated in an earlier decision that a shop rule which is permitted to lapse through nonenforcement may not be reinstated by summary disciplinary action against an employee for an alleged infraction of it. Reinstatement of such a rule should be preceded by some kind of notice to the employees that it is once again in force. Absent such a communication, employees may reasonably draw the inference that nonenforcement over a sustained period means that the rule is no longer in force.

* * *

B. Implicit Rights and Responsibilities

1. Arbitration Cases

In the following two cases, Wallen found an implicit employee protection against discharge except upon a demonstration of just cause, even where the contract is silent with respect to discipline and discharge.

Coca Cola Bottling Company of Boston and Retail, Wholesale, and Department Store Union, Local 513, 1949

* * *

The clear terms of agreements must be respected no matter how distasteful the results to one of the contracting parties. And while the caveat emptor approach to labor negotiations may leave much to be desired from the standpoint of developing sound relations between management and its employees, it cannot be deemed an adequate reason for deleting from a contract an onerous provision which an inadequately informed negotiator agreed to or adding to a contract a beneficial one which he overlooked.

In short, if this contract clearly and unequivocally removed discharges from the realm of the grievance and arbitration procedure, as arbitrators we could do naught but honor that language. But this contract does not by specific language reserve to or confer upon the employer the right to discharge at will. The claim that such a reservation exists rests not on a clear, unambiguous statement but on inferences drawn from several of its provisions. On the other hand the contract does not by specific language confer upon the union the right to have discharges made subject to the grievance and arbitration provisions. The present issue, then, revolves not around a dispute respecting compliance with the agreement's terms but around a dispute as to its meaning. Having determined that the instrument's words do not state the exclusion of discharges from arbitration, we must next determine whether such an inference is reasonable from the language the parties employed.

A contract is an instrument whereby the parties assume reciprocal rights and obligations. Some obligations of the parties are not expressed but nonetheless are implicit in the instrument's written terms. It is the proper part of contract construction to determine those meanings that reside in the logic of the contract and that are necessary to preserve its integrity. Not only its segments, but the instrument as a whole must be examined to ascertain the parties' intent.

An examination of the contract as a whole leads to the conclusion that the meaning urged by the company cannot be imputed to it. For to do so would destroy the instrument's integrity by reducing several of its important provisions to a nullity. For example, Article IX guarantees to employees a measure of job security by providing for layoff and recall according to seniority. If the employer has the unrestricted right to discharge, as the company claims, the job security provided by Article IX is meaningless for its guarantees could be nullified by the exercise of that right. An employee could be discharged immediately upon recall in order that a less senior employee could be reached. Likewise, the provisions of Article XI dealing with the adjustment of grievances could be defeated by the use of the unlimited power of discharge. It would be unreasonable to conclude that the parties intended that these provisions, important pillars of the contract, could be so easily nullified.

But further than that, the interpretation urged by management is inconsistent with the entire logic of the agreement. For the collective bargaining agreement is an instrument one of whose basic purposes is job security, as the guarantee of layoff and recall according to seniority contained in this contract attests. Can one say it was the intent of the parties on the one hand to guarantee job security in the matter of layoffs and on the other hand to deny it in the matter of tenure? Hardly so. No labor organization (with possibly a few rare exceptions) could justify such a position and few employers are so naive in the present state of industrial relations practice, as to expect it. And if the company in this case did actually expect it, counsel would almost certainly have sought to make specific reference to the unrestricted right of discharge in the contract.

In our opinion, the meaning of the contract, when viewed as a whole, is that a limitation on the employer's right to discharge was created with the birth of the instrument. Both the necessity for maintaining the integrity of the contract's component parts and the very nature of collective bargaining agreements are the basis for this conclusion. Inasmuch as this limitation is an implied term of the contract, discharges are subject to the grievance procedure and arbitration.

* * *

Draper Corporation and United Steelworkers of America, February 7, 1967

In the next case, the agreement required just cause for discharge, but was silent with respect to discipline short of discharge. Wallen responded to the company's assertion that just cause need not be proven for disciplinary suspensions.

* * *

The proposition that the company may discharge only for just cause but may discipline by suspension for other than just cause runs counter to logic. Parties are free to make illogical bargains. But if they choose to make a bargain that flies in the face of logic and runs counter to universal custom and practice, it must be so clearly expressed as to evidence that intent unmistakably and unequivocally; short of that, the language they write must be interpreted in a manner that supports the logical rather than the illogical alternative.

* * *

In addition to the implicit employee protection against discipline and discharge except for just cause, Wallen in applying this principle, also established an implicit employee obligation: that of providing his employer "a fair day's work." The following cases demonstrate how Wallen applied this concept.

Clarostat Manufacturing Company, Inc., and International Union of Electrical, Radio, and Machine Workers, CIO, Local 242, August 13, 1954

Let us deal first with the union's argument that because the plant rules, incorporated by reference into the agreement after being developed by discussion between the parties, do not list inefficiency as grounds for discharge the employer has foregone the right to discharge inefficient employees. The list of offenses for which the discharge penalty would be warranted is not by its terms an exclusive catalogue of offenses for which employees may be terminated. It is a listing of offenses which the parties agree are sufficiently serious to warrant discharge. There may be others on which the parties are not in agreement as to the appropriateness of the discharge penalty and which were for that reason not listed. No list of plant rules can be expected to catalogue the many varieties of human behavior against which the employer's normal power to discipline may be levied and the omission of one variety does not mean that with respect to that offense this power has been relinquished.

An inefficient employee is subject to the employer's power to discipline and, in a case where the evidence warranted, it could constitute just cause for discharge. The chronically inefficient employee fails to live up to the bargain that is implicit in his contract of employment to give in return for his wage an acceptable level of production.

What is an acceptable level of production? In day-work plants with no established production standards it is embodied in the concept of a fair day's work. This, in the absence of other standards, is that amount of output that falls within a reasonable range of the output of the group with which the employee works. If an employee working under substantially the same conditions as others gives output reasonably close to the average of the group, and there is no evidence that the output of the entire group is inordinately low, then that employee is giving an acceptable level of production.

* * *

Fabet Corporation and Gloucester Sea Food Workers Union, Series 1572-1, International Longshoremen's Association, June 23, 1949

* * *

Implicit in the agreement is the obligation to give a fair day's work in return for a fair day's pay. In return for his wages an employee should work at a normal and reasonably consistent pace which will neither undermine his health nor deprive management of the benefit of his capacities. The deliberate failure of employees to give a fair day's work is a breach of discipline subject to management's normal disciplinary powers.

* * *

. . . . Evidence or testimony of an excessively slow working pace, of loitering or idling, of excessive relief time or time away from the work station, and the like would be needed to buttress the claim that the worker's below-capacity output was deliberate. Data showing that several employees were producing the same amounts would be regarded as tending to establish limitation, but only under circumstances where the production represents less than a fair day's work and where the uniformity of output is maintained for a reasonable length of time. Equal output as between several cutters during a short period might conceivably be the result of more than normal output by some, given to match the normal output of others. In short, while one of these several types of evidence tends to raise a suspicion of production limitation, a reasonable combination of several types is required to establish by a fair weight of the evidence that degree of guilt to justify the penalty of discharge. And the burden is on management in such cases to prove its case by a fair weight of the evidence.

* * *

Sylvania Electric Products, Inc. and International Union of Electrical, Radio, and Machine Workers of America, CIO, Local 608, September 8, 1953

Let us deal first with the company's contention that absent a specific contract provision, management has a right to set the level of production required for continuation on the job. Unless limited by specific agreement, the right to determine the adequacy of performance levels resides in management, provided it is exercised reasonably to require no more than a fair day's work as shown by measurements of adequate performance such as time studies or the prevailing standards of performance in similar tasks and provided it takes into account inherent employee handicaps of which management had prior knowledge. We must reject categorically the company's claim to the right to continually revise upward the level of production that could be required of employees which it claims to possess, at least in theory. . . . The right to determine production levels, where not set by specific agreement of the parties, may not be exercised to require of employees more than is fair and reasonable as those terms are established by reference to other objective criteria.

What are such criteria? Let us assume for the moment a day-work job on which no established production standards are in existence. Actual performance of the employees on the job has averaged x pieces per hour and this average has been produced (with variations in some days and weeks) for a long period of time. Management in that case could require the employees over a period of time to boost their average to x plus five pieces per hour if it could sustain the burden of establishing that its new requirement does not cause the employees to exceed the bounds of a fair day's work. This it could attempt by time studies, by reference to prevailing performance standards on similar or related jobs in the plant. In short, in such a case the past level of production creates a presumption of adequacy in terms of a normal day's work, but this presumption is rebuttable by evidence tending to establish that it is below a commonly accepted standard of normality. If management successfully rebuts this presumption, if it is established that the individual employee was not hired with knowledge that he is a subnormal producer (a handicapped employee), and if it is demonstrated that ample opportunity has been given the employee to achieve the reasonable level of output, then the application of reasonable disciplinary measures would be in order and would be sustained. It should be stressed that the failure to achieve such reasonable level would not be measured by performance on a single day or week, but rather by performance over a sustained period of time.

* * *

In summary, then, 75 percent of superior operator standard (in the case at hand) would appear to be the level of a fair day's work which management can reasonably expect but which it cannot compel employees to exceed. Management would have the right to exercise its normal powers of discipline in the case of employees who, after having had ample opportunity to learn the job, fail or refuse to achieve this level of output.

Whether management has the right to "classify any one employee who has been assigned to a job on standard but has never attained 75 percent of standard as a job failure and to remove him from the job" is a question which cannot be answered with a simple yes or no. If the failure to achieve this level of production had been persistent rather than sporadic, if it was not due to any inherent handicap of the employee previously known to management, if the employee's average performance is at or near this level even though there are reasonably short spans when she fails to achieve it, if there are no production conditions beyond the employee's control acting as deterrents to the attainment of a fair day's output, if there have been reasonable attempts to get the employee to give a fair day's work by the prior imposition of lesser forms of discipline such as warnings, reprimands, and penalty layoffs and these have produced no results, then the application of further disciplinary measures, which could include removal from the job where found appropriate in the particular case, would be in order because the employee's unwillingness or inability to produce at the level of a fair day's work will have been demonstrated. If, on the other hand, the failure to achieve 75 percent of superior operator standard is occasional or sporadic, if production conditions interfere, if it is due to an inability to produce of which management had prior knowledge, if prior attempts to induce increased output through lesser forms of discipline had not been attempted, then the fact of an employee's unwillingness or inability to produce at the level of a fair day's work will not have been demonstrated and the answer to the question would be, in that case, in the negative.

* * *

In the following case Wallen explicitly set forth his views regarding the inherent right to a certain measure of job security for employees which is provided by the collective labor agreement. The case involved the replacement of bargaining unit employees with nonunit employees, with the company asserting that it was exercising a prerogative granted under the management rights clause.

New Britain Machine Company and United Electrical, Radio, and Machine Workers of America, CIO, Local 207, April 7, 1947

* * *

The basic purposes of collective labor agreements are well known. One is to fix wages, hours, and working conditions for employees whom they cover. Another is to provide the employees with a measure of job security through rules governing layoffs, rehiring, and transfers. Job security is an inherent element of the labor contract, a part of its very being. If wages is the heart of the labor agreement, job security may be considered its soul. Those eligible to share in the degree of job security the contract affords are those to whom the contract applies. In the case at hand the article governing recognition clearly sets forth that the contract applies to watchmen but not to guards, and Article I, D with equal clarity limits the benefits of the agreement to "Employees covered by this agreement as defined by this Article."

The transfer of work customarily performed by employees in the bargaining unit to others outside the unit must therefore be regarded as an attack on the job security of the employees whom the agreement covers and therefore on one of the contract's basic purposes.

The company urged that the clause governing rights of management justified its action in transferring work customarily performed by watchmen to other workers outside the unit. The management clause is designed to give management the freedom to conduct its affairs in the interest of efficient production, but this right may be exercised only within the framework of the limitations imposed by the contract. That clause cannot be utilized as carte blanche to defeat one of the basic aims of the contract.

If one of the purposes of the contract as a whole, and of the seniority provisions in particular, is to assure the bargaining unit employees a measure of job security then such security would be meaningless if the company's view in this case were to prevail. For it would mean that without regard to prior custom or practice as to the assignment of work, the company could continuously narrow the area of available job opportunities within which the seniority clause functions by transferring duties performed by bargaining unit employees to employees not covered by the agreement. Not only the seniority clause but the entire agreement could thus be vitiated.

* * *

In the next case management claimed a right not specifically delineated in the agreement. The contract did not contain a management's rights clause, and the company asserted that it needed to change its operating procedures. The union insisted that such changes be jointly agreed upon, or arbitrated, before implementation and refused to work under the new procedures. Wallen held that management had the inherent right to make such decisions, that the work refusal was a contract violation, and that the union's appropriate response would have been to grieve resulting inequitable working conditions after implementation of the changes through the grievance procedure.

Novelty Shawl Company, Inc., and Textile Workers of America, CIO, Local 75, September 8, 1946

* * *

Implicit in every collective agreement is the right of management to conduct normal business operations and make normal management decisions and the right of the union to have a voice in such decisions of management as would impose arbitrary changes in working conditions previously established. When these rights are not explicitly defined, a contract may properly be construed to protect for each party the rights set forth above.

In the instant case, the rights of the parties with respect to changing loom assignments are not specifically spelled out. Since the right of management to manage and the right of the union to have a voice in matters that would arbitrarily alter working conditions meet head-on in these controversies, it becomes necessary to place a construction on the contract that appears reasonable under all the circumstances and that does the least violence to the implicit rights of either party. The arbitrator is of the opinion that the contract must therefore be construed as follows: First, when a new construction is introduced or an old one is drastically altered or there is a change in job conditions, the company has the right to fix the loom assignment and the union is obligated to give it a reasonable trial. If the union believes it to be excessive, it shall, while continuing to work the loom assignment, invoke the procedures of Section 4 of the contract. Second, if a loom assignment is instituted by the company and is not protested by the union after a reasonable time, it may not thereafter be changed by the company, in the absence of a change in job conditions, without prior negotiation with the union and the following of the procedures provided in Section 4.

* * *

The inherent right of management to conduct its business operations efficiently and effectively and the implicit employee right to some measure of job security, both highly esteemed by Saul Wallen, come directly in conflict in arbitration cases dealing with the subcontracting of bargaining unit work. The rest of this chapter examines Wallen's treatment of this difficult issue.

2. *How Issues of Subcontracting and Plant Removal are Handled by Arbitrators**

When an arbitrator says that under an agreement containing no express limitation on the right to contract out, the question of the right to contract out is not black or white, the average management or labor representative still sees red. To him the silent contract is shrilly articulate.

To the employer or his spokesman the contract's silence shouts an intent to preserve for him the untrammeled exercise of his reserved rights to determine, in the name of efficiency, what work should be done by his own employees and what should be done by other parties with whom the union has no direct relationship.

To the union or its spokesman the silent contract is not silent at all. The recognition clause designates the union as bargaining agent for the employees engaged in production and maintenance work. The seniority clause confers on them the right to such work when it exists to be done. The union security clause guarantees the union as an entity. The wage clause puts a price on the work to be done. Singly or in concert, these

**Industrial and Labor Relations Review* 19 (no. 2, January 1966): 265-272.

The Nature of the Agreement

provisions bespeak an intent to retain for the bargaining unit all production and maintenance work, the union argument runs. If the right to remove some of the work from the unit and have it done by others is recognized, it follows that all of it can be removed, leaving the union with an agreement that is a mere shell.

Fortunately for the institution of arbitration and for labor relations generally, a second look changes the perspective. For when pressed, it is the rare management that claims an *unlimited* right to contract out.

Some years ago a tire company executive argued before me that a silent contract gave him the right to do as he saw fit about letting out maintenance work. I asked him whether by the same logic he could not contract with someone else to supply him with production workers to man his tire-building machines and produce tires at a lower cost. His reply was "Oh, we wouldn't do that!" Why not? It would be cheaper and in that sense "more efficient." And if he never limited his reserved rights to determine whether to use his own or someone else's employees to produce his goods, why shouldn't he *want* to do so.

His inability to make a reasoned reply stemmed from an innate recognition that even though his contract made no specific reference to the subject of subcontracting, one of its unstated assumptions was that the right to contract out is fettered by the obligation not to defeat the contract's underlying aims and purposes.

So is it with union spokesmen when pressed on the point. They usually start with the argument that contracting out violates the recognition clause. Does that mean that all contracting out is barred? "Yes!" they say. What if there is a breakdown of a magnitude or character which the employer's maintenance force cannot handle? "Oh, that would be different!" What if that force could do the work but not without a delay that would be costly both to the employer and to other employees? "Well, there is no intent to bar the letting out of work in those circumstances!" What if the employer does not have the facilities or equipment to do the work, while the outside supplier does? "That presents another kind of problem!"

Thus qualifications, compelled by the logic of the productive process, necessarily modify the allegedly unqualified right.

BALANCING RIGHTS AND RESPONSIBILITIES

The long and the short of the matter is that the very essence of a collective agreement implies *some* limitation on the power to contract out work and that with the signing of a labor agreement, the right previously held is no longer absolute. At the same time, where the agreement is silent on the subject, such implied limitation as is inherent in the writing is a country mile from an outright prohibition. This represents the general thinking among arbitrators.

The concept that the labor agreement by implication represents a balance between the right of management to arrange for the conduct of the work of the enterprise and the right of the union and its members to receive the benefits of the labor standards created through collective bargaining stems from the logic of the productive process in a society which sets off rights against responsibilities.

Business is often a conservative force on social questions. But when it comes to production, it is as radical as it can be. To the enterpriser feeling the sting of the competitive lash, there is no such thing as the status quo in technology or in the organization of production. He hunts feverishly for new materials, for new machines, for new ways of organizing work. When he finds them, he does not hesitate to uproot the established way of making or doing things in order to replace it with a better way.

On the other hand, trade unionists and trade unions are often the pioneers, the radicals, in changing social institutions. But they tend to be the conservatives in their approach to changes in the methods of production. The status quo represents, they think, job security and certainty; change, presented in terms of the promise of a glowing long-run future, is often accompanied by an uncomfortable, if not menacing, tomorrow.

It is these feelings and attitudes which make the subject of discussion so sensitive and contentious. The employer fights for retention of his right to innovation and change. The worker and his union cherish and seek to protect their hold on certainty and security.

The innate logic of the implied-obligations view of the collective agreement is that it reconciles this conflict by recognizing that society needs the benefits of management's productive radicalism but that it must not be employed to mask an attack on the security of the work force as a whole.

It is axiomatic that a contracting party is not privileged to engage in a course of conduct designed to nullify its agreement. My friend in the tire manufacturing business was under no illusion that having recognized the Rubber Workers Union as the bargaining agent for his production workers, he could avoid the consequences of that act by having a labor contractor come in to do the same work at the same machines, even if they were paid the same, much less lower, wages. A labor contract may not *guarantee* job security or hold out a promise that *all* the work to be done for the employer will be done by people under its coverage. But it would be worthy of scant respect if it were construed to be a promise to recognize the union and to apply its standards only if the employer, in his sole discretion, decides to have the work done by union members and

The Nature of the Agreement

not by others. This would be akin to saying that the employer's undertaking to meet the contract's terms involves no real commitment whereas the union's undertaking to abide by its terms is enforceable.

But to say that a silent contract may imply some limitations on subcontracting is not to say that it bars it. On the contrary, the contract's silence shows that there was no outright cession of the authority. By signing an agreement which says nothing about subcontracting, the employer can be adjudged to have done no more than agree not to use the right in an unreasonable way to reduce the scope of the unit or thwart the agreement's stated terms. But short of that, the right to contract out work can continue to be exercised.

The argument that the recognition, seniority, union shop, or other clauses in the agreement *automatically* bars the contracting out of work fails because it collides head on with the realities of our business system. The employer was free to add or delete jobs from his work force as his concepts of technology or of priorities in the organization of work changed. When he assumed the obligation of union recognition for the purpose of collective bargaining, he assuredly did not assent to a total surrender of that flexibility or to the assumption of a set of rigid restrictions on his right to innovate.

But with the inception of collective bargaining, he perforce acquired a relationship with a new institution. That institution inevitably became a factor in his business calculations because, by entering into a contract with it, he assumed an obligation to respect its integrity and to refrain from so exercising his powers as to significantly impair its ability to function. That sort of mutuality is the essence of contract. Hence, latent in the collective agreement is an obligation not to act so as to thwart the realization by the other party of its benefits.

This balance between rights and responsibilities in the matter of subcontracting is essential if the flexibility of our productive system is to be maintained and reconciled with the legitimate aspirations of workers and unions for security. It is, in point of fact, the dominant view expressed by the courts and the National Labor Relations Board; by the parties themselves in their bargaining agreements when they negotiate limitations on the subcontracting right; and by the mainstream of arbitrators in construing labor agreements in disputes over subcontracting practices. To put it in a more homely way, there is general recognition that on this subject the labor agreement must be viewed neither as a strait jacket nor as one of the seven veils. Rather it should be regarded as a well-fitting girdle, strong enough to contain bulges but yielding enough to permit bending.

* * *

3. Additional Cases

Anaconda American Brass Company and United Automobile Workers of America, Local 1078, November 28, 1961

* * *

.... I, along with many other arbitrators, have held that the recognition and seniority clauses do not constitute *automatic* bars to the contracting out of work and thus have overruled union arguments that the mere existence of a contract with a union bars contracting out under all circumstances. As a result, the contracting out of work has been upheld more often than not where done without intent to undermine the union or evade the terms of the agreement but in pursuance of a legitimate management goal not circumscribed by the agreement. Thus a company sending work out or having work on its premises done by a contractor because its own people did not have the skills, or the equipment, or the time, or because access was gained to a technique or process not in the company's possession, or because it was cheaper to purchase a ready-made item rather than manufacture it oneself has been upheld as a reasonable and proper exercise of the reserved rights of management.

In such cases the contracting out represented an exercise by management of its reserved rights which did not frustrate one of the basic purposes of the agreement. Here, by contrast, the bringing in of the contractor's employees to replace bargaining unit employees at their own workplace and to perform the identical work at a lesser wage than that agreed upon by the parties to this agreement constitutes a negation of one of the basic purposes of the agreement between American Brass and the UAW. For, after all, when the parties to this contract bargained out a wage scale they set a price to be paid for the performance of certain work on the company's premises. By thereafter removing the classification that performs this work from the unit and having that same work performed on the premises by someone else's employees at lower rates, the company negates the agreement it made with this union. The fundamental purpose of a labor contract is to set a price for labor. Having committed itself to pay the negotiated price, the employer may not turn around and have the identical services performed on his premises at a lower price.

If after having signed an agreement containing rates of pay for the classifications in, let us say, the casting and metal storage departments, the company thereafter contracted with someone else to supply the labor for all of those very classifications at lower rates of pay, it would surely have breached the agreement it signed with this union by the simple device of negating it. That, to a lesser degree, is what occurred in this case. The company's purpose here was not to gain access to a better way of producing its product; it was solely to secure the advantage of a less expensive supply of labor. But it had committed itself to paying the rates specified in the agreement for the work done on its premises. Hence its action of eliminating the janitor job from the unit and having a contractor's employees do the identical work on its own premises at a lower rate of pay and under inferior conditions was a breach of the contract with the union. While the company's desire to reduce its costs in order to meet foreign competition and thus to preserve jobs for its own employees is laudable, it may not accomplish this by a unilateral negation of the agreement's terms.

* * *

Chase Brass and Copper Company and United Automobile Workers of America, Local 1565, November 30, 1961

* * *

. . . . Granted that there is no stated limitation in the contract on the right to farm out work. Granted further that the union tried to get such a limitation and failed. Nonetheless it does not follow that an *unlimited* right to contract out is implied thereby. For contracting out is not a uniform thing. Under a contract silent on the point management unquestionably retains a wide latitude in the matter. But even in such a case its powers are not unlimited. If it engages in contracting out in such a scale so massive as to jeopardize the very existence of the agreement or if it contracts out solely for the purpose of evading the very wage, seniority, or other provisions it contracted to observe, it may engage in a violation of the agreement *as a whole* without specific reference to any of its parts. In short, an agreement silent on the subject implies, at most, a right to contract out work reasonably and without intent to evade contractual obligations. An allegation not patently frivolous that a particular case of contracting out exceeds these limits is arbitrable and deserves scrutiny of the merits.

* * *

Third, the recognition clause on which the union relies does not *automatically* bar subcontracting. Possibly it can be construed to do so where there is evidence that it was undertaken with the intent of evading the obligation to deal with the union or where contracting out is so massive as to effectively negate recognition of the union. But absent more it cannot be construed to withhold from management the right to exercise in good faith the business judgment whether to make or buy, whether to gain access to a better method by contracting out or whether to do so by making a capital investment so that its own employees will be given the work, whether to contract for skills not available in the plant or whether to engage them by adding to the work force, whether to accelerate production by sending work out or to accept a slower schedule in the interest of stability of its own work force.

Next I note that the company's action here was not undertaken to evade meeting the wage levels it contracted to pay but rather to gain access to an *improved method* of handling the rubbish after it is collected in the plants. Because of the contractor's more efficient equipment he is able to accomplish with two men in two and a half hours what the four or five bargaining unit employees took full shifts to do, namely move the accumulated rubbish from the plants to the rubbish burner. And at the same time it is apparent that to get the same result with its own employees the company would have to make a significant capital outlay of $46,000 or more and then not have the chance to use the equipment at full efficiency as the contractor is able to do by virtue of performing the same service for other customers. As this agreement is written, I find nothing in it that would empower me to withhold from management the opportunity to effect the considerable economy this superior equipment affords (it estimates a saving of $13,000 a year) or, in the alternative, to require it to lay out a significant capital sum to achieve it.

There was no evidence that the company's move here was to gain access to labor at lower wages than it is required to pay. In this respect, the case at hand stands in sharp contrast to *Anaconda American Brass Co.* vs. *UAW* decided by me a few days ago (unpublished but, like *Tropic of Cancer,* undoubtedly privately circulated) in which I held against the company when it replaced its bargaining unit janitors with a contractor's employees who did exactly the same work, employing the same techniques and equipment, but at a lower rate of pay. There the intent was to avoid the impact of a wage commitment. Here the intent is to secure the advantage of superior technology not available to the company except at a considerable investment of capital.

* * *

Southwestern Bell Telephone Company and Communication Workers of America, District 6, December 8, 1964

*   *   *

I believe there is in fact inherent in collective agreements limitations on the right to contract out work. It is basic contract law that a party may not enter into a contract and then engage in a course of conduct which will deny the other contracting party the fruits of the bargain by frustrating the agreement or rendering its performance impossible. The covenant of good faith and fair dealing that is implicit in every agreement in itself is a ban to the contracting out of work which would serve to diminish the scope of the bargain the parties stuck. Not even the most zealous advocates of the reserved rights theory maintain that a contract silent on the subject permits contracting out without limit. And while unions often argue that contracting out is wholly barred unless specifically sanctioned by a contract, when pressed they concede that in some circumstances, such as absence of skills or equipment or inability to meet time limits, contracting out of work is appropriate despite the absence of specific sanction.

In other words, inherent in a labor agreement otherwise silent on the subject is a tacit understanding that the right to contract out work exists but that its exercise is limited either by explicit understandings set forth in the agreement or in the parties' past practices or by implicit understandings as revealed by the history of their bargaining. The more definite and concrete the evidence of these understandings, the more specific will be the delineation of the areas in which the parties intended management to retain discretion on the subject from those in which management's rights are circumscribed. In the absence of such evidence or where there is such evidence supplementing it, the general limitations of good faith, absence of intent to destroy the bargaining unit, and related criteria apply.

The problem in each case where the parties have not spelled it out explicitly is to delineate the scope of the bargain implicitly struck on the subject of contracting out. Under contracts where the bargaining history or specific clauses permit few inferences as to the scope of the bargain the presumptions favor a broader latitude for contracting out than under ones where the history of negotiations or specific clauses support the inference that a greater degree of limitation was intended.

*   *   *

Chapter III

Individual Rights and Obligations in a System of Industrial Discipline

A S PREVIOUSLY *indicated Wallen subscribed to the belief that one of the greatest benefits of the arbitration process was the substitution of a "rule of industrial law" for the potentially arbitrary and capricious "rule of the boss," especially with regard to employee discipline.*[1] *This chapter will examine Wallen's views on the objectives of the system of industrial discipline and the rights of the employer and individual employees in such a system.*

The first section of this chapter includes arbitration decisions in which Wallen discussed the purposes of industrial discipline. As will be seen he emphasized the corrective and educational objectives of discipline rather than the punitive. He believed discharge was appropriate only for those employees who were totally incorrigible and unresponsive to corrective discipline, unless the employee in question was a positive detriment to the safety and efficiency of the workplace or was obviously unqualified and unable to perform his duties.

Wallen also found discipline warranted as a corrective measure in cases where employees' off-the-job conduct jeopardized valid employer interests, including instances where the conduct affected the reputation of the employer, indicated the likelihood of future on-the-job difficulties, or inconvenienced the employer because of absenteeism or creditor harassment. In all of the cases in this section Wallen attempted to balance valid employer interests with certain basic employee rights.

---

[1] Southwestern Legal Foundation, *Labor Law Developments, Proceedings of 12th Annual Institute on Labor Law* (Washington: BNA, 1966): 160-161.

Individual Rights and Obligations 87

The second section of this chapter consists of decisions in which Wallen expounded on what he believed were essential, basic employee rights in an industrial disciplinary system. These include the right to procedural due process; expedient, noncapricious, and appropriate penalties for transgressions; the right to representation; and the right to equal treatment or nondiscrimination in the workplace. The difficult distinction between the rights of an individual and the limitations placed upon individuals acting in concert is also examined.

Finally, several cases are included that illustrate Wallen's treatment of discipline where extenuating circumstances justified special consideration in determining degree of guilt and the appropriate penalty or remedy.

The decisions demonstrate Wallen's strong commitment to (a) the importance of seniority rights as a form of job security for the individual employees, (b) the consideration of extenuating factors beyond the individual employee's control in evaluating the equity of industrial discipline, and (c) the moral obligations that an employer may have to a physically or mentally handicapped employee who formerly rendered useful and faithful service and who was capable of being rehabilitated.

A. Purpose of Industrial Discipline

1. In-plant Conduct

In the following cases Wallen discusses the circumstances under which employee performance on the job justifies discipline or discharge.

Continental Airlines and The Flight Hostesses, Air Line Pilots Association, International, December 13, 1966

* * *

.... Discharge is not the only disciplinary measure open to management and common sense would dictate that the discharge power be exercised when there is reason to doubt the efficacy of other steps aimed at correcting an employee's behavior. The company, after all, incurred a cost of many thousands of dollars in recruiting and training Miss S_____. If for the greater part of her service she performed satisfactorily and if there is reason to believe that the transgressions for which she was discharged were aberrations not likely to be repeated, it would make sense to save the sum so invested. The purpose of industrial discipline is not to punish but to correct, and the discharge power should be exercised either when correction is not likely to be accomplished or when the initial offense is generally recognized to be so heinous that complete separation is the only logical course.

* * *

S.W. Card Manufacturing Company and United Steelworkers of America, AFL-CIO, December 31, 1956

* * *

The disparity between M_____'s output and that of the rest of the department was so great as to show a lack of effort on his part to produce up to standard. And while his illness may have accounted for some part of his poor performance in the four weeks prior to his discharge, there is nothing in the evidence to set aside the conclusion that it was a minor factor. The lack of effort, however, stemmed from a phenomenon well known to those with a knowledge of industrial relations. M_____, who in his fifteen years here had not worked on incentive standards, was consciously or otherwise resisting their introduction. It is not uncommon for such resistance to be encountered during the initial installation of an incentive system. It frequently stems from one or more individuals who by temperament find themselves in opposition to changes in their job environment. Management should not be surprised by such resistance and it acts properly when it devises ways to overcome it.

The least satisfactory way to overcome such resistance is by peremptory discharge. For this has the effect of securing an acceptance of the incentive system by the group involved through fear rather than understanding. It lays the groundwork for further and sometimes greater resistance to standards during the subsequent administration of the incentive system. It causes an economic loss both to the employee involved in the form of benefits and job security and to the company in the form of wasted manpower and training costs. And it bespeaks a failure to grasp and deal in an enlightened way with an aspect of worker psychology which can and should be handled by less drastic means.

The foregoing does not imply that management should do nothing when one or a few employees, resisting the installation of an incentive system, withhold proper effort input consciously or unconsciously. Management should act and its actions need not be limited to sterile and ineffectual warnings. They should properly encompass efforts at education of the employee involved, the development of cooperation from the employees' spokesman on the local and national union level, close supervision of the employee involved to make certain that he knows that management is evaluating his performance, and the use of management's disciplinary powers to the degree necessary to correct the recalcitrant's attitude. And if there is reason to conclude that an individual is temperamentally unsuited to work on standards (and there are some such cases) then management would be wise to use its power to transfer rather than discharge. But this is a far cry from the mere issuance of an incident report followed by summary dismissal.

In short, I find that while there was ample grounds for action by management in M_____'s case, inasmuch as his attitude was one of resistance to incentive standards rather than one of cooperation with this change in the department's operations, the action management took was hasty, premature, and not in the best interests of anyone concerned. Greater efforts to get M_____ to cooperate instead of fighting the standards were in order. Consultation with union officials, closer supervision of the employee, and possibly the use of discipline short of discharge would in all likelihood have resulted in a change in the employee's attitude and the securing of his cooperation.

* * *

American Textile Company, Inc., and Amalgamated Lace Operatives of America Branch A-6, Levers Auxiliary Section, March 7, 1956

* * *

. . . . The hazards to oneself and to others in a plant with power-driven machinery are real. Avoidance of accidents requires a work force sufficiently mature to treat such equipment with the respect their inherent hazards require. A person who capriciously starts or stops machines, even if done with no ill intent, endangers himself and others. Not only management but also other workers have a stake in accident prevention. Inasmuch as accidents in most instances have their roots in carelessness, it is sound practice to remove chronically careless and irresponsible persons from an environment where their actions are likely to cause damage.

. . . . Management need not wait till an accident occurs to divest itself of an unsafe employee.

* * *

Brown and Sharpe Manufacturing Company and American Federation of Technical Engineers, Local 119, AFL, July 24, 1954

* * *

Upon rereading the testimony and evidence presented, the arbitrator is impressed with the sincerity of Mr. M_____'s desire to continue as a screw-machine tool draftsman and also with the company's efforts to train him and give him the opportunity. There was no lack of opportunity to advance in this work. The company needed skilled draftsmen and had in fact undertaken an extensive training program with the expectation that some of the men trained would develop into Class 1 and 2 draftsmen. Mr. M_____ did not so develop; nor did he meet the requirements of a competent Class 3 draftsman. That is no reflection on him as a person nor on his potential to develop in other fields of endeavor (including other types of drafting). The arbitrator (if he may interject an analogy out of personal experience) once had a deep-seated desire to play the piano. He has no musical talent whatsoever and it has been of untold advantage to him, both financially and in terms of personal happiness, that he was discouraged in this ambition.

* * *

2. Extraplant Conduct

In the following cases the employee's responsibility to his employer while off the job is discussed. Where legitimate interests of the employer are interfered with, Wallen discusses the appropriate use of discipline and discharge.

The Bridgeport Gas Company and United Mine Workers of America, Local 12298, January 5, 1967

Individual Rights and Obligations 91

* * *

DISCUSSION

At the outset we note that the company discharged A_____ ostensibly because of the publicity he received when a newspaper article, which identified him as a Bridgeport Gas Company serviceman, stated that he allegedly set fire to the cellar of his home and then fled with a sawed-off shotgun and pistol. The only evidence submitted to prove that this in fact occurred was the newspaper story. The union points out that the matter was dropped by the police and A_____ was not arrested, tried, or convicted. The company's rejoinder is that this is immaterial.

While there may be circumstances where an employee involved in a scandal for which he is not arrested, tried, or convicted may nonetheless properly be discharged because his continued employment would place his employer in ill repute, the facts of such a case must plainly demonstrate the existence of just cause for such a discharge. Even in the arbitration forum the accused is considered innocent until proven guilty. This means that the company must sustain the burden in proving by at least a preponderance of the evidence that the employee was culpable and, if the acts complained of did not arise out of the employment relationship, that the publicity so affected his usefulness to the company as to justify his discharge.

* * *

Thus there is no basis for a holding by me that A_____ committed some *act* that is prejudicial to his employer. Certainly the company did not prove the commission of such an act. It showed only that someone had *alleged* that he had done so. The worth of that allegation has not been established. For all the record shows, the source of the allegations could have accused him falsely or could have been mistaken.

This leaves only the question whether the newspaper report linking A_____'s name with the company's was in itself just cause for the man's discharge. Plainly it was not. To hold that it was would leave any man's livelihood to the vagrant mercies of reporters and editors. Mere mention in a newspaper, without more, can scarcely be deemed just cause for discharge even assuming the truth of the dubious proposition that customers are always prone to obliterate the distinction between the allegation and the deed.

* * *

In short, there is no evidence that A_____ was guilty of the behavior the company sought to impute to him as its basis for his discharge. Nor is there proof that the newspaper stories reporting an allegation of misconduct, but no more, either have been or are likely to be prejudicial to the company or to impair A_____'s ability to function as a useful employee.

* * *

Southern Bell Telephone and Telegraph Company and Communications Workers of America, Local 3401, March 20, 1964

* * *

Management cannot be the guardian of its employees' morals. If a company retained only the wholly rectitudinous on its payroll, it would have to part with the services of a surprisingly large number of people ranging from sweepers to executives. On the other hand, management is not required to retain on its payroll persons whose off-the-job conduct is likely to bring opprobrium on the company or to jeopardize its relations with its customers or the public. L_____'s conduct was low, filthy, and repulsive. It reveals a man lacking in refinement who may be wholly unacceptable socially to most people. But that alone does not make a man unfit for continued employment. Does his retention harm the employer's reputation or endanger its relations with those whom it serves? To substitute the canon of social unacceptability for this standard would be to deny the right of the coarse and unrefined to earn a living along with those of more conventional manners and conduct.

In applying what I deem to be the proper rule to the case at hand, I note first that in none of the public reports of the case was L_____'s affiliation with Southern Bell mentioned. Hence the company cannot complain that its name was linked with the behavior of this employee and that its reputation and standing was thereby diminished. Furthermore, even if it were widely known that L_____ worked for this company, it is to be doubted that that fact would redound to its discredit. The public knows that there are many strange people in the world and that their association with a company which employs scores of thousands of persons is not a reflection on the employer. It is to be doubted that the public holds Southern Bell to the standard of accountability that management advances in this case. It is for this reason that I deem of little significance the fact that L_____ is known by his neighbors and acquaintances to be a Southern Bell employee.

The company is correct in maintaining that L_____'s actions must be viewed in the light of the nature of its business and of his job. It is, after all, a public utility which must undertake to avoid exposing its customers to unwanted attentions, molestation, or danger. And L _____ as an installer-repairman is required to go into many homes during the day. But the question to be answered in weighing these considerations is whether, given the acts which resulted in L _____'s discharge, there are reasonable grounds for believing that he is likely to menace or embarrass subscribers whose homes or offices he may enter. I find that there is no evidence that this man is prone or likely to conduct himself in an offensive manner under such circumstances.

In the first place, in fifteen years of service there was never a hint or suspicion that he engaged in improper conduct while working in a subscriber's home. If the assertion that he was overcome by an urge to disrobe and participate in the stag show is accepted as the truth, it does not follow that he is likely to engage in a similar course of conduct elsewhere. He never displayed offensive behavior toward subscribers before. His single act at the stag show, committed in vastly different surroundings and under vastly different circumstances than those present during his hours of employment, is simply not sufficient to warrant the finding that a similar occurrence is likely during periods when he is under the constraints of his job.

Second, there is no evidence or indication that L _____ is a psychotic personality of the sort whose disorders manifest themselves in a *compulsion* to engage in abnormal behavior.

* * *

L _____'s discharge is based on the hypothesis that he *may* engage in improper conduct in a subscriber's home. Unlike the *Young* case, there is no evidence that he is *prone* to engage in such conduct.

As a consequence I find that L _____'s discharge was not for cause and I shall direct his reinstatement in conformance with the provisions of the agreement.

* * *

Ford Motor Company and United Automobile Workers, Local 600, August 2, 1957

* * *

The sole issue here is whether an employee who is absent because he was confined to jail may be disciplined for such an absence in the same manner as he might be disciplined for other unauthorized absenteeism. The answer is in the affirmative. An employee who by his own misconduct is confined to jail is as much responsible for his misbehavior as one who is absent because he chooses to go on a bender or chooses not to work for any reason. In either case his behavior has caused him to be remiss in his obligation to his employer to report for work regularly. An employee may not engage in antisocial conduct which causes him to be remiss in his job obligations and at the same time invoke the consequences of that conduct as justification for his absenteeism. His absence because of confinement to jail had its origins in his own behavior. Surely the union would not argue that a man could be repeatedly jailed for drunkeness, for example, without facing the consequences of chronic absenteeism in his employment relationship.

* * *

Eastern Airlines, Inc., and Air Line Pilots Association, International, June 23, 1967

* * *

A pilot with over twelve years of service and a good flying record whose foolish essay into the world of a business about which he knows little caused him to come to grief but who nonetheless tried and succeeded in repaying most of his creditors should, in our judgment, be handled by means short of discharge if the company can be assured that it will not be harried in the future by creditors trying to get its help to collect their debts. While M⎯⎯⎯'s mishandling of his finances has without doubt put management to considerable inconvenience, we are of the opinion that if he is given responsible outside leadership he can yet remain a good pilot while shielding Eastern from further annoyance by those to whom he still owes money. If our judgment is correct, a competent pilot in whom Eastern has a considerable investment will be salvaged. If time proves us wrong, M⎯⎯⎯ can then be classified and handled as beyond redemption.

In short, while M⎯⎯⎯ is close to the line, we think that his long, satisfactory service in other respects, his evident desire to meet his obligations, and his success in scaling down his debts together justify deeming his final termination to be without proper cause. We shall direct his reinstatement subject to the conditions set forth in the decision below.

DECISION

The discharge of Captain M⎯⎯⎯ was not for proper cause. He shall be reinstated subject to the following conditions:

1. If, within sixty days from the date of signing hereof, the pilot or the association in his behalf presents written evidence to the company that Captain M_____ has either freed himself of his outstanding obligations or has made proper arrangements with his creditors to liquidate them on an orderly basis, he shall be reinstated subject to the usual conditions to which returning pilots are subject.

2. His reinstatement shall be without back pay but without loss of seniority.

Taft-Pierce Manufacturing Company and International Association of Machinists, District Lodge 64, December 2, 1959

* * *

An employee cannot at one and the same time work for an employer and compete with him for business. By their very nature these postures are antagonistic. The employee who competes for business with his employer fails to fulfill the pledge to work for the basic interests of his employer on which the established wage is promised.

The degree to which there are antithetical interests in a given case will vary with the nature of the business involved, the nature of the job involved, and the possibility of access to confidential information.

* * *

The following interesting case was decided before the Taft-Hartley Act was passed (the effect of the decision has been nullified by that statute). Wallen found employer discipline to enforce an employee's obligation to remain in good standing with his union to be a valid exercise of discipline.

American Telephone and Telegraph Company, Long Lines Department, and American Union of Telephone Workers, January 8, 1947

* * *

1. The action of a union in disciplining a member is subject to scrutiny by an arbitrator appointed under a collective agreement between the union and the employer only on limited, specific grounds. These grounds are the following:

   (a) That the disciplinary action taken was because the employee refused to commit some act which would violate a law or be against public policy.

(b) That the disciplinary action taken was for the employee's refusal to violate a collective agreement between the union and the employer.

(c) That the disciplinary action taken is not in accordance with the constitution and by-laws of the union.

* * *

The concept of a labor union as a voluntary association, with the right to adopt its own rules and regulations and enforce their observance on its members by disciplinary measures is grounded in the common law and has been affirmed by the courts in cases too numerous to cite. This concept is conveniently summarized in the case of *Polin* v. *Kaplan* 257 NY 277. The doctrine is that the constitution and by-laws of such an association are in effect a contract which defines the terms of membership and the conditions under which membership may be removed. The courts have held that they will not override the judgment of the association in the matter of such removal except in cases where a transcending community interest clearly requires it. Arbitrators have held in like fashion.

One such transcending interest is the protection of the community from the use by such associations of their power to expel to coerce members into taking actions violative of the laws of the land or running counter to public policy (*Abdon* v. *Wallace*, 95 Indiana Appellate 604 [1932]; *Bossert* v. *Dhuy*, 221 NY 342, 117 NE 582). Arbitrators have ruled in a like manner (*Link Belt Speeder Corporation* 17 LRR 580). The appropriateness of such a limitation on the exercise of power is obvious.

Another such consideration exists where a union uses its power of discipline against a member because he followed his normal activities pursuant to carrying out the terms of a collective agreement between a union and an employer. To permit the untrammeled use of disciplinary power under such circumstances would be to tolerate the undermining of the social interest by discouraging the faithful observance of labor agreements. This point of view is basic to the decision of Umpire Harry Shulman in *Ford Motor Company and UAW* 14 LRR 2625 (March 29, 1944) and the decisions of other arbitrators in such cases as *Sheffield Steel Corporation* 28 War Labor Reports 121.

A third type of interest that has prompted the courts and arbitrators occasionally to pass upon the actions of unions in dealing with their members is where the action taken is beyond the union's authority—that is, where it exceeds the powers contained in the constitution and by-laws. The community will intervene if the procedures followed in determining the conflict between the individual and the organization have not been fair.

With these exceptions, the power to discipline a member for infractions of the basic rules of an organization has been regarded as a matter between the member and the organization. In such a matter even the courts will not ordinarily interfere, at least until the remedies provided within the framework of the organization have been exhausted.

More than mere precedent justifies this doctrine. The maintenance of intraunion discipline is necessary to the development of sound, stable unions capable of playing a wholesome role in the field of industry. The very power the abuse of which is alleged today may be the means by which an employer is assured stable relations and freedom from unrestrained contract violations tomorrow. It may be the buffer between the employer and power-hungry union factions willing to use any weapon, including employer harassment, in their struggle to win control from a more temperate and far-sighted leadership. The power of discipline is an inevitable counterpart of democracy; and healthy, disciplined democracy in trade unions is essential to our political and economic well-being.

* * *

The war-time history of maintenance of membership reveals its purpose. It was granted by the War Labor Board to aid union leaders in coping with internal union dissatisfactions arising from the war-time administration of union agreements without losses of union membership. It was granted also to free union officials from the need for concentrating on the day-to-day activities essential to the maintenance of a union so that they could turn their energies more fully to the task of encouraging the production of goods for war purposes. It was granted as a means whereby the application by responsible union leadership of democratically arrived at decisions is made possible without a weakening of the union. In the words of the board majority in the *Little Steel* cases under maintenance of membership:

> If the union leadership is responsible and cooperative then irresponsible and uncooperative members cannot escape discipline by getting out of the union and thus disrupt relations and hamper production. If the union leadership should prove unworthy, demagogic and irresponsible, then worthy and responsible members of the Union still remain inside the Union to correct abuses, select better leaders and improve production.

It is clear from the history of maintenance of membership under the War Labor Board that the clause goes beyond the mere maintenance of dues and protection from raids by rival unions. It was intended to give workers a free choice in deciding the nature of their relationship with their employer and with the union that holds the bargaining rights under the law. After the choice has been made this provision, in the words of the *Little Steel* majority, inhibits individuals' freedom of action in the interest of "the larger liberty of the members in a secure and stable union." The winning of that "larger liberty" necessarily implies the acceptance of the restrictions imposed by the group majority.

The War Labor Board, through maintenance of membership, sought to require that workers who elected to join or remain in unions live up to all of the responsibilities such a choice imposed, including the responsibility to abide by the will of the majority of their organization. Only if the majority will imposes requirements that the law be violated or public policy be flouted or the contract with the employer be broken is the convenant created by the acceptance or retention of membership weakened. In the absence of such requirements, the doctrine underlying the clause is that the democratic action of strong unions create a balance of strength between workers and employers, and that balance is in the long run mutually beneficial to all segments of society and is a factor in the achievement of industrial peace. Union strength and responsibility lies not only in the maintenance of healthy treasuries but also in the ability to translate the majority will into effective action. These objectives were all intended to be within the purview of the maintenance-of-membership clause.

But, it might be argued, how can one reconcile the use of the maintenance-of-membership clause in this case to foster industrial warfare with the goal of industrial peace that is one of its avowed objectives? The question is rooted in a misconception of that provision's basis. Maintenance of membership is no automatic guarantor of industrial peace. During the war it was granted only to unions observing labor's no-strike pledge. But its goal was the development of that type of union strength and responsibility that is a necessary precondition for the maintenance of good relations between labor and management. It was not and is not a substitute for a no-strike clause.

* * *

B. Employer and Employee Rights and Responsibilities

The cases in the following three sections reveal Wallen's strong commitment to the enforcement of basic employee rights in the workplace. The first section relates to the employee's right to fair treatment, including some semblance of due process in the employer's exercise of its disciplinary power and protection from the abritrary and capricious use of such power. The second section includes cases in which Wallen discusses the employee's right to representation during the disciplinary process as well as in the grievance procedure. The third section relates to the employer's responsibility to treat employees equally in the workplace. Wallen's treatment of this issue reflects not only his commitment to the concept of equality, but also his unusual sensitivity to the problems of minorities and women in the workplace.

1. Right to Fair Treatment

Beacon Tanning Company and Leather Workers International Union, Local 21, June 13, 1960

* * *

DISCUSSION

That D⎯⎯⎯ did a poor job on the pack of skins that led to his discharge is not denied. It is evident also that his work in the past has ranged from passable to downright unsatisfactory on occasions.

But against these facts is the fact that the company chose to tolerate his brand of workmanship for eight years, that it unabashedly admits that it chose to live with his poor work a year ago when it was inconvenient to fire him, that it did nothing beyond giving him routine talking-tos to compel this man to be more careful in his work, and that it decided to lower the boom on him only when he could easily be dispensed with because of slow business.

Despite the fact that D_____'s record is unimpressive, I cannot regard this method of handling an employee to be either just or good business. Certainly it did not take eight years to find out that this man is a poor buffer. And when the company did observe that his work was poor several years ago, it should have taken steps short of discharge but stronger than group reprimands to impress upon him the importance of performing responsibly on every pack of leather. It could and should have warned him the first time, followed it with a penalty layoff the next time, and, on failure to improve, then fired him. This is the principle of corrective discipline which I brought to the company's attention in at least one prior case. Discipline in a plant should not be invoked only when convenient. It must be applied consistently and as a matter of policy if management wishes to avoid the taint of discrimination or the charge that it acts capriciously.

I shall therefore order D_____'s reinstatement, the time he lost to stand as a penalty layoff for the poor work he turned in. He is put on notice that this is his last chance to survive in this plant and that having gotten two chances, one after he was found deadheading and this one after turning in poor work, he can expect no further consideration if he turns up before me again.

* * *

Kennecott Wire and Cable Company and International Brotherhood of Electrical Workers, AFL, Local 1450, March 7, 1955

* * *

This is a most unfortunate case in which the employee's inefficiency was made apparent. M_____'s limitations are obvious. They are not of his own making but they are nonetheless real and it is easy to understand why supervision, used to directing [the employees] in a general way with the expectation that they will display initiative and understand orders easily, [may] find it difficult to work with a man of M_____'s limitations. M_____'s inefficiency in the sense that he is unable to meet the normal requirements of intelligence and understanding needed even for unskilled factory work was established to our satisfaction. The needs of orderly plant administration justify his termination.

On the other hand, management hired and retained M_____ past the probationary period. It could have observed his shortcomings earlier and terminated him without recourse. By failing to do so it led the employee to believe he had a degree of tenure. The right to hold a job is contingent upon adequate performance, it is true; but here management erred in hiring and keeping a man who plainly was incapable of such performance.

We do not feel justified in compelling the company to retain a man who is obviously inefficient. On the other hand we believe the company bears some of the responsibility for the difficulties he will face upon termination. Accordingly, we hold that while his termination was in order, it should have been accompanied by payment of a sum to tide him over during an adjustment period while he finds work more suited to his abilities.

* * *

The B.F. Goodrich Company and United Rubber, Cork, Linoleum and Plastic Workers of America, CIO, Local 5, April 7, 1952

* * *

To engage in physical violence in a plant is to commit a breach of discipline for which the severest kind of penalty is usually in order. And where two employees become involved in a fight in which blows are exchanged, it has been properly held that equal penalties apply, except in cases where the aggression is unprovoked. But the penalty in such cases is imposed on both men for *fighting*—for *exchanging* blows on company property. By definition a fight requires two contestants. Inasmuch as fighting in a plant cannot be justified, both contestants should be deemed equally guilty. In such cases one participant usually defends his role in the fight with the claim that the other struck the first blow. It has been recognized that when two men trade blows, the exchange may have its origins not in the striking of the first blow but in provocative acts prior thereto. The finding of provocation in such cases is an offset to the claim of self-defense. The fighters in such cases are equally guilty, not because one provoked a blow and the other struck it, but because they both engaged in the forbidden act of fighting.

* * *

We think that verbal and physical assaults are distinct and different kinds of aggression that do not automatically call for the same penalty. When men stopped belaboring each other with stone axes and began to rely more on verbal insults as a means of working off their aggressions, they took at least a partial step toward civilization. The law recognizes that although both are punishable, an assault is more serious than an insult, no matter how foul. In a civilized society the security of person is paramount; and, while one has a right to freedom from verbal as well as physical abuse, the standards of punishment for the former are not *automatically* as severe as for the latter. So should it be in industrial life.

The foregoing is not to say that, while a man who commits an assault in a plant will almost always be discharged, one who provokes the assault by insults will never be. It merely holds that the discharge penalty does not *automatically* apply in such cases and that in deciding them account may be taken of all the relevant surrounding circumstances.

* * *

The B.F. Goodrich Company and United Rubber, Cork, Linoleum and Plastic Workers of America, Local 318, August 21, 1962

* * *

DISCUSSION

Over the years the arbitrators have held that the theft of valuable company property is an extremely serious offense, subjecting the culprit to the likelihood of severe penalties. In most cases of bald theft of something of value the discharge penalty has been upheld.

This is as it should be. The losses from theft by employees impose severe losses on industry and, through it, on society as a whole in the form of economic costs which the consumer ultimately pays for. As strong a deterrent as is reasonably consistent with justice to the individual is appropriate in such cases.

In some cases the arbitrator has found extenuating circumstances to be present and he has modified the discharge penalty. The taking of scrap or articles of small value, while not condoned, has been weighed in some cases against the employee's total record and the nature of his motivation in engaging in the act. This, too, is as it should be. The penalty of discharge for theft is a sound general rule but, like all rules, cannot be applied mechanically or without the exercise of sound judgment.

* * *

Connecticut Telephone and Electric Corporation and International Union of Electrical, Radio, and Machine Workers, CIO, April 3, 1954

Individual Rights and Obligations

* * *

The right of the company to discharge is circumscribed by the requirement that it be for just cause. Is the failure of an employee to meet a more precise visual standard than he was required to meet when hired just cause for his discharge? We are of the firm opinion that it is not, unless the jobs themselves have changed so that higher visual efficiency is required to perform them at a minimum acceptable standard. Let us pose an analogy. Suppose that management decides that a job be performed by persons five feet six inches or taller and it hires a number of men, some five-feet-six-inches tall, to do it. Suppose further that they perform the job routinely, that it is not changed, that defective work is not specifically traced to them, but that management, wishing to improve quality and believing that if the job were manned by men no less than five-feet-eight-inches tall quality would improve, discharges the shorter men. We do not think that action would be justified under a contract limiting discharges to cases of just cause. The men met and continued to meet the prerequisites of the job fixed by the employer at the time of hire. The claim that the defective work is traceable to the short employees was not substantiated. There is no evidence that any of the shorter employees was less effective on the job than the taller ones. No attempt was made to show that the shorter men were incapable of meeting minimum acceptable standards of quality and output. The mere supposition that there is a connection between quality and height does not constitute just cause for discharging the short men. Only convincing proof that these individuals have been unable to produce satisfactory work might constitute cause.

The analogy is applicable to the instant case. The aggrieved employees have not been charged with being incompetent workmen as individuals. The company claimed only that their work was generally inferior, without attempting to show in any case that it was so inferior as to justify the termination of the employee. It then made the assumption that the fact that these employees had defective vision, as measured by its newly introduced standards, means that they were responsible for the defective work produced in the preceding eleven months of the year. This is quite an assumption. The defective work may have resulted from a variety of causes such as carelessness by employees with perfect vision, lack of proper supervision, faulty materials, engineering problems, and the like. The mere fact that there is defective work on the one hand and employees with defective vision on the other may raise presumptions as to the reason for the defective work but does not, standing alone, constitute proof that those employees were responsible for it.

We find that, in the absence of changes in job conditions which cause new physical requirements to be essential to the performance of the changed job, the company may not discharge employees who met its physical requirements at the time of hire and who continue to meet the same requirements. Discharge in such a case would not be for just cause for the employee continues to meet the terms and conditions of employment originally fixed by the employer. The best the company can expect to do in such a case is to establish higher physical requirements for new employees.

* * *

2. Right to Representation

General Cable Corporation and International Association of Machinists, AFL-CIO, Lodge 2101, January 27, 1958

* * *

Basic to the grievance procedure is the right to representation in the handling of grievances. The grievance procedure presumes that the employee is not well equipped to act as his own representative and that the skill and authority of the union will support him in taking up a dispute with management. Employees are entitled to representation and it is incumbent upon management to facilitate rather than thwart this right.

* * *

The B.F. Goodrich Company and United Rubber, Cork, Linoleum and Plastic Workers of America, Local 281, February 24, 1967

* * *

... the functions of training, counseling, cautioning, or directing workers are supervisory functions in which the union is not involved. It may become involved, if, in the performance of these duties, the foreman handles the employee unfairly or violates his rights under the agreement. But the steward's involvement then begins *after* the act which results in a complaint, not before. The function of discipline through warnings, suspensions, or discharge is also a matter for supervisory initiative, with the qualification that at the time the discipline is levied the employee has a right to representation. Representation at this point is not for the purpose of negotiating the action to be taken. It is for the purpose of assuring observance of the employee's procedural rights. Negotiations over the propriety of management's action is appropriate in the grievance procedure, which may be invoked *after* management acts, not before.

* * *

3. Discrimination

Texaco, Inc., and Oil, Chemical, and Atomic Workers International Union, January 16, 1969

* * *

I turn next to two other union objections which must be answered. First is the charge of discrimination. No direct claim was made and no evidence inferentially supports discrimination on account of race which, though not specifically banned by contract, is subsumed under the law. And indeed T_____, a minority group member, appears to have been hired and handled without regard to color.

It can be argued that this very evenhandedness, this failure to give special *counseling* and assistance to a minority person, 23 years old, in his first factory job, and undoubtedly especially sensitive to handling which a white would regard as routine but which a black might react to more subjectively, does not do justice to the problem of integrating minority people into factory employment. A case can be made for special consideration, for special counseling for minority workers, and for sensitivity training for supervisors who may unconsciously act out attitudes which are counter to company policy. But it is not possible to construct separate rules and standards for these cases. A wise management will take steps to give its newly hired minority people and its supervisors special training in order to avert the need for application of the penalties attached to violations of these rules. However, it cannot be required to repeal those rules for any group.

* * *

Southern Airways, Inc., and Air Line Stewards and Stewardesses Association,
September 14, 1966

* * *

The second reason—that airlines sell "atmosphere" in addition to transportation and that the use of single stewardesses is part of the sales promotion program—probably lies closer to the true reason for the company's rule. The logic on which this proposition is based is dubious. An attractive girl loses none of her charm when she marries; in fact, it may be enhanced. While something might be said for the argument that a small segment of the traveling public may be influenced in its choice of a carrier (where it has a choice) by the fact that its stewardesses are attractive, it is highly doubtful that any but the most predatory of males bother to consider whether they are "unencumbered." Moreover the predatory ones are not likely to be deterred if they are "encumbered."

The crucial significance of this sales promotion argument, however, lies in whether the impact of a finding that stewardesses on Southern may marry without forfeiting seniority is likely seriously to impinge upon the company's sales promotion program. A little reflection shows that it is not likely to do so. If the aim of the program is, as the company's brief states, to build the image of stewardesses as young, attractive, and unencumbered, the marriage of a young girl does not cause her to forfeit her youth any more than it makes her less attractive. But, more important, since the company's right to hire single girls only is not gainsaid and since only a minority of stewardesses are likely to want to continue flying after marriage, the likelihood that the *average* stewardess will present the image of being encumbered is small. And since the "image" sought to be projected is that of an average or composite of the entire work force, it is hard to see how the marriage of some stewardesses is likely to create the impression that most are married. For the passenger lured on board by the prospect of the chase, the presence of a few encumbered ones among the quarry is likely to be an obstacle which merely adds zest to the hunt.

In short, assuming the efficacy of a sales promotion program that seeks to project the image of stewardesses as young, attractive, and unencumbered, a rule against marriages by incumbent stewardesses would appear to be unreasonable because it would cause a forfeit of their seniority without contributing significantly to the objective sought. Hence it cannot be deemed a bona-fide occupational requirement of the job.

* * *

4. Individual *vs.* Concerted Rights

In this section Wallen distinguishes between the rights of individual employees to contest employer conduct affecting working conditions and the rights and responsibilities of employees, acting in concert, to take similar action, particularly where the pertinent collective bargaining agreement contains arbitration and no-strike clauses.

Creese and Cook Leather Company and Leather Workers International Union of America, Local 21, October 27, 1964

* * *

It is true that there have been instances in the past where individual employees have elected to waive their rights to new machines and to exercise their seniority only on the old operation where it continued to exist. But these instances involved individual choices on the part of particular men who felt ill adapted to the technological change or who believed there were better work opportunities under the old method than under the new. This right, where a company in effect maintains an old job and also creates a new one such as occurs when a pasting unit is installed but some leather continues to be toggled, is recognized. But it is an *individual* right which may be invoked by the individual choice of the men whose seniority entitles them to such choice. It may not be invoked in *concert* for the ulterior purpose of forcing managements' hand on rates on the new job. So invoked, it becomes nothing more than a type of work stoppage; it is a group action to put pressure on the company for another purpose rather than an individual selection of alternative employment.

Furthermore, the transparency of the group refusal to work the automatic stacker job and to choose instead the old method is revealed by the fact that there is so little of the old-type work to be done, on the average no more than one hour per day per man. The men are thus claiming what amounts to nonexistent jobs, a fact of which they are well aware. That they do so as a means of maintaining pressure for the change in a piece rate already set by arbitration is plain.

* * *

Fitchburg Paper Company, Division of Litton Industries, and United Papermakers and Paperworkers, Local 12, June 1, 1966

* * *

DISCUSSION

This case presents two questions: first, is an individual employee required to report for early start-up one hour prior to the start of the work week? Second, may a crew *as a group* refuse to report for start-up in order to compel concessions on some matter of dispute between the parties?

It is to be noted in the first instance that the one-hour early start-up has been a feature of this plant's (and, so far as we know, the industry's) operations for many years. And this is entirely natural. The jobs involved run on continuous five- or six-day operations. There is a weekend shutdown. Certain essential preliminary tasks must be performed before normal production can be resumed. If not done prior to the beginning of the normal shift, the bulk of the work force will have no work available, hence, will work a short day the first day of the week. Hence, in order to permit management a full day's production and to permit the men a full day's work, it has long been the custom to have the machine room crews come in one hour early Monday morning to get the equipment ready for production at 7 A.M. This is neither unusual nor surprising; in fact, it is a feature of factory life in many industries and occurs as a matter of course, without specific contract sanction any more than punching the clock or reporting to the foreman.

It is true that employees were not always *compelled* to report for start-up work. Where an employee was scheduled for it but had a reason for not doing so or where, if he had no reason, someone else was available, his presence was not insisted upon. But this concession to voluntarism did not relieve employees of all obligations in the matter. For implicit in the voluntary arrangement heretofore observed was the availability of substitute personnel. It was assumed if one man refused, another would volunteer. The nature of the basic practice, however, is that where there are no volunteers, management may require the junior qualified employees to come in for early start-up. This is sanctioned by both the nature of the problem and by long-standing custom. The interests of both management and other employees have over the years impelled recognition of an implicit obligation on this point.

That the matter became a source of conflict only once before, in 1961, is due to the fact that the need was always recognized and volunteers to replace those unable to report early were always available. The specific

Individual Rights and Obligations 109

arrangement that beater room employees would be obligated to report for start-up made in 1961 was not, in realistic terms, a recognition that they had a right not to report. It was an agreement that whereas previously a beater room crew member had the right to refuse to report for early start-up if a substitute was available he now is required to be available for such work.

Established practices not sanctioned by specific contract language but not barred by it and arising out of the logic of the work relationship are invoked frequently by unions as working conditions intended to be preserved, not supplanted by, the agreement. This is as it should be. The customary ways of doing things not negated by an agreement's specific terms are subsumed. But management, as well as unions, has a right to rely on this principle. Management's reliance thereon in this case is well placed.

Second, in any case even if start-up work were wholly voluntary, a collective refusal to volunteer in order to exact concessions on other problems would be in the nature of an interruption of work banned by Section 19. Such individual right to refuse work as may be inherent in the agreement was intended to be motivated by purely individual reasons, not by a desire to join with others to compel a solution to a problem by group action or inaction. The settlement of grievances or other disputes during the life of the agreement is supposed to be accomplished by means of the grievance procedure and arbitration, not by group refusals to perform work. And if the problem is one not compassable by those procedures, it must remain to be handled in negotiations at expiration time.

5. Extenuating Extracontractual Considerations

The following two sections reveal how under certain circumstances Wallen looked beyond the contract and applied the concept of equity in resolving disputes over discipline or other employer conduct which prejudiced employees. Thus, where the disciplined employee had both seniority and a relatively satisfactory work record, these factors were given substantial weight by Wallen in determining the appropriateness of a disciplinary penalty. Similarly, where the conduct which resulted in discipline was the result of factors beyond the employee's control, Wallen took this fact into consideration in measuring the equity of the discipline imposed.

In the second section, the cases demonstrate Wallen's compassion for physically and mentally handicapped employees. Wallen believed that where such employees have previously demonstrated that they could perform their jobs satisfactorily, the employer had the responsibility to encourage and assist in their rehabilitation, if that appeared possible.

Witch City Tanning Company and International Fur and Leather Workers Union, Local 21, July 25, 1949

* * *

M_____, a dry trimmer, with seniority from June 14, 1940, was laid off due to lack of work on February 15, 1949. On February 21, while still on layoff, he told his foreman he was quitting his job to enter school to study for the priesthood. He reiterated this statement to the bookkeeper and refused a leave of absence. On February 23, the other trimmers were called back. On March first he phoned the plant and on March fourth he visited the plant asking for his job back. He was told he would be hired as a new employee and he was put to work on March seventh.

The crew and the union executive board thought this loss of M_____'s seniority to be unreasonable and on April 22 the union wrote a letter to the company requesting reinstatement of his seniority. The company did not reply.

There is no question in my mind that under a literal application of the contract, M_____ forfeited his seniority. I have rejected the union's argument that a man cannot quit while on layoff, as well as its claim that the company's failure to answer its letter of April twenty-second changed the situation. However, I can see no point that would be served by the company's refusal to grant the man his seniority under the exceptional and peculiar circumstances of this case. The company stated frankly that M_____ had been a loyal, competent, and industrious workman. It will encounter no objections from the crew if his seniority is reinstated; on the contrary they support his stand. The company advanced no reason, other than its technical position under the agreement, for its refusal to restore his seniority; M_____'s departure was not an act of caprice or irresponsibility. He left out of high motives and returned only after he found himself unable to meet the great responsibilities required by a life devoted solely to religion. It would hardly be just if his worthy purpose, now defeated, was also to cause him the loss of his employment standing. The restoration of his seniority will therefore be ordered.

However, this is an exceptional and unusual case. As a general rule management has a right to rely upon an employee's statement that he is quitting and the union is hereby put on notice that in the future the strict provisions of the agreement must be applied by the arbitrator in cases of this kind. . . .

* * *

Sylvania Electric Products, Inc., and International Union of Electrical, Radio, and Machine Workers, CIO, Local 608, October 3, 1953

* * *

At issue in this case is the validity of the company's action reinstating eight employees of the Huntington plant who had allegedly resigned during a six-week strike in order to obtain temporary employment elsewhere.

The Facts

An agreement between the parties dated September 11, 1951, expired on September 10, 1952, and a strike ensued on October third. It continued for six weeks until November 15, 1952, when a strike settlement agreement was signed. This agreement provided that all employees would be recalled on the basis of the seniority they held immediately prior to the strike. It held further that there would be "no discrimination or retaliation against any employee of the company because of any occurrence relating to the strike."

During the course of the strike numerous employees obtained other jobs. While some employers who hired them did not insist on a formal termination of the strikers' relationship with Sylvania, some employers required prospective employees to formally resign their jobs at Sylvania. Eight of the strikers submitted such formal resignations during the strike. When the strike was ended all were notified of its conclusion. Five of the eight men returned to work on November 17, 1952, the day the plant reopened. Two returned on the next day while one requested and was granted permission to remain at his temporary job until a replacement could be found. He returned to Sylvania three weeks later.

The union in arguing that these employees are not entitled to credit for their prior service upon their return to Sylvania cited Article 10, Section 7, which states that "continuous service shall be regarded as broken by: . . . (b) a voluntary quit or resignation." These employees resigned voluntarily, consequently their service was broken at the time of resignation and their reemployment must be as new employees, the union maintained. In response to the company's claim that it had obligated itself to reinstate strikers without discrimination, the union replied that this provision was intended to protect employees who might have incurred management's displeasure during the course of the strike but not employees who quit their employment during the course of the strike.

The company maintained that the no-discrimination, no-retaliation provision, included in the strike settlement agreement at the request of the union, was intended to restore all employees to the status they enjoyed prior to the strike without regard to any individual action taken during and relating to the strike. The eight employees who resigned during the strike were reemployed just as all other employees who took other jobs during the strike without tendering a formal resignation were reemployed. This was the intent of the strike settlement agreement. These men, like other strikers who took jobs elsewhere, were under the same economic compulsion to maintain their homes and feed their families, the company maintained. Their resignations were only to aid them to secure employment. The fact that they were unfortunate enough to have to go through the sham of resigning should not be held against them.

DISCUSSION

The arbitrator can find no merit in the union's contention. These men, like numerous other strikers, had to find other employment during the protracted strike period in order to support themselves and their families. They ran into difficulties in obtaining jobs. They could get them only by tendering a formal resignation to Sylvania. Other employees who took jobs elsewhere during the strike period were more fortunate. They did not have to tender such a formal resignation. It would be unfair in the extreme to tell these men that they had lost their seniority rights when they returned to work only because of this formality. It is obvious that the resignations were not made with the intent of severing all employment connections with Sylvania. As soon as the strike was settled the men returned to work promptly except in one case where a special arrangement was worked out with the company. Their employment elsewhere was, as was true in the case of other employees who were involved in this dispute, a temporary expedient designed to carry them through a difficult period, rather than a resignation in the sense that that term is ordinarily used.

Decision

The grievance is dismissed. . . .

* * *

H.K. Barnes Leather Company and International Fur and Leather Workers Union, Local 21, CIO, August 7, 1947

* * *

. . . . The arbitrator has regarded this case from all of the angles involved, *human as well as contractual.* [Emphasis added.] It is true, as the union claims, that the contract is silent with respect to the rights of men promoted from the bargaining unit into the ranks of supervision . . . who subsequently return. It is also generally true that the guarantees of the contract extend to persons falling within its scope and not to those not covered by it. It must also be recognized that the unrestricted right to place foremen into the bargaining unit and have them carry their accumulated seniority would jeopardize the opportunity for jobs of bargaining unit workers.

On the other hand, D_____'s case presents an acute human problem. He has worked here for forty-five years which is twenty years more than any other employee in the plant. To say that he should lose all the benefits that those long years of service have earned for him merely because he spent a few months as a regular foreman instead of a working foreman would be extremely harsh and unfair. Furthermore, the questioning of D_____ and union representatives revealed that, while D_____ got a withdrawal card, he was not adequately notified by the union that the granting of such a card to take a job outside the bargaining unit would cause him to lose all of his accumulated seniority in the event of his return to the bargaining unit. It seems to me that where such an action takes place in the case of an older man with many years of service, the union is under a strong moral obligation to give the man involved adequate warning of the significance of his request. It is evident that this was not done in the case of this man. For these reasons, the arbitrator will rule that D_____'s seniority should date from September 1902.

I wish to stress that this decision is not to be considered as a precedent for cases of this type. It has been decided on the basis of the special facts here involved. Certainly, the demotion of foremen who have never been in the bargaining unit or who left it a number of years ago would present a vastly different problem [from] the case here involved. This decision can therefore not be construed as validating such actions under this contract....

* * *

Shahmoon Industries, Inc., and United Steelworkers of America, AFL-CIO, January 23, 1959

* * *

.... In an earlier day, when unions had to fight tooth and claw to exist and when supervisors were used as shock troops deployed by a hostile company to decimate union ranks, there may have been justification for the view that when a man became a supervisor he joined the enemy and cut off all ties with the union group. But in the present state of industrial relations, characterized by substantial acceptance of and even accommodation to unions, there is no longer substance to the view that the bargaining unit worker who accepts a promotion to foreman has made himself an outcast. He has done no more than accept a different status in what is essentially a common enterprise in which the long-range interests of the parties are parallel. While the man who makes such a move relinquishes most of the protections of the collective bargaining agreement, in all equity one link—the right to seniority retention—should not be deemed severed unless clearly required by the agreement's terms. I find no such clear requirement here.

* * *

Firestone Tire and Rubber Company, Firestone Store, and United Rubber, Cork, Linoleum and Plastic Workers of America, Local 7, January 14, 1964

* * *

.... The accumulation of petty annoyances and minor irritations that tend occasionally to anger people in their working relationships is known to all of us. None of us has been exempt from feelings of frustration in our work with the result that we say to ourselves "I'm disgusted! I quit!" While people generally control such impulses, occasionally the thought bursts into words. But having vented themselves, these feelings disappear and the employee's true feelings, that of a desire not to interrupt his service and jeopardize his livelihood, assert themselves.

When such an incident occurs, we witness an action that is clothed in the forms of a quit but is not characterized by an intent to quit. And that,

I believe, is what happened to S_____. Under the stimulus of a series of irritations arising out of his being shuttled rapidly between assignments, he finally exploded into an "I quit" in the middle of the shift. But within ten or fifteen minutes, before he left the premises, he had reconsidered. M_____ sensed that the man had no real intention of quitting and had no difficulty in getting him to volunteer to return to work. He brought him to H_____ who, it appears, might have been willing to drop the matter after P_____'s call but who apparently was thwarted by his superior's dictum that "when a man quits, he quits."

The facts are that in the real sense S_____ walked off the job during the shift but without intent to resign his employment, that he quickly reconsidered, but that he was by then locked into the forms of his act. I do not believe that he was in a real sense a quit. On the other hand, he walked off the job during the shift. For this discipline is in order. Inasmuch as the time he lost stemmed from this improper act and inasmuch as the company can scarcely be blamed for seeking to rely on the forms of his actions, I shall direct his reinstatement but without back pay.

* * *

Firestone Tire and Rubber Company and United Rubber, Cork, Linoleum and Plastic Workers of America, CIO, Local 336, October 19, 1954

* * *

DECISION

There is no doubt that the five employees, by failing to report for work after senior men at the last minute claimed the same week for their vacations, violated the letter of the agreement as it then existed. The agreement provision giving senior employees priority in the selection of vacations then contained no time limit on the exercise of the right and had in fact been administered to permit last-minute displacements.

On the other hand, the chagrin of these five at not being able to fulfill long-cherished plans is understandable and must be viewed with some sympathy by any reasonable person. They must for weeks have been sighting, in their imaginations, deer down the barrels of their rifles, listening to the crackle of a fire, and visualizing four aces in every other hand. To have such a pleasant prospect rudely shattered at the very last moment is not pleasant.

While the loss of the vacation of their choice may have been a rude jolt, it did not justify the absence of these five men. After all, they got no more nor less than what the agreement gave them when their seniors claimed the same week. But the circumstances of the case should have been taken into account in assessing the penalty. We think that, all things considered, a one-day penalty layoff would have been enough to make the point that a disruption of operations was uncalled for.

* * *

Republic Steel Corporation and United Steelworkers of America, Local 1033, December 26, 1967

* * *

DISCUSSION

.... In the ordinary case of an assault on a supervisor there is little question but that the discharge penalty is in order. Management must be assured that its supervisors will be able to function without fear for their personal safety. An employee whose self-control, even under considerable provocation, is so limited that he is prompted to resort to fisticuffs is hardly equipped to withstand the stresses of factory life and in the usual case his removal from employment is justified if he assaults a foreman.

* * *

But even this would not in the ordinary case mitigate the gravity of the offense of assault on a supervisor. We are given pause, however, by the second component of this case, namely the use by P_____ of racial epithets in response to F_____'s verbal insults directed at him.

If supervisors in industrial plants should have learned anything from the turmoil over civil rights and over the justified demands of Negroes for equal treatment of the past decade, they should have learned that it is absolutely essential to refrain from racial slurs in talking to employees of another color or ethnic background. A supervisor who has not mastered that simple truth and who cannot forbear from giving voice to his innate prejudices can scarcely lay claim to the fullest measure of the immunities that should attach to his status. A racial insult, in the fragile and tenuous state of race relations currently, can be as dangerous as a match in a hay loft and is a provocation that no one should engage in.

When the matter at hand is thus viewed, one cannot justify F_____'s act of striking P_____ but one can understand the nature of the pressures generated by the entire incident. In no cases are assaults on supervision justified, and when they occur a severe measure of discipline is in order. But where, as here, the foreman had such a definite part in creating the atmosphere in which it occurred, I must in all fairness take that into account in determining the degree of discipline that is in order.

* * *

J. Flynn and Sons, Inc., and Leather Workers International Union of America, Local 21, January 28, 1957

* * *

DISCUSSION

Anyone familiar with industrial relations and with the interior of a factory knows that some language is used there which is not heard in a drawing room. And most men in a plant are accustomed to being addressed by their fellows from time to time in terms which, if not employed jocularly or in a friendly spirit, would be regarded as "fighting words" and lead to strong reactions. Such talk is inevitable between men doing hard physical work and, if kept in bounds and uttered in the proper spirit, constitute no basis for animosity either between workers or between workers and foreman.

But there are two circumstances in which the same kind of talk is taboo. One is when strong language is employed in an aggressive, angry spirit; the other is when those words, uttered in that spirit, are combined with disparagement of another's race or color. The man who lacks the self-control to curb whatever prejudices he has along those lines risks the strongest kind of reaction.

F_____'s addiction to strong language, his brusque and aggressive manner and mode of speech, and his repeated reference to the race of those whom he addressed were an open invitation to the strongest kind of response especially from a person like B_____ who appears to have an especially marked, though understandable, sensitivity in this area.

Despite the foregoing, I cannot in good conscience say that B_____'s action was justified. For an industrial plant would indeed be a chaotic place if men were allowed to respond to provocations, real or fancied, with blows and then to be entirely free of the consequences of their loss of self-control. Physical violence, and especially violence toward supervision, must be severely dealt with if management is to be expected to live up to its responsibility to provide a safe place to work. In the ordinary case the discharge penalty for such behavior is upheld.

But this is not the ordinary case. The background and circumstances I have described in all equity call for some lesser degree of discipline. It should be severe enough to impress upon B_____ the absolute necessity for keeping his temper and under no circumstances to use his fists in the plant. At the same time it should take into account the more-than-ordinary provocation which was present here. And finally, it should serve as a warning to F_____ that his speech and manner, if not corrected, can cause him and his employer needless difficulties.

With the foregoing in mind I have determined on B_____'s reinstatement as of February 4, 1957, a week hence, without back pay. The loss of pay from November 30 to that date is intended to impress upon him the absolute need for self-control. His return to the plant is designed to impress on F_____ the absolute necessity for changing his attitude to one of respect for all persons and to have such respect reflected in his speech. It is intended to impress on management that it, too, has a responsibility to see that F_____ mends his ways.

* * *

The General Tire and Rubber Company and United Rubber, Cork, Linoleum and Plastic Workers of America, Local 9, January 28, 1963

* * *

DISCUSSION

W_____ was so soundly asleep, the photograph submitted in evidence shows, that he would have made a splendid ad for Beauty-rest mattresses. And since the company runs a tire plant, not a men's dormitory, its chagrin at this state of affairs is understandable.

In fact, sleeping on the job, where it is of a deliberate character, is a dischargeable offense and that penalty will ordinarily be upheld. But justice should be tempered with mercy in appropriate cases and this appears to be one such. The man's health and hapless condition, my conviction that he is truly contrite for his improper action, and the fact that he has already lost two and a half months' pay convince me that if given a final chance, he will stay out of trouble. If I am in error his subsequent behavior will reveal it and he will have to stand the consequences.

* * *

Beggs and Cobb, Inc., and International Fur and Leather Workers Union, Local 22, January 30, 1953

* * *

DISCUSSION

The records of these men are indeed bad and the company is to be commended for its forbearance in carrying them on its payroll as long as it has. Management seems to have been fully aware of, and has given more than reasonable consideration to, the human problems involved. It has taken steps short of permanent separation from their jobs to try to get the men to change their habits and come to work regularly and in good condition. That these steps have failed so far was not due to any lack of diligence on the part of the company.

On the other hand, the arbitrator is stirred by the fact that S_____ has nearly a lifetime of service with this company. To separate a man with so many years of service one must be convinced beyond all doubt that some less drastic step will not serve to cause him to change his habits. Likewise M_____ has undisputed talents as a workman which it would be a shame to lose if there is a lingering doubt about his ability to rehabilitate himself. The arbitrator does not mean to imply that long-service men can never be discharged, but he does say that discharges in such cases should be invoked only after a full conviction that all hope is gone.

The arbitrator has determined to place the full responsibility for the continued employment of S_____ and M_____ on these men themselves. Their return to work without back pay will be ordered on condition that their continued employment, in the event of misconduct of any character or of absenteeism for any reason except proven illness, will be at the will of the company. Should such misconduct or absenteeism occur, the company shall have the right to discharge them and they will not have the right to appeal to the arbitration machinery of the agreement.

In the arbitrator's view these men, knowing that their fate is in their own hands, will either change their ways or will shortly demonstrate that they are unable to do so. Should the former eventuality occur, the company will not have lost two otherwise satisfactory employees. Should the latter eventuality occur, the company will no longer be burdened with their continued presence.

* * *

Aluminum Company of America and Aluminum Workers International Union, November 16, 1960

* * *

Management should not be required to keep forever a hopelessly careless or inadequate workman . . . . At the same time if there is a reasonable chance that a workman's career can be salvaged by imposing a penalty short of discharge, the result, if it comes to pass, benefits both the company and the employee. The former saves its investment in recruiting and training the man. The latter saves his equity in his job.

* * *

Premier Worsted Mills (Bridgeton Division) and Textile Workers Union of America, CIO, Local 423, January 7, 1947

* * *

D_____ was employed by the company on October 29, 1945, as a marker in the sewing room at a wage of $34.60 a week. The maximum number of markers employed in the past was ten; at present nine are employed, this number in the company's judgment being sufficient to handle the present volume of work. Mrs. D_____ is married and has two children. Her husband is employed. They live in a rural area some five or six miles from the plant. Also living in the household is her father who ordinarily cares for the children while the parents are at work. However, during the racing season at the Narragansett Race Track the father secured employment at the track for the duration of the meet which extended from September 27 to November 16.

Prior to September twenty-seventh Mrs. D_____ had asked Mr. H_____, the overseer of burling and sewing, for a leave of absence. Mr. H_____ testified that the request was for a three week's leave and that no mention was made of a return at the end of the racing season. Mrs. D_____ testified that her request was for a leave for as long as necessary for her to find someone to care for her children but in no event longer than the racing meet, at the end of which her father would return. Mr. H_____ stated that he informed her that his authority to grant leaves longer than one week had been curbed by the office, which alone could grant longer leaves. He told her to take one week and ask the office for more time. Thereupon, on September 24 Mr. N_____, international representative, spoke to Mr. M_____, who is authorized to grant longer leaves, and asked for a longer time. Mr. M_____ didn't specifically limit a leave to one week but indicated that three weeks was too long.

When Mrs. D_____ did not appear after a week, H_____ asked the office to send her a letter informing her that if she failed to appear for work on October 11 she would have been considered as having left the company's employ. This was sent on October ninth and Mrs. D_____ testified she received it on the afternoon of the eleventh. Following Mrs. D_____'s failure to appear H_____ hired another marker who was working on the third shift in another plant. Mrs. D⎯⎯ stated that she didn't respond to the letter because she got it late on the eleventh, had not been successful in getting someone to care for the children, and had told company officials that she would in any event return no later than the end of the racing season. On November twelfth she called H⎯⎯ saying that her father would be back on the sixteenth and she was ready to report for work on the eighteenth. She was told her job was filled. She reported on the eighteenth but Superintendent B⎯⎯ refused to put her to work.

It was testified that prior to July fourth all reasonable requests for leaves of absence up to six months were granted by the overseers. Around July fourth the rule was changed, limiting the overseers' authority to granting one-week leaves and permitting only the office to grant longer leaves. This new rule was not posted or communicated to the union or the employees; it was explained verbally to the overseers. It was prompted by the abuse of the more liberal practice by some workers. The contract is silent on provisions for leaves of absence.

In deciding the issue I have considered three factors. One is that the company needs reasonable assurance of a stable labor supply and may make reasonable rules to insure such stability. The second is that where previous rules or practices are changed notice thereof should be given to workers and their bargaining agent and their reasonableness may be the subject of discussion between union and management. The third is that family women, who constitute a substantial proportion of the supply of textile labor, have especially difficult problems that should be treated sympathetically.

In this case the reason for Mrs. D⎯⎯'s leave was not challenged as frivolous or unnecessary. Any mother faced with her dilemma in a period when domestic help is scarce would have taken her course. But the fact that in the past reasonable leaves of absence of extended duration were given, coupled with the fact that the imposition of stricter standards after July fourth was without notice or discussion, leads me to the conclusion that the refusal to grant her a leave longer than one week was arbitrary. The textile industry has always employed many women and during the war they helped the industry do a magnificent job of production. The dependence on women as a source of labor carries with it the obligation to deal leniently with the disabilities peculiar to their employment. The problems arising out of child care is one of them. The mere fact that the labor market is now looser than it was a year ago does not lessen this moral obligation. Mrs. D⎯⎯'s reason for her absence is no less worthy than that of a worker on leave for extended illness. Furthermore she had reason to rely on the more liberal past practice in the matter of leaves which was changed without notice.

These considerations must be blended with the company's needs for assurance of a steady labor supply. If Mrs. D⎯⎯ had stayed out for reasons of personal convenience instead of absolute necessity, her reinstatement would, under these circumstances, not be in order. But the necessity for her action is clearly established. The change in leave standards without notice should not bar her return to employment. That return, however, will be without back pay in view of all the circumstances of the case.

* * *

6. Rehabilitation of Handicapped Employees: Employer Rights and Responsibilities

American Airlines, Inc., and Transport Workers Union of America, January 20, 1964

* * *

On the merits of this case, we note that this company has an enlightened and generous policy for dealing with employees afflicted with alcoholism problems. It is to be commended for this. If its efforts are successful in even a few cases, the results are worthwhile both in human terms and in the economic sense. On the other hand, even a generous policy must have limits. Management cannot be expected to carry hopeless cases on the dim chance that a miracle might occur. Its interests in efficient operations must be balanced against its humanitarian concern for individuals.

We note that H⎯⎯ has been given several "last chances" and that his imminent or actual discharge was twice rescinded. We can scarcely blame local supervision for feeling it had gone the limit in this man's case.

But the touchstone for consideration of such cases, it seems to us, is whether at a given time the prospects for rehabilitation have brightened or whether they remain the same as they had been. If the company's enlightened policy is to be meaningful, it should be not unwilling to accept the possible inconvenience which may be involved in giving a man whose prospects for rehabilitation had improved another opportunity, provided there are grounds for believing that his situation has in fact changed for the better.

On this score, the board was impressed by H⎯⎯'s frank self-appraisal at the hearing and by S⎯⎯'s solid support of the individual which was based on a need to have the subject realize that his only hope was self-help. It seems likely that the profundity of the experience H⎯⎯ had in the mental hospital has impelled him toward such self-help. At least the chances, in our opinion, are sufficiently good for us to ask the company to take the small risk involved.

At the same time, if H⎯⎯ does have a relapse, we are not disposed to require the company to again go through the entire process of the grievance procedure and, possibly, arbitration in order to divest itself of a man who has already had many chances. Hence we shall order H⎯⎯'s reinstatement without back pay only on condition that he give the company a signed letter of resignation with a blank date, to be filled in by management at its option in the event H⎯⎯'s performance or attendance is not maintained at an acceptable level.

* * *

Curtiss-Wright Corporation and United Automobile Workers of America, Local 669, March 5, 1958

* * *

While the company should not be expected to continue in its employ indefinitely a man whose health prevents him from discharging the duties of his job, it is reasonable to require it to string along with a long-service man so handicapped if there is a reasonable expectation that his situation will improve.

* * *

Aluminum Company of America and Aluminum Workers International Union, Local 405, October 13, 1961

* * *

DISCUSSION

Article IX gives employees [who are] subject to force reductions displacement rights if qualified. This, of course, includes physical qualifications. Management has the right to pass on qualifications in the first instance subject to the union's right to seek review of its determination in the grievance procedure.

In making its determination the company may take into account the question whether the employee is able to perform the job safely. Indeed it has an obligation to make such a determination for it must avoid exposing employees to undue hazard both for the sake of the employees and their fellows and for the purpose of protecting itself from exposure to liability. Where management's judgment in this regard can go either way, prudence dictates error on the side of safety.

But to say this is not to say that virtually all jobs are barred to one-eyed men in the company's employ. In determining such a person's qualifications the company should try to strike a reasonable balance between maximum safety and the needs for and rights of these persons to continued employment. The ultimate in safety might dictate their being barred from employment entirely. This is an unrealistic approach in a world in which men must work for a living. On the other hand, workers so handicapped cannot fairly expect consideration for jobs where the chance of injury to their good eye is real and tangible.

What is required in such cases is an approach which recognizes that, while there are always some risks in factory jobs, places must be found for people so handicapped (in line with the seniority provisions of the agreement) in which the risk is relatively small even though not totally absent. And, wherever possible, steps should be taken in the form of special safety measures to further reduce the risk in such cases.

* * *

Aluminum Company of America and Aluminum Workers International Union, Local 110, November 16, 1964

* * *

While the company's annoyance at Miss G_____'s absences and claims of inability to do press work and at her actions of March 9 are understandable, our appraisal of the medical evidence in her case is that, whether of traumatic or psychosomatic origin, this employee is indeed subject to pains and peculiarities that have severely limited her ability to function as an employee. Contrary to the company's belief, it is not likely that she is in a physical or emotional state that would permit her to assume the full range of duties of her job were she of a mind to do so. On the contrary, her physical and emotional patterns combine to produce an inability to turn in normal performance on her job.

Miss G____ is, therefore, not a disciplinary case in the usual sense, to be dealt with at this time by the usual disciplinary devices of penalty layoff or discharge. Rather her problem is one to be classed as an illness or injury, traumatic in origin and psychosomatic in its present manifestations. On March 9,1964, it would have been appropriate to place her on sick leave of absence. The manifestations of pain, real or fancied, she displayed at that time as well as the statement of the physician to whom the union sent her both show that she was not then in a condition to perform her work in a normal manner. At the same time, if her condition will respond to therapy, she is entitled to an opportunity to obtain it. Only if therapy proves unavailing will there be justification for final termination.

I shall therefore direct that Miss G____'s termination be rescinded, that she be placed on a sick leave of absence as of March 9, 1964, and that she remain in that status until her ability to work normally is restored or it is established that her inability to do so is chronic.

* * *

The Bassick Company and International Union of Electrical, Radio, and Machine Workers, Local 229, June 14, 1960

* * *

One of the rules prohibits employees from "coming to work under the influence of alcohol. . . ."

There is no question but that P____ violated this rule. The basic question is whether discharge was merited in this case "taking into consideration all of the factors, including previous violations of the same or other rules."

In this connection I note first that P____ had never been disciplined, before he was discharged, for either this or any other rule transgression. The company acknowledges that his conduct and performance were excellent until the poststrike period and excuses its failure to invoke discipline short of discharge, when P____ began to show signs of drunkenness and low efficiency, on the ground that he was the union president at the time. This excuse is hard to accept. It implies that if he had not been the union president he would have been given discipline short of discharge before the extreme penalty was invoked. But because he was the president supervision merely talked to him about his work and behavior and made discharge the first overt act of discipline taken in his case. The company implies, in effect, that it favored P____ because of his union position, but I scarcely see how it did so. By firing him without giving him the chance to correct his conduct under the impact of a penalty short of discharge, it in reality withheld from him the opportunity for self-correction that is implicit in its stated disciplinary policy and that would have been reasonable and proper in his case.

The fact is that while there was just cause for a reasonable measure of discipline in P_____'s case, his discharge was not justified. His prior record was entirely clear. By management's admission his production was outstanding. The deterioration in his output and his in-plant behavior extended over a relatively few weeks, from December 22, 1959, to January 13, 1960. Then at his own request he went out on an excused absence in a conscious effort to eliminate the source of his improper in-plant behavior. Here was concrete evidence of a desire to end the erratic behavior and inefficiency with which the company was properly concerned.

His first attempt at a cure was not successful. After eleven days he quit the hospital and resumed drinking. He returned to work and a few days later lapsed into the condition that resulted in his discharge.

At this point he was entitled to the assist that a more moderate application of management's disciplinary powers might have given him. Having tried once to break the grip of alcohol without succeeding, it is entirely conceivable that a disciplinary layoff rather than discharge might have spurred him to conquer this scourge, regardless of whether it is an illness or a manifestation of weakness. Certainly if management had suspended instead of discharging P_____ and he subsequently became rehabilitated, its disciplinary policy would have been amply vindicated by virtue of having aided the employee while at the same time salvaging for the company the benefits to it of retaining a highly efficient workman whom it spent money to train.

P_____'s actions subsequent to his discharge resulted in a significant improvement in his condition. The company may be right in saying that his physician's prognosis is not yet one of a definite cure. But as of now he is not drinking, he is faithful in following the regimen prescribed for him and he is wholly fit to work efficiently. To refuse to give him the benefit of the doubt in these circumstances would be as unreasonable as it may prove to be wasteful.

Of course, it is entirely possible that the company's action of discharging P_____ was the spur he needed to renew his efforts at a cure. If so, he should be eternally grateful to his employer. But in the present state of the matter there is no compelling reason for that action to stand. On the other hand, there is a solid basis for expecting that this employee will resume his former role as an efficient, capable workman. Should this prove to be wrong and there is a resumption of the type of behavior that led to his discharge, management still retains the right to deal with his case under the terms of its stated disciplinary policy.

For the foregoing reasons I shall direct P_____'s reinstatement, his record to show a one-week penalty layoff for violation of the company rule dealing with intoxication and to show the remainder of the time he lost as a leave of absence for illness. Back pay was not requested and is not granted.

* * *

The B.F. Goodrich Company and United Rubber, Cork, Linoleum and Plastic Workers of America, Local 5, March 22, 1962

* * *

An inability to work steadily, even if due to illness which the employee cannot help, if chronic and sustained, may constitute cause for discharge. The logic is simple: If an employee is unable to render in a consistent way that function or service for which he is engaged, he is unable to fulfill his obligation in a relationship which is reciprocal. That inability can be cause for discharge even though the element of misconduct for which discipline, in the sense of suspension or discharge, is ordinarily levied is absent. It is not enough to say that a man cannot help being ill. The employer cannot help it either. At some point an employee whose health frustrates his ability to fulfill his duties to a reasonable extent ceases to be an employee solely because he cannot render the service that the term implies.

* * *

The B.F. Goodrich Company and United Rubber, Cork, Linoleum and Plastic Workers of America Local 43, December 19, 1963

* * *

DISCUSSION

Cases of this type are always gambles. On the one hand, one hesitates to require management to continue to tolerate an employee who has been a hindrance rather than a help. On the other hand, one hesitates to turn out an employee, even though his record has been poor, if one feels that there is indeed a chance that, if retained, he will become a useful member of the plant and community and a credit to his family.

There are few certain guides to a judgment in such cases. If one goes overboard out of sympathy for the grievants, management is perforce loaded down with incorrigibles. If one goes overboard out of sympathy for the plight of supervision, men who might otherwise become useful to the company and to themselves may well be sacrificed.

One can only decide these cases by as careful an appraisal of the possibilities as can be mustered. And often this becomes a matter of "feel." In this case we were impressed by the possibility of a likelihood that, with proper guidance, C⎯⎯ may shape up. We are sensitive to the fact that management has gone far in tolerating him despite his erratic attendance. At the same time it was also acknowledged that when at work, this man was a good employee and not a source of trouble. We have the union's earnest profession of a continuing interest in the case to the end that he will be watched. And we have a pledge from the union that if he falls from grace, C⎯⎯ will have "had it."

Weighing all of these factors, it is our judgment that a chance remains that C⎯⎯ will become a worthy employee. But we recognize that he needs help in his family situation and in coping with his drinking problem.

As a consequence we shall award his reinstatement without back pay on the following conditions:

(a) That he, with the union's guidance, place himself in the hands of a family welfare agency in the Greater Los Angeles area which will provide guidance and assistance in coping with his family problem. Such assistance can be obtained by making contact with the Community Chest organization, the Family Service Association, or the AFL-CIO Community Services Committee in the Los Angeles area.

(b) That he seek assistance from an appropriate agency in dealing with the problem of alchoholism.

(c) That in the event his absenteeism continues, his termination will not be subject to appeal.

* * *

The B.F. Goodrich Company and United Rubber, Cork, Linoleum and Plastic Workers of America, Local 318, April 5, 1965

* * *

In these circumstances, where there is a direct and undeniable connection between the employee's mental illness and the act leading to his discharge, is discharge proper or should the employee be handled as an ill person despite the antisocial consequences of that illness? The answer is not easy, for management does have an obligation to protect its employees from hazards it can reasonably be expected to foresee. On the other hand, an employee whose irrational actions are the direct outgrowth of an illness, mental or otherwise, is entitled to the consideration under the contract usually given ill employees.

After long consideration I have concluded that there are two aspects to be dealt with here. The first is the employee's entitlement, if ill, to the benefits of the employee benefit program. If H_____ had been ordered confined to Vinita but had assaulted no one, he would have been eligible for the benefits. The fact that his derangement led him to assault P_____ does not, as I see it, in itself cancel the right to these benefits.

The second aspect concerns H_____'s fitness for work. He is mentally ill and in his present state he is neither available nor fit for work. Whether he ever will be is conjectural. If and when he is discharged from the mental institution, his condition may be such that a complete cure has been accomplished. On the other hand, his prognosis may be poor and the danger of a relapse may be great. These questions will have to be faced at that time and the answers will turn on the medical and psychiatric findings. Both his own and company physicians will have the chance to make such findings and if they differ, the agreement provides a means of breaking medical deadlocks. In view of the nature of the illness, doubts should be resolved in favor of safety.

The company's action of final discharge as of October 30, 1964, then, was improper in H_____'s case because his was not the act of a man who can be held responsible for his actions. At the same time, given the current state of the art of treating mental illness, it was premature to say that H_____'s condition is incurable. Finally, he was and is ill and is entitled to the benefits the agreement provides in such cases.

* * *

Warner Gear Division, Borg-Warner Corporation, and United Automobile Workers of America, Local 287, June 12, 1967

* * *

G_____'s case presents much more difficulty. In fact, it involves one of the most difficult problems I have ever encountered in the area of discharge for cause.

This is not because G_____'s case, when judged by his actions alone, is a difficult one. On a recital of the cold facts and on those facts alone, G_____'s conduct could not possibly be condoned by reinstatement to his job. He fought with B_____, was injured, then deliberately and with forethought later sought him out, stabbed him and sought to injure him further by throwing heavy gears at him.

What makes the case difficult is the understandable rage that must have built up in the man after he lost his teeth, a rage that must have been fed by his subconscious reactions to the loss of his fingers in the plant in 1963. That anger resulted in an explosion of violence that led to his hospitalization and treatment. There is the inevitable tendency in such a case to reason that because G_____ lost his fingers in the plant, because he again suffered grievous injury in the altercation with B_____, and because these emotion-charged experiences, added to what was apparently an underlying psychological weakness, led to his subsequent act of violence in seeking out and stabbing B_____, G_____ was subjected to pressures beyond his control for which he should not now be held responsible.

There is much to be said for this line of reasoning. G_____'s response to the accumulation of anger and frustration that must have raged within him was a violent, antisocial act which at the moment of occurrence he lacked the resources to control. It was this fact which saved him from the toils of the law and directed him toward the therapy of a psychiatric hospital.

But the question before me is not only whether G_____ was responsible for his actions at the time but also whether he can be depended upon to avoid a repetition of this conduct in the future. This question is a real one for the company, the union and the arbitrator for it is the responsibility of all of us to be concerned not only with G_____'s problem and that of his family, but also with that of those with whom he seeks to work. Both the union and company owe it to the generality of employees to see to it that they can work safely, without danger to their person from one whose psychological defenses are so fragile that he is prone to respond to others with the extremes of violence.

When the case is placed in this perspective the question becomes "Is the man capable of handling his environment without the danger of a recurrence of the same pattern of behavior?" If there is some risk, is it fair to ask others to assume part of it?

On the record before me, I do not belive that G_____ is at this time prepared to resume work in this environment. While the V.A. Hospital authorities advised in a letter that he is capable of resuming full-time employment, it is to be doubted whether the nature of the plant environment was considered in detail. The man can, the doctors say, work safely for his livelihood. But it is to be doubted whether his return to this particular atmosphere at so early a date would be advisable or in the best interests of either himself or his fellow employees.

At the same time his final termination would be unfair to him at this time. His act was patently one which grew out of a psychiatric illness which may well have been induced or increased by his unfortunate experience in the plant in 1963. Yet he has shown improvement and his prognosis, according to disinterested psychiatrists, is good. I think he can be safely considered for future employment if the improvement in his mental health continues and competent psychiatrists so recommend.

As a consequence I shall hold that G_____'s termination is not sustained at this time, that he shall be considered as on medical leave of absence until January 1, 1968, that in the interim the union arrange for him to receive care through a community mental health center or other appropriate agency or psychiatrist, and that he may then apply for reinstatement if in the opinion of a competent psychiatrist, jointly selected by the parties, his health justifies it. Reinstatement, of course, will be without back pay.

In so ruling in this highly unusual case, I wish to emphasize that this decision in no way condones or forgives in-plant violence where the tie-in with a disordered mental state is not as manifest as it is here.

* * *

Chapter IV

The Mediation Process

ALTHOUGH SAUL *Wallen achieved his reputation primarily as an arbitrator, his outstanding talents as a mediator were also generally recognized.*[1] *In this chapter, Wallen's views on the process of mediation, not only as a technique to assist parties in reaching an accord on contract terms, but also as a technique which could be used propitiously in factfinding and grievance arbitration hearings are revealed.*

In the first speech reproduced below Wallen outlined his views on the role and benefits of the mediation process in general.

The second section is an excerpt of a Report to the President by a 1964 Emergency Board chaired by Wallen which was created to investigate a railroad shop craft dispute. As this excerpt indicates, Wallen altered drastically the usual emergency board procedures in order to facilitate mediation of the dispute which was contemplated by the Railway Labor Act but rarely, if ever before, attempted. While his efforts were not successful, they evoked the following comment:

> He very nearly succeeded. It matters little to history, though I suspect it mattered to Saul, that in this case his mediation efforts did not succeed. It might have mattered greatly to history, although it mattered not at all to Saul, that these parties rejected him for future assignments. And he certainly succeeded in shaking up the practitioners in the railroad industry.[2]

The final piece is an excerpt from an article Wallen coauthored analyzing the variety of grievance arbitration systems present in American industry. In describing the impartial chairman system, Wallen defined the role mediation could play in such a system. Although Wallen used mediation in a few instances where he served

---

[1] James C. Hill, "Remarks at Funeral Service For Saul Wallen," p. 2.
[2] *Ibid.*, p. 5.

as a permanent umpire with the parties' acquiescence,[3] as an arbitrator he did not normally mediate, particularly when the parties were unwilling. As he states, "There is no one 'best' or 'right' approach to labor arbitration, as a few people seem to have argued in the past. An arbitration system must be adapted to the basic characteristics of the industrial relations environment in which it must operate."[4]

1. *A Sparrow Who Got Caught In a Badminton Game: The Role of the Mediator in the Collective Bargaining Process**

The term "mediator" needs definition. An apt one is "a mediator is a sparrow who got caught in a badminton game."

It's not a bad definition. If the mediator moves too boldly or too fast, he frequently gets a hell of a whack in the region of his tail feathers. And in many cases, the mediator is tossed back and forth between the parties, used by them not to achieve a settlement but to postpone one.

If you believe, as I do, that collective bargaining is a method of compromising two competing and often ill-defined equities and that it is practiced by parties who, by the nature of the institutions they represent, place primary emphasis on their own notion of the balance of those equities, you can appreciate that there is a role, often an important role, for one who aims to reconcile these warring interests.

The role of the mediator in collective bargaining has a special importance because where there exists an equality of power between management and the union the prospects of a brutal clash of wills between two strong protagonists can wreak havoc on one or the other and, in the long run, on both. Where a strong union and a strong management face each other and each is conscious of the other's strength as well as his own, the role of a third party in helping devise a formula that will reflect a balance of these strengths can be crucial. He becomes essential

---

[3]Marcia L. Greenbaum, "Saul Wallen: A Lifetime Commitment to Problem Solving," *Issues in Industrial Society* 1 (no. 3, 1970): 51-52.
[4]Charles Killingsworth and Saul Wallen, "Constraint and Variety in Arbitration Systems," *Labor Arbitration: Perspectives and Problems, Proceedings of the 17th National Academy of Arbitrators* (Washington: BNA, 1964): 80.
*Speech delivered to the Air Line Pilots Association Negotiating Committee Seminar, Chicago, December 13, 1967, from a manuscript found in Wallen's files.

because, by the very nature of each party's strength, neither may be able to advance compromises it knows must be made, lest the other party regard such a proffer as a sign of weakness or wavering.

In this context, the mediator can play an important role. He can become the repository for private modifications of previously publicly taken positions. His job is to keep such modifications made by one side private until he has secured from the other party an acceptance in advance of the modified terms. Thus, the mediator can bring about agreement on a compromise basis which, if advanced by one party unilaterally and directly, could be rejected because its tender might be regarded merely as a prelude to further concessions.

But before he reaches this stage in the negotiations, a skillful mediator can play several other roles which cannot only help him settle a dispute but, ideally, help the parties settle it directly between themselves.

One such role is to aid the parties to define and clearly spell out their demands and thereby the nature of the issues that divide them. Bargaining demands and the other party's replies are often advanced in general terms and, in the hurly-burly of negotiations are imperfectly analyzed or understood. If he does nothing else in the case, a mediator can often contribute to a settlement by sharply questioning and eliciting from each party details as to the true nature of the demand or counterproposal. Once the true dimensions of an issue are thus established, a way can often be found to solve the dilemma it presents. The astute negotiator will try to utilize the skills of the mediator to think out for himself and to convey to the other side the dimensions of a particular bargaining demand.

Mediators have another task that they can profitably fulfill. I call it making little ones out of big ones. By this, I mean taking some overall, generalized issue, analyzing its origins and background, and breaking it down into its essentials in the hope that, thus reduced in scale, the problem becomes soluble.

A CASE IN POINT

Examples are legion. One that comes to mind is a case where a general claim for an hour's reduction is advanced because of the special impact on working conditions of a particular type of equipment or other particular condition. A mediator can often induce the parties to break down the problem and to deal with it at the point of maximum impact.

Having helped analyze and establish the dimensions of the parties' demands and having helped the parties to break them down into their more and less essential components, the mediator's task is to help the parties find an area of agreement. The demands of the parties, Arthur

S. Meyer wrote in a perceptive article on "The Function of the Mediator in Collective Bargaining," may seem to be reaching for the moon but the settlement must be made within narrow limits fixed by custom, history, the changing times, and the power content of the situation.

"The demands of the parties," Meyer wrote, "may be represented by two large circles that barely touch, but the important fact is that they do usually intersect and that it is this common segment which represents the not impossible area of agreement. The precise point of accord may fall anywhere within the field, but it cannot appropriately fall outside of it."

To this I would add that the circles themselves are not fixed but movable, depending on the ebb and flow of events and the changes in the parties' power relationship. This in turn can be influenced by the passage of time, the economic hardship of a strike, the pressures of public opinion or of government, the degree of union or management solidarity or the extent to which the strikers or the management receive outside support, whether in terms of strike benefits or mutual aid pact funds.

The role of the mediator is to size up the confluence of these forces, at the right point in time to detect the degree to which the circles intersect, and to shape settlement proposals that fall in the overlapping field.

How should the mediator be handled by the contending parties? I shall assume for the purpose of discussing this point that demands have been exchanged, that there have been direct but fruitless negotiations between the parties themselves and that a strike deadline looms in the reasonably near future. I shall assume also that neither party wants a strike but [both] want a settlement short of one as close to his original terms as possible.

I say that I shall assume neither party wants a strike with full knowledge that this is not always the fact. There are occasional situations in which, because of internal power struggles on one side or the other or because of the far-reaching and revolutionary demands resolutely made by one party and as resolutely opposed by the other or for some other reason, a strike is inevitable, and one or both parties know it. In such a case, the mediator can do little more than prepare the ground for the settlement that must come after a period of bloodletting.

But where a strike is not inevitably in the cards, a mediator can be helpful in achieving a settlement if given the proper assistance by the parties.

The first thing he needs in order to be useful is not only a list but a full explanation of, and an education in, the meaning and significance of the specific issues. If he has some background in your industry and some experience with your contracts, it should not be too difficult to acquaint him quickly with the implications of the important issues.

Next, he should secure from you some idea of your true list of priorities among the issues on the table. Here you must help him in a little charade. Obviously, the party who made the demands is not going to label a significant number of them unimportant and thereby weaken its initial bargaining position. Nonetheless, the mediator knows that while all the demands are of equal importance, some are of more importance than others. He will seek to elicit from you, and by indirection and without commitment you will do well to convey to him, some order of priority of essentiality among the issues. After he has done the same with the other side, there will evolve a picture of the make-or-break items that have to be reconciled if a contract is to be made without a strike.

The mediator will then explore with each party its reactions to these dominant issues. Ordinarily he does not expect, nor will each party give him, its final position early in the game, preferring to do this close to the moment of truth when rejection must be weighed against the unpleasant alternative of a strike. But in these explorations, a sensitive mediator dealing with sensitive negotiators will divine the extent of elasticity in positions on particular issues. From the knowledge thus gained, he may be able later to put together a balanced proposal that will look better to both parties than the strike alternative.

In talking with the mediator in these latter phases of the negotiations, the important thing for negotiators to remember, it seems to me, is to reject proposals (if they merit rejection) firmly, but to leave escape routes open. The most pitiable case is that of a negotiating team that has said no so emphatically and unconditionally that it has the devil's own time changing its answer when compelled to by later events.

In my own view, the most effective mediator is not the one who is content merely to ride the shuttle between the parties, conveying to each offers or ideas put forth by the other. He is the one who innovates by trying out combinations of ideas on each party in turn, to see if a given combination evokes enough mutual interest to merit more intensive explorations. If you are dealing with such a person, you should aid him by not abruptly shooting down a tentative idea that in its overall design falls within your true area of expectancy, merely because it fails to meet your every demand. I don't mean that you must display instant enthusiasm but in collective bargaining there may be significance in the difference between acceptance on the one hand and nonrejection on the other.

Mediation is most useful when there is equal bargaining power. When the power relationship is unequal, the stronger side will often try to utilize the mediator merely to arrange surrender terms. But even here, properly employed, the mediator can be helpful. Even where one side is the more powerful, it is often prompted to agree to terms of settlement not sharply inconsistent with those being concluded in the industry generally. The mediator, with the negotiator's help, can develop, explain, and argue for this standard often in a way that the weaker party cannot in direct negotiations. In appropriate cases, a mediator can be handled in a way that will advance your cause, not because it is yours, but because it is the right and just thing in the light of prevailing conditions.

COMPLICATIONS BY MANAGEMENT

I should like to close by commenting on one way in which some labor organizations, including yours, and some managements complicate a mediator's task. I refer to those matters which fall within the ambit of collective bargaining but on which unions and sometimes managements adopt fixed, immutable positions in their internal government. They then take a "Nyet!" position at the bargaining table, using the shield of company policy or convention action to blunt all maneuvers leading to compromise.

There is one large corporation in America that has made this philosophy the bedrock of its labor policy. It is a philosophy known as Boulwarism and it may be paraphrased thus:

> We, the corporation, have a responsibility toward the stockholders, the public, and our employees. As custodians of that responsibility, it is up to us to decide what is a fair return to stockholders, a fair price for the consumer and a fair wage for our employees. In dealing with our unions, we have carefully and in good faith analyzed all factors and have reached a position that deals justly with all three groups. Therefore, in negotiating our labor contracts we do not haggle. We lay down our first offer and that is our final one, not to be changed in any of its important essentials.

All of American labor and the greater part of American industry reject this approach to bargaining because it is a negation of the term. Its danger lies not in the fact that it eliminates haggling and horse trading. The danger is more profound. It lies in the fact that one element in our society—in this case the corporation—has arrogated to itself the responsibility of determining how the fruits of productivity are to be shared. If the government undertook to say how much was to go to profit, how much to the consumer in the form of prices, and how much to the worker in wages, we would call it something less than democracy and rightly so. The same is true when a corporation seeks to exercise this power.

KEEP LOOSE

In this society, the goal is to decide such questions by negotiation, consensus, and, hopefully, compromise. I do not intend to equate the tendency of some unions to legislate, in advance of negotiations, conditions of employment in which management should rightly have a voice with Boulwarism, but the analogy is not wholly imperfect. And as far as mediation goes, such fixed position makes the mediator's task impossible. I can only express the hope that in approaching all issues that are embraced by the term "wages, hours and working conditions" both parties will keep loose and not lock themselves in.

2. The Board's Procedures*

Section 10 of the Railway Labor Act charges emergency boards with the duty to ". . . investigate promptly the facts as to the dispute and make a report therein to the President within thirty days from the date of its creation." This board created by the president on March 17, 1964, was appointed on March 27 and met with the parties on March 31, 1964, to receive their opening statements and consider the procedures to be followed in its investigation.

When the board asked the parties to estimate the amount of time they expected to consume in the presentation of their cases, it was informed that a total of about forty-two four-hour days of hearings would be required. While the act does not specify the manner in which the board is to carry out its investigation, the parties have long shown a preference for lengthy, rather formal hearings of a quasijudicial nature in which most witnesses read their testimony and in which mountains of exhibits containing data, some of current value and some of historic significance only, are filed. Prior emergency boards have for the most part accepted this pattern of procedure.

We believe, however, that these procedures deviate from the intent of the framers of the Railway Labor Act. The provision for a report in thirty days must have been made in contemplation of a flexible procedure suited to the problems of each case in which all suitable means of information gathering would be employed, including written statements of the facts; informal discussions with the parties, together and separately; and direct and cross-examination of witnesses where necessary or appropriate. The framers of the act could not have intended that disputes be heard and reports be written in thirty days from

---

*"Report to the President, Emergency Board No. 160," Saul Wallen, chairman; Jean T. McKelvey, member; and Arthur M. Ross, member; August 7, 1964.

the date of a board's creation without conferring on the board the discretionary power to determine the quantum of evidence it requires and the necessary means for obtaining it.

In an attempt to reduce the long delays that have become a feature of disputes handling under the act, the board informally advised the parties in this case that it contemplated requiring the submission of the parties' direct and rebuttal cases in the form of documents and exhibits, after which it proposed to take testimony on those areas in which a factual controversy was thus revealed and to hear summary argument on the disputed issues. However, the parties, long accustomed to their own way of procedure, objected in part on the ground that they had prepared their cases in contemplation of the full-hearing type of procedure. For this reason the board issued the following procedural ruling:

> Emergency Board No. 160 enters into the record the following ruling on the procedure to be observed in the hearing of the dispute between the parties:
> 1. Each party is to be limited to a total of seven days to present its case in chief and its rebuttal evidence or testimony.
> 2. Each party is to be limited to a total of one day for presentation of oral argument.
> 3. The time consumed in cross examination shall be charged to the party doing the cross-examining.
> 4. Written briefs may be filed at the option of the parties.
> 5. In order to permit the most efficient utilization of the allowed time, the Board encourages the parties to submit background or other non-controversial evidence in exhibit form.
> 6. A day of hearing will be six hours, exclusive of recesses. Hearings will commence at 9:00 A.M.
> 7. Hearings will commence on May 4, 1964, in Chicago, Illinois, at a place to be determined. The Organizations' case in chief will be presented during the course of these hearings in Chicago. Thereafter the Carriers' case in chief will be presented in Washington, D. C. at a place to be determined.
> Per order of Emergency Board 160 by Saul Wallen, Chairman.

Even this expedited procedure, however, permitted the presentation of a considerable amount of extraneous material only remotely related to the issues. The fact is that, while some of the documents introduced as exhibits and the testimony of some of the witnesses were valuable in enabling us to grasp the issues, our mediation sessions with the parties constituted a more economical and efficient method for developing the facts concerning, and the implications of, the issues in the case.

It is our hope that future emergency boards will take the initiative in developing procedures suitable to the particular case and will reinstate the flexibility that is inherent in Section 10 of the act in carrying out their investigatory function. We believe that disputes will be settled more expeditiously and more economically if this is done.

* * *

---

3. *Constraint and Variety in Arbitration Systems**
by
Charles C. Killingsworth and Saul Wallen

* * *

The impartial chairman was given a broad grant of authority. All disputes arising during the term of the agreement, "including but not limited to" questions of interpretation or application of the agreement, were within his jurisdiction. He could not change the terms of the agreement; but, if he found that either party was using its rights under the agreement "oppressively," he could remedy that. The primary method of dispute settlement was mediation.

It is important to understand what "mediation" means in this kind of system. It is often assumed that mediation must be a process of splitting the difference, compromising principle, and ignoring contractual rights and obligations. Anyone who has this view of mediation is likely to find that having an issue mediated by an experienced impartial chairman like George Taylor is an unsettling experience. Taylor has said that the essence of mediation is to develop "the consent to lose." Where the principle or the contract right is clear, the task of the chairman may be to persuade the losing party to accept that fact. But where the contract is unclear—as in the "just cause for discharge" concept—or where it simply does not cover a particular dispute, then the task of the impartial chairman is usually to develop a consensus which will clarify or supplement the parties' formal contract. The skillful chairman tells the parties that he can and will decide an issue himself if necessary, but that

---

*Labor Arbitration: Perspectives and Problems, Proceedings of the 17th National Academy of Arbitrators (Washington: BNA, 1964).

the solution is more likely to be mutually acceptable if they agree upon it themselves; he helps them to explore alternatives and may greatly influence the outcome, but decisions on this kind of problem are basically the product of negotiation. Where the contract is brief and phrased in general terms, such guided negotiation will usually be the principal method of resolving disputes. Over time, as the contract becomes more elaborate and precedents accumulate, the emphasis may shift.

* * *

Chapter V

Industry and Society

SAUL WALLEN *strongly believed that organized labor and management were, as members of society, responsible to it for their actions. As an arbitrator, mediator, and executive director of the New York Urban Coalition, Wallen had much opportunity to expound his views in this regard. Wallen wrote extensively on the public interest in labor-management relations. This chapter contains excerpts of his arbitration decisions and speeches which pertain to this issue.*

The first section of the chapter contains two arbitration decisions in which Wallen took into consideration the interest of the public in the outcome of such disputes. In the first case, Wallen had to rule on the discharge of an allegedly unqualified pilot. In this unusual case, Wallen found that management's responsibility to the public to assure safe personnel and equipment gave it greater latitude in determining just cause than is ordinarily the case. In the second case, in reviewing the discharge of an employee who refused to wear safety glasses on a dangerous job, Wallen found that the employee had a community responsibility to avoid becoming a ward of the state because of unnecessary injury on the job due to his own negligence.

The public interest in labor-management disputes was of paramount importance to Wallen when he served on several presidential emergency boards. The second section of this chapter contains excerpts of an article written by Wallen that related his views regarding the nature of the "emergencies" under the Railway Labor Act and Taft-Hartley emergency procedures.

The last section of this chapter includes several of Wallen's papers and speeches delivered after he became executive director of the New York City Urban Coalition. These deal primarily with the problems of, and industry's responsibility for, the employment of society's unemployables. Of particular interest is a brief letter of Wallen's responding to one of the Coalition's critics. This letter beautifully reflects the intensity of Wallen's commitment to the Coalition and, more importantly, to the resolution of the many urban problems for which he believed all members of society had a responsibility.

1. Arbitration Cases

National Airlines and the Air Line Pilots Association, International, August 1, 1950

* * *

The ordinary collective bargaining agreement usually circumscribes the employer's common-law right to discharge by requiring that it be only for just cause. In the usual discharge case under such agreements management, which initiates the discharge, carries the burden of proving that cause for the action exists. As for quantum of proof, cause must be established by a preponderance of the evidence. If the evidence leaves the existence of cause in doubt the burden has not been sustained. In the instant agreement Section 28 governs discipline and dismissal of pilots. It provides for notice of discipline or dismissal and for investigation and hearing at the pilot's request. The tenor of the entire section is that a pilot will be disciplined or dismissed only if cause exists and that the investigation and hearing is provided in order that a determination may be made whether there was just cause for the discharge. Airline pilots, like others working under collective agreements, have sought and achieved a measure of job security, of protection against the exercise of the unfettered right to discharge held by employers at common law.

In ordinary employments this doctrine is applicable with a minimum degree of difficulty. Its essential fairness has been recognized by management and unions alike. It has evolved and survived because the cost of an erroneous judgment in a doubtful case is not usually great. However, the carrier in this case asserts that because it is charged by law with a positive duty to perform its services with the highest degree of safety in the public interest its action on the discharge of pilot personnel should not be reviewable in the usual sense but only with respect to whether it was discriminatory, arbitrary, malicious, or capricious. One is constrained to agree that because of the nature of the industry and of airline management's safety responsibility a lesser degree of proof of a pilot's lack of qualifications is in order than is true in other fields of employment. But if management is to have the benefit of this lesser standard in the interests of carrying out its responsibility for the safety of the public, its actions must be free of all taint of arbitrariness, capriciousness, favoritism, or discrimination and the evidence must be convincing that the pilot, and not extraneous factors, was responsible for the acts on which the charge of incompetency was based. Only then would there be some justification for resolving doubts as to pilot competency in favor of management and against the pilot; for if errors are made under such circumstances they would be in the interests of safety.

But where there is evidence that the action of discharge is tainted with motives other than a concern for safety or that the acts of the pilot on which the incompetency charge is based were the result of other causes, the degree of proof required to establish a pilot's lack of qualifications increases. More than mere reasonable grounds for the carrier's action must be shown. A lack of ability must be demonstrated by a fair weight of the evidence. Otherwise, errors might be committed not in the interests of safety, which is proper given the nature of the industry, but in support of a malevolent intent or an erroneous conclusion. This rule is necessary to prevent a carrier from using its obligation in the matter of safety as a shield for attacks on the job security of pilots and, at the same time, to prevent pilots and their organizations from using the charge of discrimination to cloak a lack of flying technique and judgment.

* * *

What is an unsafe pilot? Certainly not one who at one time or another fails to observe some aspect of the voluminous regulations governing his craft. On that basis practically all pilots could be deemed unsafe in the same way that practically all motorists are guilty at one time or another of traffic code transgressions. An unsafe pilot is either one whose record over a period of time shows a progressive failure or inability to maintain his mastery of flying techniques or exercise sound judgment or one who at a given time commits acts that violate such important basic tenets of aviation safety as to clearly demonstrate that he lacks the judgment to continue to be a pilot.

* * *

Union Carbide Corporation, Linde Division, and International Brotherhood of Teamsters, July 31, 1967

* * *

P_____'s refusal to wear safety glasses and his unilateral determination that sunglasses would do was as foolish as it was dangerous. The headache excuse, often invoked by those who do not wish to be saved from their own folly, is transparent nonsense. One can suppose that P_____ reasons that they are his own eyes and he can, if he wishes, risk them as he pleases. This simplistic reasoning does not fit a society which imposes on the employer and on the community as a whole the cost of care of those disabled in the course of their employment. P_____ and others owe it to the community, to their employers, and to themselves to avoid injury by taking reasonable safety precautions.

* * *

2. *National Emergency Disputes**

I propose to open this talk with a sweeping general statement. Since World War II and except for the period of the Korean War, there has been only one dispute that truly created a national emergency. That was the one-day national railroad strike in 1948, which was ended even as President Truman was engaged in handing the problem over to the Congress.

Many other disputes in this period were labeled as creators of national emergencies but none truly met the test of dire *imminent* paralysis of the nation's life or defense posture.

For example, the thirteen-state Pennsylvania Railroad strike in which the Transport Workers' Union is now engaged, according to today's *New York Times* (September 7, 1960), has not stopped the flow of products to the nation's major markets. The sixty-three-day Louisville & Nashville Railroad strike of several years ago inconvenienced but did not paralyze the area that the line served. The airline strikes of 1958, which involved Capital, Eastern, TWA, and American in turn, did not keep many people at home.

Yet nearly all of those disputes were the subjects of declarations of national emergency by the president of the United States under the Railway Labor Act.

It is noteworthy that the term "emergency" is not defined in the Railway Labor Act or in the Taft-Hartley Act but is left to the judgment of the president to determine. In an earlier day there was little reason to define the term. Any extensive paralysis of the railroad system, even in a

---

*Labor Law Journal 12 (no. 1, January 1961): 61-66.

particular area of the country, created a crisis in transportation which effectively cut off shippers from receivers of goods and thwarted travel between cities. Modern technology, however, has changed all of this. The nation's highway system has grown so tremendously and the availability of over-the-road trucking has increased to such an extent that it is now possible, when railroad transport is shut down, for goods to be shipped by truck. Passengers, previously dependent solely on the railroads, travel now largely by airline and when either or both of these are shut down, intercity buses and private automobiles still remain a means of rapid transportation.

Nonetheless, the White House is still called upon under the Railway Labor Act and, occasionally, under the national emergency provisions of the Taft-Hartley Act, to intervene in labor disputes on the ground that an imminent dispute will create a national emergency. The result has been that the office of the president has often been used, sometimes by labor and sometimes by management, to secure governmental intervention in disputes in the hope that the power and thrust of the other side will thus be blunted. Such intervention often occurs in the guise of dealing with an emergency when in fact no realistic emergency actually exists.

PRESIDENTIAL INTERVENTION

Presidential intervention in last year's steel strike in the form of a Taft-Hartley injunction also left much to be desired in terms of its timing. Was there an emergency when the president intervened? Or was the nation inconvenienced without yet being imperiled? The opinion of Justice William O. Douglas in the Supreme Court case involving the challenge to the president's right to invoke the Taft-Hartley Act in that dispute was that, if the country faced an emergency because the supply of steel was cut off from plants working on defense contracts, the government should do no more than order a resumption of production in the few plants whose output would be vital to meet its defense needs and not intervene massively by requiring the entire industry to resume production before the dispute between the parties was settled.

What are the consequences of this improper use of the word "emergency" as a basis for the intervention by government in major disputes?

One consequence has been the increasingly frequent rejection of recommendations of emergency boards appointed by the president to hear disputes under the Railway Labor Act. Knowing that strike action would not in fact create an emergency, some unions have been impelled to use emergency board recommendations as a basis from which to negotiate upward during a strike. The debasement of the emergency features of the Railway Labor Act and the too free use of the emergency features of the Taft-Hartley Act have in more cases than necessary bred disrespect for the recommendations of boards of inquiry.

PUBLIC'S ATTITUDE

The fact is that there is an ambivalence in the public's attitude toward governmental intervention (other than as mediator) in labor disputes of national magnitude. Should the government intervene only if there is a true emergency in the sense that the national safety is immediately imperiled or should the government intervene if there is a significant disruption in a normal routine of a segment of the population as a result of a strike or strike threat even though no true emergency is created thereby?

These questions are important because today we have no policy on them. Each dispute is handled ad hoc. Western Airlines, for example, went through a ninety-day strike of pilots in 1958 while the administration withstood pressure from the company, the union, and . . . a bloc of western congressmen and senators for the appointment of an emergency board. This, despite the fact that the shutdown of that airline greatly inconvenienced the many communities served by that single airline. On the other hand, Pan American Airways, threatened with a strike by the Brotherhood of Railway Clerks in 1960, succeeded in getting the White House to appoint an emergency board over the objections of the Brotherhood of Railway Clerks, even though the effect of a strike on that property would have been to hurt the company's business at the peak of the tourist season but not to unduly inconvenience the tourists, who had many alternative means of getting home from their European vacations in the summer of [that] year.

These questions are important also because the answer will have much to do with the development of more effective methods for dealing with disputes of this type. The dispute which involves mere inconvenience to the public lends itself to a variety of treatments short of an imposed settlement. The one which truly involves an emergency may require the drastic treatment of an imposed settlement (or the threat of one, as in the 1948 railroad strike) to meet the overriding national interest.

Furthermore, the present Railway Labor Act depends largely on public opinion to force acceptance of emergency board recommendations. What does public opinion mean in a strike which inconveniences but causes no real hardship to a relatively minor segment of the nation over issues of which the public is hardly aware, dealt with in reports which they never read, embodying solutions they scarcely understand?

There is one practical reason for anticipating that government will tend to intervene in disputes which fall short of creating a true emergency as long as they have a significant impact on the national economic life. That is politics. Under our party system, government cannot afford to sit by indefinitely while labor and management engage in a protracted brawl of national import. The vote-conscious politician cannot permit it except in relatively minor disputes of narrow impact. The impulse of government, as custodian of the peoples' well-being, is to act. In an earlier day, when governmental philosophy was not attuned to the role of custodian of the peoples' well-being, government was inclined to act only where civil commotion made action imperative. Today people look to government to play a decisive role even in circumstances where the situation is drastic, though not dire.

Further, a persuasive case can be made for the proposition that a country living in a near-permanent state of international tension, engaged in the competitive race with an adversary who boasts he will bury us, can ill afford the luxury of untrammeled labor disputes and that its government must take positive action even where the peril is long range rather than immediate.

Finally, in many cases not involving a national emergency, both labor and management long for and welcome suggestions leading to settlement after an airing of the issues, though they often are in no position to say so publicly.

Thus the tendency, as I see it, is for governmental intervention short of compulsory arbitration in major disputes which do not create true national emergencies. The trouble has been that we have neither acknowledged this to be our policy nor applied it consistently.

What is needed, then, is a statement in the laws which would give realistic meaning to the [word] "emergency" in the Railway Labor Act and to the phrase "imperil the health and safety" in the Taft-Hartley Act to the end that disputants will know in advance whether or not their dispute is likely to involve governmental intervention. If bargainers are firmly convinced that government is not likely to intervene, they will tend to bargain realistically with full cognizance of the likelihood of a strike or a lockout. If, on the other hand, they bargain with one eye cocked toward the likelihood of governmental intervention, questions arise about the nature of such intervention in major disputes.

These are the alternatives:

(1) Compulsory arbitration. No one wants it and there is no serious body of opinion in support of its imposition.

(2) Factfinding with recommendations. We have it now under the Railway Labor Act, but not under the Taft-Hartley.

(3) Factfinding without recommendations. This is the current procedure when a national emergency is declared under the provisions of Taft-Hartley.
(4) Mediation only.

If we rule out compulsory arbitration as undesirable, I believe that factfinding with recommendations is the formula most likely to succeed where mediation has failed. But in my judgment the present method of accomplishing this under the Railway Labor Act is yielding diminishing returns. Witness the strike of the International Association of Machinists which represents the airline mechanics. In 1958, six airlines and the machinists were joined in a proceeding before an emergency board appointed by the president of the United States. This board recommended a 21 cents-per-hour wage package. The machinists rejected the recommendations, went out on strike and were successful in winning wage increases ranging from 48 cents to 54 cents per hour. Similarly, emergency board recommendations on the Long Island Railroad, on the Pennsylvania Railroad, and on Eastern Air Lines, involved in disputes, the pilots and the flight engineers were rejected. Strikes resulted in all of these cases.

The record of rejections in the last few years of recommendations of emergency boards under the Railway Labor Act emphasizes the argument that there are serious flaws in the act and that it should be revised. Those who favor the preservation of the act in its present form might argue that the recent railroad settlements, on which the operating brotherhoods and the railroads agreed to final and binding arbitration and in which the nonoperating brotherhoods accepted the emergency board recommendations, demonstrate that the act continues to be effective. I submit that the success of the act in dealing with the recent threatened crisis on the railroad was due to special circumstances. The strategy of the parties was deeply affected by the pressure of the railroads for revision of work rules.

It is unlikely that the disputes would have taken the same course had the brotherhoods not desired to split off the question of wages from the question of work rules.

The fact is that negotiations and mediation in major disputes under the Railway Labor Act and in some disputes not covered by that act have been conducted against a reasonable certainty that factfinding with or without recommendations is likely to follow.

Hence there has been little disposition on the part of the parties to compromise or to yield prior to the appointment of emergency boards or factfinding boards. Furthermore, as the experience on the airlines in 1958 shows, emergency boards, acting like boards of arbitration, have not taken sufficiently into account the relative strength of the parties. Recommendations, even generous ones, by emergency boards have little possibility of acceptance if one of the parties is convinced that rejection and resort to strike action will yield substantially greater benefits. If there is too great a disparity between what can be secured through strike action and what can be secured from recommendations of an emergency board, the strike weapon is likely to be used.

PUBLIC NOT REACHED

In addition, the recommendations of emergency boards do not have sufficient circulation among the public or even among the employees on the property affected to sufficiently mold attitudes of workers or of the public to bring about a settlement.

Finally, recommendations in disputes going to emergency boards or factfinding boards generally are made at a stage in the history of the dispute in which positions have become fixed and rigid. It might make sense to reform the emergency board procedures of the Railway Labor Act and to introduce features into the Taft-Hartley Act along the following lines:

A problem in many disputes is the failure to define and list the issues in a public way early in the dispute. Mediation can and often does accomplish this end, but in a major dispute it is difficult for the mediator to summarize and advertise the issues in such a way as to make the public aware of their precise bounds. Take, for example, the dispute over Section 2B in the steel contract in 1959. For months the dispute dragged on and the public had no notion of what 2B was. Even the best of the newspaper reports had difficulty in pinning down and clarifying the true nature of the dispute. Only after many months of negotiations and strike action, culminating in the appointment of the Taylor board under the Taft-Hartley Act, was the precise nature of the Section 2B problem recorded and reported in terms that the public could begin to understand. For reasons which remain obscure to this day, the companies failed to pinpoint the true nature of the problem confronting them. At the same time the unions had no immediate interest in doing so. The probing and searching of Dr. [George] Taylor's factfinding board finally did much to illumine the problem.

It might be well, therefore, to introduce the use of factfinding by emergency boards relatively early in major disputes, after mediation has been tried but before the dispute has gone too far. At that stage it might be well to confine the factfinding activities to a hearing in which the issues will be listed and explained. The board could explore with the parties the relative importance of the several issues and list them in a preliminary report, ranking them in categories of importance. This preliminary report could then be turned over to the parties and to the mediators as a basis for a resumption of direct negotiations within specified time limits.

All of the issues placed by the board in categories of major importance which are not settled in the subsequent negotiations could then be heard by the same emergency board on their merits. But instead of making flat recommendations for their disposition, the emergency board could recommend reasonable limits within which the parties could reach a voluntary settlement. Such a report might rule out some demands as wholly unreasonable, recommend the granting of others as wholly reasonable and recommend alternative possibilities of settlement within limits for still others.

This second report could then become the basis for a further resumption of direct negotiations and mediation. In the meantime, the board or an appropriate government agency could be given the task of preparing a one-page summary of the recommendations; of sending a copy of the summary to each employee affected, at his home; and of having it advertised in the national press. A strike would be permitted after the foregoing procedures had been exhausted. In that event the employees, the employers, and the public would be able to know and understand the precise nature of the strike issues.

It might be argued that this procedure is not dissimilar from the procedure now followed by emergency boards under the Railway Labor Act. I think, however, that there are important differences. Under the approach suggested above, the important issues would be segregated from the less important ones. The important issues would be carefully defined in a way which collective bargaining now often fails to define them. The parties would be obligated to bargain on the issues thus defined before they are made the subject of recommendations by the emergency board.

Today much of the bargining that precedes the creation of an emergency board is pro forma and diffuse. This procedure would strip the issues down to the barest essentials, put them in terms that all concerned—including the public—could understand and provide a rallying point for public opinion.

3. Industrial Relations Problems of Employing the Disadvantaged*

This subject, "Industrial Relations Problems of Employing the Disadvantaged," in its broader reaches is one of profound significance for both practitioners and students of labor relations.

Out of the turmoil of the thirties and early forties, there have developed orderly procedures for the determination of wages, hours, and working conditions and for the resolution of day-to-day disputes. These procedures have served the society well. They have not been free of conflict; nor have they resolved all the questions that have arisen over the decades, some of which we have so far found impossible to answer. Nonetheless, the institution of modern industrial relations, which so many in this audience helped to create, shape, and make function, has by and large achieved the dual goals of accommodating necessary change while maintaining economic and social stability.

Now, however, we are faced with a new condition of massive social change which presses inexorably on established institutions—collective bargaining, trade unionism, and industrial relations not excepted. Can these particular institutions respond to these pressures by reshaping themselves to accommodate to the new condition? Or do we face a clash of contending forces that can yield only the destruction of one or the other?

Since I am not a seer or a pundit or a guru, I can neither predict with assurance nor accept with equanimity what time will bring. The future is clouded and uncertain. One has the feeling and sees the portents of impending change without sure guides as to the nature and direction of change. All one can do at this time is point up and classify the signs of change and the problems they overlay in the hope that, if fully understood, means can be developed to reconcile change with ongoing values.

But first we must appreciate how our present circumstance is different from what went on before. After all, this is not the first time that Negroes have entered the industrial labor force in significant numbers. During World War I, again during World War II, and through the postwar prosperity of the forties, there was a significant migration of blacks from the rural South to the industries of the North. Many of them were, if not disadvantaged in the current sense of the term, at least

---

*Arbitration and Social Change, Proceedings of the 22nd Annual Meeting, National Academy of Arbitrators, Gerald G. Somers, ed. (Washington, D. C. : BNA, 1969) : 65-75.

uprooted, thrust into an alien environment, and the first to suffer the vicissitudes of the labor market. Their entry into the labor force and into factory life was not without conflict. Nonetheless, it did not create the explosive possibilities for industrial relations that the current situation presents.

The reason for the difference, I think, lies in the new consciousness, self-pride, and resolution of identity that is the chief feature of the current black revolution. Today's Negro, able to live with himself, able to accept his own blackness, and resolved to rely primarily on his own strength, now wants "in"—"in" to jobs, "in" to apprenticeships, "in" to unions—not as just another worker but as a black worker. And as a black worker he wants the institutions he is entering to adjust to the special inequities and disabilities arising out of the long economic and social inferiority imposed upon him by a largely hostile white society.

The industrial relations problems associated with the employment of minority workers in larger numbers, a goodly proportion of whom come under the rubric of "the disadvantaged," can be classified for purposes of discussions under several headings.

One is the problem of administering agreements. Another is the problem of making agreements, with its concomitant problem of internal union government. A third is the problem of interpersonal relationships in the plant—between supervision and disadvantaged workers and between the newly hired disadvantaged and the established work force. A fourth is the problem of entry into the trade where there are strong elements of union control.

ADMINISTERING AGREEMENTS

The reconcilement of the employment of the disadvantaged with the established norms of contract administration is a problem now frequently encountered by companies and unions. Take, for example, the National Alliance of Businessmen's program of getting employers to pledge to employ the hard-core unemployed and of compensating employers for the extra costs of remediation and skills training that must be imparted to this stratum of the population. Under the MA-3 and MA-4 contracts, the hard-core recruit is on the employer's payroll from day one. Does the contract probationary period apply to these workers even during the period of their remediation training? Even where hired directly for the line or the bench, the hard-core may need a longer period in which to become acclimated to the workplace. The conventional probation, ordinarily adequate to determine the fitness of the average worker motivated for employment and reasonably secure in his new environment, may be quite unsuited for the minority man or woman never before introduced into the world of work.

In this situation some unions have been willing to negotiate special probationary arrangements to apply to their companies' hard-core employment programs. But this has been far from universal. No data are available, and one can only speculate on the extent to which rigid agreement provisions, drawn for typical labor market conditions, have thwarted the recruitment and training of the special population that makes up the hard-core unemployed.

But the complications of the problem extend beyond labor agreement rigidity. Assuming the willingness of a union to relax contract standards for probationary employment for the hard-core, can the normal standards for the rest of the new hires be maintained? What is the impact on general employee morale of preferential treatment for specialized groups? Granted that the fact of long deprivation of opportunity now justifies compensatory arrangements for minorities, can the rest of the plant population be induced to accept this concept?

These are the kinds of questions every industrial relations manager and every union official must deal with if the problems that won't go away are to be faced realistically. Too often questions are avoided by both parties, the unions remaining unyielding in their refusal to bend old rules to new conditions and the employers hiding piously behind "union rules" in an endeavor to avoid the complications that will follow if the demands of the times are met.

Take the simple problem of in-plant discipline—observance of shop rules with regard to tardiness, loitering, remaining at one's workplace, and behavior toward one's fellow employees or toward supervision.

The average white worker who enters a plant is presumed to have had some conditioning in his background as a result of which, it is assumed, he will be able to meet the norms of conduct in these respects. Only the misfits—relatively few in number—are screened out by rules. But apply the same rules to the disadvantaged and the experience often is that they don't work—that they screen out more people than they retain.

This is neither illogical nor unexpected when one reflects on it. The minority disadvantaged (and in some sections the white indigenous poor as well) have been raised in the conviction that the larger world has no place for them. The basic facts of their deprivation have trained them in habits that are antithetical to the rhythms of the productive process. They often enter an environment they believe to be hostile, and they are often right.

Straight logic would impel a management to bend its rules to recognize the disadvantages of the disadvantaged. But if such logic is exercised, what happens to the rules? Can they be applied more generously to the disadvantaged minority employees than to the run-of-the-mill whites and still maintain their viability?

Every management that hires minority people these days faces these questions, and on occasion my arbitrator brethren do, too. They try to walk the fine line between rigid adherence to the requirements of plant discipline, on the one hand, and complete capitulation to the concept that people so long deprived need to be held to only minimal standards of behavior, on the other. The first course is mechanistic and often callous; the second is sentimental and often overpermissive. To find and hold to a middle ground that takes into account the disadvantaged worker's special background without undermining the total concept of industrial discipline is a major challenge for company and union contract administrators.

MAKING OF AGREEMENTS

The expansion in the employment of minorities may well lead to larger problems in the making of agreements. Every employer knows he is in for headaches if he has to make a contract with a union of sharp factions. And every union leader with factional division in his organization is inhibited in his collective bargaining by the compulsion to take nervous glances over his shoulder.

The awakened self-identity and self-pride of black workers tends to foster the group cohesiveness of minority unionists. This will tend to develop power blocs with their own agenda and with their own sets of leaders who have their own sets of personal ambitions.

There are disquieting signs of this polarization. It interacts, of course, with the increasing blue-collar and lower-middle-class reaction to Negro militancy and assertiveness in behalf of their needs and their rights.

These contending emotional reactions, fed by the strident cries of black ultramilitants on the left and the Wallacite reactionary militants on the right, are leading to formations of blocs within unions. Witness the proposal at the Steel Workers Union convention last fall, offered by a bloc of Negro delegates, that a certain number of posts in the union's leadership be automatically set aside for blacks. The idea was rejected by the delegates, but it is symptomatic of the development of power bloc union politics based on race.

In other unions, black caucuses are being formed to marshal the views and exert the pressures of minority workers on the larger group. At best, such caucuses can work within the structure to advance legitimate claims of the minorities for total union attention. At worst, they can become divisive power centers to the detriment of all concerned. I was told of one extreme case recently where a contract made between a university and its organized building service employees was ratified by the majority—the majority being all white and the minority being all black and Puerto Rican—with the minority then manning picket lines. What was the university management to do? It could not very well yield. The replacement of the dissidents—a sizable number—was fraught with dangers, especially in these days on a campus with its potential for a student-worker nexus.

I don't know how this story came out, but I cite it as an extreme example of the potential trials industrial relations may encounter in the current situation of the growth of minority employment coupled with the push of Negroes for their rightful share of the society's abundance. The development of the DRUM movement at the Dodge Hamtramck plant, the FRUM movement at Ford, the Concerned Transit Workers in Chicago, and among blacks in Division 241 of the Amalgamated are other straws in the wind.

Employers are perhaps less able than unions to influence the course of these events. The latter must find ways to intergrate into union leadership the spokesmen of these emergent elements. This leadership must be won over to a concern for the needs and aspirations of all unionists, not the blacks alone. And this can be done only if the established leadership simultaneously begins to turn to a redress of the special disabilities long suffered by minority people in their work environment—to a removal of long-existing, though often informal, limitations on promotion opportunities, to the creation of training programs that will help remove the "ability" obstacle in the promotion clause.

These and many other obstacles to a fuller integration of blacks into union life and into the higher reaches of occupational structure must be removed if the kind of polarization that can otherwise lead to factional splits and, conceivably, attempts at dual unionism is to be averted. Most important, there is a need for the conscious development of responsible minority people for leadership roles in the union structure.

INTERPERSONAL RELATIONS

The expanded employment of the disadvantaged has been the result, in most cases, of top management decisions among the larger employers to meet this vast, long-neglected social problem. Those decisions were the outgrowth, in turn, of a combination of pressures that created in large industry a concern with the problem—legal pressures, labor market pressures, civil disturbance pressures, and demographic pressures that made it plain that in the major urban centers the labor supply and the market of the future will be heavily minority.

But top management decisions, as you all know, have a way of becoming diluted, abraded, or misshapen between their promulgation and their execution. Hence the best intentioned of policies are often imperfectly carried out.

They usually founder on the rocks of human stubbornness and prejudice that are not removed by the issuance of ukases from on high. The case of the employment of the disadvantaged is no exception. Just because the chairman of the board has finally decided that we must find a place for those in the society longest the victims of our collective neglect, it does not follow that the foremen in Department 42 will follow suit. They are the products of their own emotions, prejudices, and backgrounds.

These, in turn, often determine whether management's desire to integrate the disadvantaged into the work force will be successful. And success in this respect will not be happenstance. It will come only if the emotions and prejudices that militate against success are exorcised.

This problem of the interpersonal relationship between supervisors and the older work force, on the one hand, and minority workers in general and the disadvantaged in particular, on the other, can be met by well-designed long-range efforts to counsel and educate the minority workers' supervisors and fellow employees in the origins and history of their special problems and the psychology of their attitudes and behavior. Only with this sort of deeper understanding is a program of employing the disadvantaged likely to succeed.

The challenge for personnel and industrial relations executives is to seek out or devise such programs and apply them not only to supervisors, but also to the rank and file in the plant. This is no small order, but one is reminded that it can be done by the fact that a whole generation of foremen in the forties and fifties, at first hostile to unionism and later cowed by it, were trained into an understanding of the proper role of foremanship vis-à-vis this huge new force.

ENTRY INTO TRADES

The final area of industrial relations that is fraught with problems arising out of the needs of the minorities to take their rightful place in the field of employment is in those trades and crafts where entry is controlled by apprenticeship or hiring hall arrangements.

Whenever one speaks with people not close to the labor scene—black or white—the question is inevitably encountered: "What of the building trades?" The building trades seem, in blanket fashion, to have become the bête noir of those of both races who profess to be anxious to advance the status of minorities.

There is, of course, a history of reluctance or refusal by some building trades unions to admit Negroes. It ran hand in hand with discrimination in hiring policies which existed for many years in nonunion plants and in industries where unions have little say about hiring.

Slowly (too slowly), however, these restrictions are breaking down and barriers are beginning to be lowered. While it is a fact that only about 4 percent of the nation's apprentices in the urban areas are minority group people, there are signs of forward movement. The IBEW's Local 3, under Harry Van Arsdale in New York, has made fine strides in recruiting Negro and Puerto Rican workers into membership via the apprentice route. A number of other building trades unions—the laborers, the carpenters, and others—have not had bars to entry into the trade.

Under the spur of the EEOC and of the provision in the Model Cities program which calls for "maximum opportunities" for employment of ghetto residents on Model Cities projects, the Building Trades department of the AFL-CIO and the national building trades employers associations have recommended to their respective local bodies that they negotiate a trainee classification in the crafts for Model Cities projects with a sliding scale of rates leading to attainment of journeymen's scale. C. J. Haggerty, in a letter to Secretary [Willard] Wirtz on February 1, 1968, promised "maximum utilization of responsible civil rights organizations willing to join in a cooperative effort . . ." of support for minority recruitment.

But in the last analysis, the fate of these encouraging efforts will rest with the local building trades unions. And these, in turn, vary greatly in their willingness to remove racial barriers to minority participation in building trades employment.

The building trades scene, then, is one of slow, spotty progress in the matter of employment of minorities—this in the face of the likelihood of vastly expanded building programs if the nation decides to become serious about tackling the job of eliminating its slums.

The industrial relations implications of this state of affairs are obvious. Given the new Negro militancy, the likelihood of large-scale construction in ghetto areas by all-white crews is not great. But unless a significantly greater number of blacks, Mexican-Americans, and Puerto Ricans are admitted into the work force, the possibility of turmoil in these industries cannot be denied.

There is a tendency to view "the union" as the entity that discriminates. This view, of course, is superficial. I know of a number of craft union officials who are willing to move faster in the matter of minority employment, but who encounter such implacable opposition from their rank and file that they put their jobs on the line if they advance the idea.

At the extreme of a range of possibilities are proposals for the establishment of black building trades unions. This would be a most unfortunate development for the society, for the labor movement, and for employers, and no one at this point in time believes that it is a likelihood. Nonetheless, it is being talked about in minority circles. The best hope is that progress in integrating minority people into the construction crafts will be sufficient to stem any such movement.

CONCLUSION

These, then, are some of the industrial relations problems that loom in the continuing national effort to further the employment of minority people and the disadvantaged. It may be that the potential crisis will turn out to be more apparent than real—that minority people, while developing and cherishing their cultural identity, will blend their efforts for economic advancement smoothly into the programs of the larger labor movement. Much will depend on how unions and employers act to encourage and foster these trends.

This blending of the minorities smoothly into the larger labor movement is a result devoutly to be wished. But to the extent that there are other tendencies at work, it is not likely to be achieved without difficulties that will be felt by all involved in industrial relations.

4. *Urban Problems and the Private Sector**

We are a people of drastically changing moods. For years we looked only to government to cure our social ills. Business was regarded at best as indifferent, at worst as hostile to social change in the New Deal days. Government was the instrument by which it was wrought.

In the postwar decades and until recently, there was wider recognition of business' beneficent role in the raising of living standards by maximizing production, maintaining reasonably stable prices, and raising wages and salaries, the latter not without the pressure of labor unions. But business' concern about the quality of life, about provety, about slums, about civil rights and equal employment was absent. After all, it

*Address delivered at the June 7. 1968, Meeting of the Industrial Relations Research Association, Southern California Chapter, Los Angeles. Manuscript in Saul Wallen's files.

was only in 1963 that Roger Blough, when asked to bring the power of United States Steel to bear on the question of civil rights in Birmingham after the church bombings there, said that it would not be proper for business to exercise its power for any particular set of social views.

Now, however, it is a new ball game. Business, particularly big business, is in the urban-problem solving business, at least philosophically, with a vengeance.

Critics of the private sector allow that this interest is long overdue. They say it reminds them of the two octogenarians, veterans of World War I, sitting and rocking on the veranda of the Old Soldiers Home. One says to the other, "Remember those pills that they used to give us in France to make us forget girls? I think they're beginning to work."

But late or not, the new involvement of the private sector in urban problems is to be welcomed because, while these problems will never be solved by the private sector alone, neither will they be solved by government alone.

Here is an example. New York City owns some eight-hundred parcels of vacant land in its twenty-six areas designated as slums. For the most part they are filled with debris, garbage, and waste, breeding rats and decay. The quality of life in these areas would be improved if they were cleared and converted into miniparks for neighborhood recreation. The cost is small—perhaps $10,000 to $30,000 apiece—to clear and landscape for a park. Moreover, the parks department has capital funds for the purpose. We at the Urban Coalition talked to the parks commissioner to spur such a program.

"If you expect us to get it done, forget it," he said. He explained the engineering bottlenecks, the necessity for approval and clearance of plans in the several layers of his civil service bureaucracy, the delays encountered at each level, the bidding procedures that by law have to be followed before the city can let each contract, the approvals and clearances that have to be obtained for each commitment of funds. He was right.

But the New York Urban Coalition is not about to forget it. We are embarking on a program to create one hundred such miniparks by persuading private-sector business donors or vanity givers each to contribute the money; getting a neighborhood community organization to sponsor, help design, and maintain each project; and getting private contractors to use the maximum amount of local labor in carrying out the project.

The great impediment to the solution of the problems of urban decay by local government lies in just this encrustation of obsolete regulations, procedural roadblocks, special-interest legislation, and bureaucratic timidity. If the City of New York builds a structure—a housing project or a single building—it cannot let a single contract to a general contractor who will then let pieces of the project to subcontractors. Because of the provisions of the Wickes Law, passed many years ago in response to pressures from both the contractors and the building trades unions, each project must be subject to bids by prime contractors within four separate categories—land clearance and foundations, structure, electrical, and plumbing. The law was passed, I suppose, to insure that contracts would be available for the many, not monopolized by a few prime contractors who might be tempted to intensify bidding by the subcontractors. But its impact on cost is considerable, and, since locally sponsored, federally financed housing must meet rather rigid cost limits, the handicap is obvious.

Another case in point is the time it takes a contractor working for the city to get paid for his services. Every bill the city pays must be approved by the controller. He has a staff to see that the work promised was performed to specification. In a city the size of New York, the work load of that office is tremendous and it takes six to eight months for a contractor to collect. The reason for these controls is laudable. After all, New York City was more than once looted by Boss Tweed and the old Tammany Ring, and the reformers who ousted them wanted to be sure it didn't happen again. But their zeal effectively thwarts a lot else from happening too. On top of this, when there is a mayor of one party and a controller of another, the charge is heard that delays are at times prolonged in order to embarrass the administration. Whether true or not, a contractor for the city must figure into his costs the cost of money he must advance to tide him over this period.

Since so much of the urban problem is a problem of housing, education, and employment and since it is precisely in these areas that government, for a host of reasons, is most muscle bound, the need for private-sector involvement is manifest.

The motivation for private-sector involvement is mixed, as one would expect in any aspect of human behavior. Management's interest in and concern with ghetto problems has deepened with the deepening of the crisis in our cities. The menace of civil disorder has galvanized into action several latent influences on management behavior in this area. The first influence is the very human concern management shares with most of enlightened America about the appalling waste of human resources in ghetto life. Michael Harrington's book *The Other America* tapped deep roots in the American conscience, in business ranks no less than elsewhere. The second influence on business behavior is the deepening concern about the impact on business of the social instability expressed in the ghetto revolt. The third is the realization that the demographic changes confronting the nation in the next few decades are inexorable, that our cities will become increasingly populated by blacks and Puerto Ricans in the East and Middle West and by blacks and Mexican-Americans in the West, that these will be major sources of our future labor supply in the cities, and that they will be the future market for industry's goods and services.

The industries that are most deeply rooted in their communities and the least mobile are the ones most committed to solving the problems of urban decay: the utilities, which cannot move elsewhere; the banks and insurance companies; the department stores. The large employers in general who have the foresight and the resources to look ahead are beginning to meet the problem. But the small or medium-sized employer, concerned with his day-to-day headaches, does not project either his markets or his manpower needs. Although short of qualified labor, he lives in the illusion that a miracle will occur and that, if he advertises enough, a qualified labor supply somehow will show up. He has neither the vision nor the resources to realize that if his future labor supply is not educated and upgraded now he may have neither workers nor customers later.

But the private sector is not just management, it is the labor unions as well. To what extent are they facing up to the requirements of the new day?

The most significant aspect of the urban problem is poverty. In one sense labor had been fighting poverty before it became fashionable. It did so by raising wages from subsistence to respectable levels in many industries. When your hospital unions raised wages of hospital workers—mostly black or Mexican-American—from a pittance to $2.00 or more per hour, they thwarted a lot of poverty as a result. This sort of thing has been the stock in trade of the labor movement, a fact which many newly aroused poverty fighters are prone to overlook. Also, some, though by no means all, unions led the way in insisting on nondiscrimination clauses in contracts and nondiscriminatory practices on the job.

At the same time, the very success of the labor movement has created vested interests that are at war with the desires of the ghetto people to advance with greater rapidity. Seniority protections, promotion ladders, prerequisites for entry into the trade are all inclined toward the workers who are already there or the sons and daughters of those who had been there. They are not likely to be black, Mexican-American, American Indian, or Puerto Rican, all of whom are now clamoring to be let into the society which for so long excluded them.

Hence much of labor leadership is caught between its professed ideal to help the underclass on the one hand and the logic of its success on the other. In the best of the unions there is a great gap between the leaders and the rank and file on the subject of race, minorities, and employment. The skilled worker who had to build up his status, skills, and standards slowly over the years feels threatened by the Negro militant who wants in now and fast. The average American blue-collar worker, sad to relate, is much closer on these questions to Enoch Powell than to Walter Reuther.

In the face of these realities it is all the more a tribute to the leadership of labor that it is willing, as so often it is, to step out ahead of its own rank and file and to sponsor programs that do not set well with them. This is not to say that much more does not need to be done. Obviously, much remains. But the quiet contributions to the solution of the urban problem made by a forward-looking minority, though a significant one, of the labor movement go unheralded, overshadowed by the exclusionary examples of that reactionary minority that refuses to face the facts and the future.

To say that the private sector is increasing its commitment to the problems of urban life, however, does not define the nature and scope of that commitment. Plainly, private funds will never be a substitute for that massive commitment of public resources that will be necessary if we are to really remedy the blights of bad housing, poor education, and an untrained labor force. Private-sector money diverted to fighting urban blight is so far clearly tax-deductible, charitable contribution money, except in those cases where the commitment coincides with an immediate profit potential.

This is as it should be. Corporate managers are custodians of other people's money. They cannot be expected to allocate these resources to goals not likely to be profitable *solely* because there is some larger social purpose to be served. Hence, despite the concern expressed by business for the problem, the direct allocation of funds by business for employment and training programs or for economic development is small and is likely to remain so.

At the same time, many businesses recognize that the Negro and other minority markets are the fastest growing in our economy, that they are likely to continue to grow, and that they are a potential source of profit. As a result more and more companies are looking for outlets for their goods and services in these markets. Their normal quest for greater volume and greater profit, operating in a new atmosphere of Negro self-identity and self-pride, is changing the forms in which expanded black entrepreneurship and minority employment are possible.

There is great emphasis today in the black community on economic development of the ghetto, on the creation of a minority business class which will own and operate minority enterprises, employ minority labor, and reinvest the profits in the minorities. One gainfully employed person in forty in the white world is a businessman or entrepreneur. In the black world the figure is one in one thousand. The objective of creating a black business class which will own and operate businesses is a laudable one. The program marshals pride, mobilizes talent, and, if successful, raises living standards of community people.

However, many of the hopes articulated for such purposes as an easy and quick panacea for the problems of the ghetto are fanciful. The process of capital accumulation in any underdeveloped sector is by its nature a slow one. To expect that the ghettos will quickly develop and generate large sums for the capital investment needed to make them economically independent is an illusion. Nonetheless, economic development in the ghetto, though likely to be on a modest, not grandiose, scale, can be important for what it does to the hopes and aspirations of community people, for what it exposes them to in the way of training and experience, and for the pride and self-reliance it is likely to instill in key members of the minority groups.

One of the first projects of the New York Urban Coalition was to devise a plan to aid and finance ghetto businesses. We surveyed the field of organizations which purported in New York to do this job and found that of the twenty-two claiming to do it, none were performing in a significant way. Hence, a task force of bankers, finance experts, and community people devised a plan to create a management assistance corporation, a venture capital fund, and a small business investment corporation to furnish risk capital, soft loans, and technical assistance to minority businessmen or would-be entrepreneurs able to develop proposals that customary commercial funding sources would find to be too uncertain to finance with funds for which they have a fiduciary responsibility.

Moreover, our staff will be engaged in developing connections between established companies seeking outlets for their goods and services and ghetto residents motivated to become distributors, franchisers, or subcontractors for such companies' products by going into business themselves. Finally, we plan to stimulate and organize cooperative ownership of ghetto establishments by minority people.

But in the black community as in the white, most people will continue to work for others for a living. Hence the field of manpower and employment will remain decisive in the fight against poverty. Here the private sector's responsibility is to provide jobs. Every Sunday there are want ads in the New York Times for about 12,000 jobs. Yet there is a constant pool in our city of about 120,000 unemployed and several times that number underemployed. Labor shortages amidst labor plenty is a phenomenon of our times.

The reasons are multiple. In part it is because there is no match between job requirements and job candidates due to undereducation or lack of skills. But many low-skilled and unskilled jobs are going begging too. Many of these are at or close to the minimum wage, have no apparent career potential, or are menial in nature and symbolize to ghetto residents the discrimination they are now fighting.

Such jobs have to compete with "the hustle." As one ghetto resident put it at a meeting of our Manpower Task Force on which some of New York's most important employers serve, "You must remember that there *is* money in the ghetto. Now, it's not the right kind of money—like from running dope, snatching purses, or worse. But it's not easy to switch from that sort of life to a 7 A.M. to 4 P.M. routine for the same dough or less." Many jobs go unfilled because people are unmotivated or have never worked before and do not understand the discipline of work. Others are held only briefly by persons, initially convinced by previous experience that the white world is hostile, who quit because of slights that are more fancied than real.

In short, the manpower problem in today's ghetto is not simply one of jobs alone. Its solution requires the promise of a job with a potential for upward mobility, the availability of motivational and attitudinal training, an input of remedial training for reading and arithmetic skills, and then skill training. Industry is slowly learning the full dimensions of the task it has undertaken, and it is slowly beginning to respond to the need.

Jobs were often not filled with minority residents living in ghetto poverty because it is the personnel officer's task to screen people *out*, not in. The result has frequently been artificially high entry requirements for quite ordinary jobs. Employers persuaded to drop unnecessary educational requirements, to overlook must criminal convictions, and to screen people *in* are finding in many cases that their work is performed as adequately by former hard-core minority people.

The Urban Coalition is involving the private sector in three other important aspects of urban decay—housing, education, and communications.

In housing the problem is so vast and complicated that we have set a relatively modest immediate goal for ourselves. We are undertaking to provide a "bottleneck unplugging" service to nonprofit housing sponsors. Many a good housing project languishes because the necessary approvals are held up at one of the many way stations on the tortuous route from conception to construction. We are assembling a staff of expediters to blast projects out of each step to the next.

There is much housing money available at the state and federal levels that is not drawn on, partly because many potential sponsors under Section 221D3 of the Federal Housing Act do not know of their potential or, if they do, have not got the experience or talent to launch a project, plan it, push it through the necessary stages of drawing plans, arranging financing, letting contracts, and the like. In my naiveté I assumed that the housing departments of the city, state, or federal governments surely had staffs performing this obviously needed function. It was always something asked for in the budget but cut out by parsimonious legislators. We believe that the private sector, through the Coalition, can provide this vital kind of linkage.

In education the job is even more complicated. Our program is two pronged. The first concerns itself with help in the training of paraprofessionals to work with teachers in ghetto schools in order to improve the by now almost ineffective communication between white middle-class teachers and their ghetto students. We are also involved in establishing linkages between high schools and the business world to improve the chances that the curricula of the former will relate meaningfully to the requirements of the latter.

The second part of our education program concerns school decentralization in New York, which all concede is necessary, but on which no two groups agree as to method. Today the city's education system, with a school population of one million children, 60,000 teachers, 30,000 administrative and clerical employees, is run by one central headquarters. The same bureaucratic paralysis operates here as elsewhere.

The communities want control of their children's education, and they want it on the basis of community administration of smaller school groupings. They want to have their own teachers, negotiate their own salary scales, decide how to divide the educational dollar between teacher salaries, educational materials, buildings and plants, etc. The teachers' union and the board of education take a dim view of so drastic a dismantling of the present structure. At the same time, all recognize that responsibility must be dispersed among smaller administrative units. Our Coalition of concerned citizens from business, labor, and the community is trying to draw up a plan that will deal with these competing concerns.

In communications our aims are two fold for the time being. One is to blunt once and for all the argument advanced by media executives, "Find me a qualified Negro editor, reporter, technician, etc., and I'll hire him." We aim to do this by setting up a program at a school of journalism and communications to quickly upgrade minority people in entry-level jobs in the communications industries for middle or top management jobs.

Our second task is to make communications people more sensitive to the implications and impact of their handling of racial stories and of the impact of their media on the 20 percent of the city that is not white. We plan to do this by joining working newspaper, radio, and television people in key spots in a dialogue with minority spokesmen and others who can acquaint them with the reactions of the community to their output.

Is the Coalition idea viable? Is the private-sector interest a passing phase, a fad, or fashion; or does it have staying power?

No one can answer with certainty, only with hope. My hope is, I think, grounded on facts. One is that the urban problem is so vast and intractable that it won't let itself be ignored.

Another is that it is impinging itself unceasingly on vital business and labor interests, giving the private sector a personal motive for involvement and action.

A third is that we have, I believe, come a long way from the polarized thirties, have passed through the indifferent fifties, and, on social questions, at least, have arrived at a balance between public and private responsibilities that makes some sense. Hence my mood of cautious hope.

---

5. Lessons from Arbitration in Dealing with Minority Problems*

The nation today is in the midst of a profound clash of forces, the sound and fury of which have not yet reached a crescendo. No one up to now—white or black; trade unionist or employer; private sector or government; integrationist or separatist; militant, liberal, or conservative—has the full answers to the profound problem of the relationship between the races in American society. The clash of forces is around us everywhere—in the streets, in employment, in the schools, in the universities, in the churches, in politics, in the unions and in labor-management relations. Before you can find the answers, you have to know the questions. And we are still grasping for many of the questions.

The feelings underlying today's turmoil, generated by the demands of the minorities for full-fledged membership in American life—for access to its standards of living, to the opportunities for growth and self-development and, at the same time, for retention of that inner pride and sense of worth that comes from group identity and group cohesiveness—

---

*Paper presented at the Collective Bargaining Forum, Waldorf Astoria Hotel, New York City, May 12, 1969. Papers found in Wallen's files.

should not be unfamiliar to anyone who has lived through or studied labor history in America.

I remember reading years ago a book by Robert R. R. Brooks called *As Steel Goes* . . . which described how the Steel Workers Organizing Committee, headed by John L. Lewis and Philip Murry, took over the company unions of the major steel producers and forced United States Steel for the first time to recognize the union and engage in real collective bargaining. Brooks had described life in a Pennsylvania steel town in those days, with its coal and iron police, its company spies, its company-controlled town government, its atmosphere of terror growing out of the fear of arbitrary discharge or, worse, of eviction from the company-owned house and of facing a labor market in which jobs were nonexistent.

Brooks recounts how, after recognition was won and the first agreement was signed, he interviewed steel workers in this town to ask them how they felt about the changes. One middle-aged worker he interviewed told him how it felt to be free:

> It was worth it. It was worth it to be able to walk down Main Street for the first time in my life and hold my head up high and look the s.o.b.'s in the eye and think "I have my rights and I have something to protect them and I don't have to keep my head bowed any more."[1]

Much of the same emotions permeate minority people in America today.

Just as the triumphs that followed unionism's earlier struggles led in some cases to excesses that were later redressed, so minority demands on the institutions of trade unionism and collective bargaining today are in some cases couched in terms that need understanding, analysis, and modification. They need modification if industrial relations is to be able to accommodate itself to the realism of trends in race relations.

The need today is to adapt the institutions of collective bargaining, trade unionism, and industrial relations to the current condition of massive pressure for social change. Otherwise we face a clash of contending forces that can yield only the destruction of one or the other.

The pressures are there, both within the labor movement and on management. They cannot be eased by wishful thinking or exorcised by closing one's eyes to them. Increasingly, the movement for a separate black identity is making itself felt in the labor movement and is pressing on unions and management for recognition, for status, for concessions.

Let me give some examples. There has been a small but ominous trend toward the creation of black unions. There are, among many

---

[1] This is a paraphrase from memory since I did not have the book before me when this paper was written. [Wallen was referring to *As Steel Goes . . . Unionism in a Basic Industry* (New Haven: Yale University Press, 1940). Ed.]

others, the Independent Alliance of Skilled Crafts in Ohio, the Maryland Freedom Labor Union, the United Community Construction Workers in Boston, the United Construction and Trades Union in Detroit, the Allied Workers International Union in Gary.[2]

The specter of dual unionism resides in these and other groups. And if unionism based on race continues to grow the entire structure of industrial relations is threatened, to the detriment of the black worker as well as the white and to the long-run harm to the interests of industry and the society itself.

The growth of black caucuses within unions has been more dramatic. The Concerned Transit Workers was formed in [Local] 241 of the Amalgamated Transit Union in Chicago and last summer struck Chicago bus operations. The push was for a greater voice in local union leadership which the dissidents charged was kept in white hands by the votes of 3,000 retired white drivers who tipped over what would otherwise have been a black majority of working drivers.

The UAW has its Dodge Revolutionary Union Movement (DRUM), its counterpart at Ford (FRUM), and gestures toward the same idea at General Motors plants. G.E.'s Hotpoint plant in Chicago has its Afro-American Employee's Committee. It has been reported that "A new nation-wide black caucus has emerged recently within the United Automobile Workers . . . headed by Robert Battle. Battle is a vice-president of Local 600 . . . at the Ford Motor Company's River Rouge works . . . ."[3] This group has told the UAW leadership that unless Negroes received "full equity in the union" it might be anticipated that "chaos could ensue" unless the representation of blacks, who claim to be one-fourth of the UAW membership, in the 100 policy-making and key staff positions [was] raised from the seven posts they now hold.

The Steelworkers Union now has a black caucus that picketed its convention and is demanding greater power in union affairs, and similar groups are emerging in steelworkers [locals].

Management is by no means immune from the headaches arising out of these developments. Organizations with separate demands tend to strike to impose those demands. Strikes of blacks to enforce demands of black groups are a growing phenomenon, to the detriment of management, unions, and often the black workers themselves. We've read about a number of these: at General Motors in Tarrytown; at Ford in Mahwah, New Jersey; at Chicago Transit System; . . . and at many others.

Some of my friends in the management of major automobile companies

---

[2] Herbert Hill, "Black Protest And The Struggle For Union Democracy," *Issues In Industrial Society* 1 (no. 1, 1969): 22.

[3] *Ibid.*, p. 25.

have expressed concern about the rise of black caucuses in the unions in their plants in various parts of the country but more particularly about the lack of communication between those groups and the established union leadership. They express concern about the absence of efforts to reconcile the interests of these new forces with the established groups in their local unions. Unlike the managements of a quarter century ago, they see no profit in dual unionism or any approximation thereof and are concerned about any developments in that direction.

But if the corporate giants have learned a thing or two in the last two-and-a-half decades, it does not follow that all of business has too. The National Right To Work Committee in January of this year financed the formation of The Black Workers Alliance in Washington, D.C. Given its history, we can safely conclude that this outfit did not take that step out of an abiding concern for the interest of Negro workers.

Moreover, one may safely conclude that in the long run medium-sized and small employers especially will be unable to resist the lure of a cheaper competing labor supply even if we assume that it is to the interest of major corporations to prefer stability to cheap labor. I was asked by some black leaders last year if I favored black unions in the building trades. When I replied in the negative because it would lead inevitably to the debasement of current wage levels, I was given the reply "So what if we don't get those $6 and $7 an hour rates? What if we get $4 or $5? That's still good pay."

That psychology is not likely to be lost on employers in labor-intensive industries. Indeed, it has long been operative in the industries having dealings with racket unions, which exploit minority workers by phoney contracts between racketeers and unscrupulous employers. These contracts place a whole work force, or nearly [such], at the legal minumum wage and provide substandard benefits. It is to the discredit of both important segments of the minority leadership and of established employer organizations that they have not joined the New York City Central Labor Council in its efforts to stamp out this evil which perpetuates poverty and exploits minority people.

To sum up, to address myself to the theme of this session, "The Minorities Problem and Its Effect on Collective Bargaining," before giving my answer to the narrower question put to me, "What lessons can we learn from arbitration in dealing with minority problems?" I would say the following: First, the minority problem is beginning to place sharp strains on trade unionism, collective bargaining, and industrial relations as it has been developed and practiced over the past three decades. Second, the often confusingly stated but deeply felt aim of minority leadership, and particularly militant leadership, is to acquire a greater share of power in unions, collective bargaining, and industrial relations and to do so rapidly. Third, the tactics and indeed the aims of some militants in the minority community, by creating the possibility of dual unionism . . . in labor ranks, create a threat to the standards of both minority and white workers. Fourth, industry should not, and large industry for the most part does not, relish the prospect of internal divisions in the work force along racial lines. Fifth, the problem of sharing power equitably with those so long excluded from access to it by disabilities the total society has imposed will tax the ingenuity, patience, good will, and intelligence of all parties and especially of established union leadership.

What lessons can be gleaned from arbitration that will be helpful in dealing with these problems? First, it is plain that arbitration as a process can at this point in time play a useful role in dealing with minority problems in industrial relations only to a limited extent. It can be a useful tool for resolving the rights of minority individuals under existing contracts. Properly administered and developed, and given greater confidence of minority unionists in the support and good will of the union officialdom, it can be the preferred choice for pursuing claims of discrimination over recourse to human rights commissions or complaints to other government agencies or the courts.

But too often the complaints of minority people in the collective bargaining scene are directed against the union as well as the employer. Moreover, arbitration is usually a means of [enforcing] rights under a contract. Minority problems in industrial relations, on the other hand, often arise out of demands either for reforms in those contracts for the benefit of the minority group or for a transfer of a greater share of union power to minority hands. Arbitration, given the present balance of forces, does not seem well adapted to that assignment at this point in time.

But what lessons have we gleaned from the arbitration *experience* that can be useful here, even if the *process* of arbitration is not now appropriate for the problems at hand?

The highest utility of industrial arbitration is as the capstone of a well-functioning grievance procedure. And a well-functioning grievance procedure, in turn, requires a highly developed system of communication between grievants and the union apparatus on the one hand and between the union apparatus and its management counterpart on the other.

I suggest that in most local unions and with most managements, this kind of communication about the relations of minority workers to their union and their employer is lacking. I suggest, further, that unions and companies begin to think about creating procedures especially tailored to bring to the surface and to their joint attention in an orderly way the aspirations and complaints of their minority members and employees.

It is time that many local unions have civil rights chairmen or committees [to improve communication with and hear complaints of minority members]. But it is probably also true that their emphasis is on the protection of *existing* legal and contract rights of minority workers and that they seldom serve as a vehicle for venting the views and aspirations of minority groups about whether and how to *expand* those rights.

It is a fact that in reasonably democratic unions the ordinary processes of the committee structure and the local union meeting can help serve this purpose. But there are variations in union democracy. The growing alienation of many Negro workers from their unions, whether the result of their response to demogogic appeals or to the unresponsiveness of existing officialdom, calls for an especial effort to establish communications which will permit their aspirations to be aired.

One other aspect of the arbitration experience should be mentioned for its particular aptness to the current subject. Effective arbitration rests on a marshaling of facts and their separation from fiction or fancy. The advantage of a more aggressive program by unions of reaching out to minority members and talking with them about their needs, their desires, and their aspirations is that they can be educated by the facts and disabused of the fictions pumped out by demagogues or uninformed self-seekers.

Finally, the single most important lesson of the arbitration experience is that it provides a structure for the airing of grievances, whether real or fancied, without which anarchy presses order. The suggestion made here is to extend a similar structure to the current complaints, whether spurious or real, of minority workers toward their unions.

Today's demagogues would split minority workers from the overall union structure. Whether intended or not, this would pit white against black in the labor market and exacerbate racial conflict. Unions, and with them managements, must, for the sake of all, make special effort to thwart this design.

6. Report of October 4, 1950, Speech to United States Rubber Supervisory Employees*

Management's responsibility to its community is as great as its more obvious responsibilities to its stockholders, workers, and customers. Saul Wallen, former industry and federal arbitrator, told United States Rubber Company supervisory employees last night.

* * *

The days when industry could make a sudden decision to liquidate without notice to its employees or the public without suffering public condemnation are gone, Wallen said.

". . . . I do not mean to imply that a company should subsidize its workers or the tradesmen in its community without showing a profit. I do mean to imply that all members of the community should be called in before such a decision is announced, in an attempt to minimize dislocations.

"Business no longer functions in a vacuum. It never did. But there is a consciousness among management of its social function as never before."

Wallen said the community's responsibility to its industries was to provide a "legislative climate with as few restrictions as possible, compatible with minimum social obligations."

To its workers, Wallen said, industry owed not only the economic promise of good wages but a rational system of rate organization providing incentives for skilled help, some answer to the "insatiable quest for security" and greater work satisfaction for all employees.

Employees who come to feel a share in the company's plan or purpose produce increasingly greater amounts than employees who routinely accomplish their tasks. Management must increasingly dramatize employees' jobs to attain the work satisfaction they are entitled to, he said.

**Providence Journal* (McLean, Va.), October 5, 1950.

7. Urban Coalition Letter

April 1, 1969

Dear _____:

Thank you for your letter of March 24 enclosing a letter from an undisclosed friend dated February 13 in which he asks, "Where is the Urban Coalition?"

I should like to meet your friend face to face and, through you, hereby extend an invitation to him to call. I can answer all his questions and allay most of his concerns.

For example, it is clearly not true that money was raised with no plans for its use. The money we raised has been put to use and not for administrative expenses alone.

We have funded Coalition JOBS to the tune of $275,000 and have raised over $600,000 from government and foundation sources to mount this year's job development effort and to create a coordinated manpower system linked to MCDA and SES.

We have granted seed money to four housing projects long stalled for lack thereof and will shortly place a good deal more of such money.

We were responsible for the creation of sixteen street academies. We have funded a program to train community people to assume responsibility under a decentralized school system. We secured from outside sources the sum of nearly $300,000 for the East Harlem Federation Youth Association, a worthwhile program of redemption and rehabilitation of delinquents through athletic, educational, and cultural activities. The money is being used to acquire a site for the first black community center in the city.

We have created a structure for private-sector involvement in . . . planning to convert Benjamin Franklin High School into a comprehensive high school with links to industry. We persuaded the board of education to advance $18,000 toward that project and have ourselves appropriated $38,500 for it.

We have made seventeen loans to minority businessmen in sums ranging from $3,000 to $150,000 each, for a total of about $650,000, and will be placing the rest of the $1.25 million appropriated for Coalition Venture

Corporation in the next few weeks. We have begun to provide significant technical assistance to minority businessmen.

We are creating a housing packaging unit which will provide technical assistance to would-be sponsors of housing projects and plan to appropriate $60,000 for this function and raise $90,000 more from the life insurance companies and savings banks.

We have developed a plan for the comprehensive redevelopment of a sizable area in the city utilizing the systems approach toward housing development and construction, a plan which has been approved by prominent persons in the construction, financial, and business community; and we are working with Jason Nathan and Ed Logue to bring it to fruition.

We have gotten the Department of Labor to commit $338,000 in funds for the East Harlem Skills Training Center, a significant effort to train minority workers for the printing trades.

We were instrumental in bringing together all elements and securing funding for the Hunts Point Multiservice Center.

The more I dictate, the madder I get. The above is a cross-section of what we have done so far, and what is in the works. Your friend asks, "Where is the Urban Coalition?" I ask, "Where is your friend?" Why don't you have him come up here and help us tackle the problems of this vast city, problems which have so far overwhelmed us all.

I believe we have made a hell of a good start and if we have not impinged on the consciousness of everyone in town it has not been for lack of trying.

I would appreciate your passing on a copy of this letter to the man who wrote to you and telling him I would be delighted to talk the matter over with him face to face at his convenience.

Sincerely,

Saul Wallen
President

Appendix

Saul Wallen as Perceived by Others

1. *Saul Wallen: A Lifetime Commitment to Problem Solving**

by
Marcia L. Greenbaum

The current crises in the cities, in the communities, and on the campuses have led many to look toward the field of industrial and labor relations for possible ways of dealing with these new confrontations. Whether the concepts of collective bargaining, and the techniques of mediation and arbitration can be transferred to such spheres is not certain and the answer may not be known for some time.

This article is not an attempt to generalize about this transferability. Rather, it is an account of how one man, who for more than twenty-five years was a distinguished mediator and arbitrator, brought these concepts and techniques to bear on one situation—the New York Urban Coalition, an organization of more than 150 business, labor, and community leaders formed in September 1967 "to enlist the energies, skills and resources of the private sector to improve the quality of life in New York."

To understand why such a coalition would seek out Saul Wallen, why he would accept such a challenge, and how he would keep such a

---

*Issues in Industrial Society 1 (no. 3, 1970) : 42-61.

tenuous amalgam together, it is necessary to understand the man, his work, and how he approached it.

To say that Saul Wallen was an outstanding mediator and arbitrator is not only to describe his professional competence but also his person. As Secretary of Labor George Shultz said at the time of Mr. Wallen's death in August 1969, "He had in abundance the essential qualities of a superior mediator and arbitrator—intelligence, patience and good humor."[1] In addition, he was a sensitive man with a unique sense of fairness. As another colleague stated, "He had a basic understanding and respect for the separate needs and viewpoints of employers and unions, and an uncommon ability to find the points of common ground."[2] As a mediator, he had an ability to view a situation objectively, grasp the problem quickly, couch it in terms that could be understood by the worker in the shop, divide it into manageable portions, help the parties come up with a range of solutions, persuade a recalcitrant party to accept one, and not only bring about the consent to lose, "but somehow, he seemed to make the losing party feel downright good about it. He did this through no magic or trickery—for he was completely without guile—but simply by the force of his open, honest and friendly personality. . . . Saul was a person everybody trusted. They simply liked him and felt comfortable in his presence."[3]

These characteristics are cited not simply to laud the man, but to explain how he operated as a middleman and to give insight into his role as head of the Coalition.

Saul Wallen was also a man with commitments—a commitment to legal, social, and economic justice, a commitment to resolving conflict, and a commitment to public service. His principal work as a neutral in the resolution of labor disputes began with World War II. He was one of a handful of young men who were recruited as hearing officers and mediators for the War Labor Board in 1942 and sent out "to investigate and report, to persuade and cajole disputing employers and unions in matters where feelings were as deep and intense as those involved in civilian riots or war."[4] In the same year he was appointed Chairman of the New England Regional War Labor Board—a position which brought him from New York and Washington, D.C. to Boston, where he was to make his home until the Coalition brought him back to New York City.

---

[1] *New York Times,* August 6, 1969, p. 39, col. 3.
[2] "Remarks at Memorial Service for Saul Wallen," delivered by James C. Hill, president of the National Academy of Arbitrators, August 6, 1969.
[3] *Ibid.*
[4] *Ibid.*

INTERUNION DISPUTES

During those twenty-five years he served on numerous government-appointed boards of inquiry, factfinding panels,[5] and emergency boards, appointed by Presidents Eisenhower and Kennedy pursuant to Section 10 of the Railway Labor Act to investigate disputes in the airline and railroad industries.[6]

A number of these disputes were essentially between two unions with the carriers caught in the middle. Saul Wallen was to hear this kind of interunion dispute often in the late 1960s after he was appointed one of three umpires under the AFL-CIO Internal Disputes Plan to hear and decide disputes between unions who were parties to the AFL-CIO No-raiding Pact. His ability and experience in resolving such disputes, between parties seemingly on the same side of the fence was later called upon at the Coalition where he served to bridge the gap between black and Puerto Rican community leaders.

His last two emergency board appointments were as chairman of Nos. 145 and 160. The former involved "11 cooperating railway labor organizations representing 73 1(I.C.C.) classes of nonoperating employees, totaling a half million persons, employed by 212 line-haul railroads and certain terminal and switching companies represented by the Eastern, Western and Southeastern Carriers' Conference Committee."[7] The latter involved a dispute primarily over job protection between the Na-

---

[5] His earliest appointments were to factfinding boards investigating disputes between Central Greyhound Bus Lines Group and the Amalgamated Association of Street, Electric Railway and Motor Coach Employees of America (1946, 1 LA 596); Western Union Telegraph Company and the American Communications Association (1946, 4 LA 251,268); and the Maritime Industry and the East Coast Longshoremen (1947, 10 LA 912, 11 LA 388).

[6] His first such appointment was as chairman of E. B. No. 103 in 1952 in a dispute between United Airlines and the Flight Engineers International Association. In 1958 President Eisenhower selected him as a member of E. B. Nos. 120 and 121 involving Eastern Air Lines and FEIA in one case and the Air Line Pilots Association in the other—two disputes closely related by the underlying issue of flight crew complement.

This was followed by his service as a member of Boards No. 123, involving a dispute between Trans World Airlines and the FEIA over a scope clause, and No. 128, involving a pay and reclassification dispute between Pan American World Airways and the Brotherhood of Railway and Steamship Clerks.

Thereafter, President Kennedy appointed him in 1961 to chair E. B. No. 140 concerning a dispute between TWA and the Transport Workers of America over the replacement of celestial navigation used by nonpilot navigators with a pilot-used Doppler and Edo-Loran system. In 1962 he was chairman of the Boeing Aerospace Board.

[7] Saul Wallen, chairman, Laurence E. Seibel, member, and Edward A. Lynch, member, "Report to the President by the Emergency Board No. 145 Appointed by Executive Order No. 11,008" (Washington: May 3, 1962), p. 1.

tional Railway Labor Conference, which represented all major railroads except two, and the Railway Employees' Department, which represented the shopcrafts of these roads.[8]

These appointments made him fully familiar with the procedures under the RLA and aware of their shortcomings as well—the improper use of the word "emergency," the increasingly frequent rejection of the recommendations of emergency boards, and the cumbersome procedures.[9] As a man of action, Saul Wallen was an advocate of the no-nonsense approach. His tendency to dispense with the customary red tape and handle matters expeditiously (traits which were to please and displease various factions at the Coalition) led him to criticize the parties in the E.B. No. 160 Report, and the procedures in a panel discussion he chaired at the National Academy of Arbitrators Annual Meeting in 1965.[10] He said:

> While the Act does not specify the manner in which the Board is to carry out its investigation . . . the intent of the framers of the [legislation who provided] for a report in thirty days must have been in contemplation of a flexible procedure suited to the problems of each case in which all suitable means of information gathering would be employed. . . .[11]

He limited the number of hearing days, required materials be submitted in briefs, and made an effort to mediate the dispute, something the law contemplates and encourages, but few neutrals had been inclined to attempt.[12]

This penchant for getting to the heart of the matter was acknowledged by him in a response to a panel discussion question about whether an arbitrator should shore up a case for an inept party:

> . . . . There is a qualitative difference between "shoring up" one party's case and finding out what the case is really about because of the inept

---

[8] Saul Wallen, chairman, Jean T. McKelvey, member, Arthur M. Ross, member, "Report to the President by the Emergency Board no. 160 Appointed by Executive Order No. 11,147" (Washington, D.C.: August 7, 1964).

[9] Saul Wallen, "National Emergency Disputes," *Labor Law Journal* 12 (no. 1, January, 1961): 61-66, publication of a speech given before the Association of State Mediation Agencies, September 1960, in which he asked a question with respect to emergency boards that might well be applied to public employment factfinding boards today: "What does public opinion mean in a strike which inconveniences but causes no real hardship to a relatively minor segment of the nation over issues of which the public is hardly aware, dealt with in reports which they never read, embodying solutions they scarcely understand?" (p. 63).

[10] "Procedures Under the Railway Labor Act: A Panel Discussion," *Proceedings of the 18th Annual Meeting of the National Academy of Arbitrators, January 27-29, 1965*, Dallas L. Jones, ed. (Washington: BNA, 1965), pp. 27-65, with Saul Wallen as chairman.

[11] "Report to the President by Emergency Board No.160," *op. cit.*, p. 2.

[12] Hill, *op. cit.*

presentation of one of the parties. This difference is developed by the way in which you ply such questions as are necessary. For myself, I am of the school that wants to find out what the case is about, even if I am courting the risk of appearing to make out a case for one of the parties. I have been criticized for this in some cases, and my response is that my feeling about the arbitration process is that I am not a referee in a prize fight; I am trying to find the facts to make an intelligent decision.[13]

He would also be criticized for this by some at the Coalition who felt he became impatient with the consensus process, made up his mind too soon, did not consult enough with his staff or make them feel a part of the decision-making process, and stubbornly refused to change decisions once they were made. Others viewed this as an asset, for it enabled him to see which course must be taken, provide leadership, decide, and act without unduly delaying the decision-making process.

* * *

CONSENSUS APPROACH

In addition to numerous ad hoc arbitration appointments either directly from the parties or through the Federal Mediation and Conciliation Service or the American Arbitration Association over the years Mr. Wallen served as permanent umpire for a number of companies and the unions with which they dealt.[50] In all of these arbitration systems he was an arbitrator-adjudicator. However, in two umpireships he initiated informal procedures in the nature of problem-solving sessions. Having served as permanent umpire under contracts between the B.F. Goodrich Company and the United Rubber, Cork, Linoleum and Plastic Workers of America from 1951 to 1955 and 1960 to 1968, he was familiar with their contracts and problems. In his last year as umpire he developed, with the cooperation of the parties, an informal procedure which provided an opportunity for case discussion prior to the formal arbitration stage. The union determined which cases should be handled at this informal level. Mr. Wallen met with the parties, frequently hearing several cases in one session, and giving an informal indication of how he

---

[13]"Procedural Problems in the Conduct of Arbitration Hearings: A Discussion," *Labor Arbitration—Perspectives and Problems, Proceedings of the 17th Annual Meeting of the National Academy of Arbitrators, January 29-31, 1964,* Mark L. Kahn, ed. (Washington, D.C.: BNA, 1964), p. 12.

[50]These included General Motors and the UAW, Ford Motor and the UAW, Scovill Manufacturing and the UAW, Warner Gear and the UAW, Sylvania Electric Products and the IUE, Western Airlines and ALPA, American Airlines and the TWUA, TWA and the IAM, General Tire and URCL&PWA, Firestone and the URCL&PWA, Mass. Leather Mfrs. Assn. and the F&LWU, Kaiser Aluminum and Chemical and the URCL&PWA, and the B.F. Goodrich Co. and the URCL&PWA.

would rule on the case if it were appealed to the formal arbitration step. This provided the necessary guidance to the parties to help them reach a settlement. It is noteworthy that all cases that reached this level were settled and none was appealed to formal arbitration.

At the Seventeenth Annual Meeting of the NAA, before he developed this system at Goodrich, Mr. Wallen had occasion to describe what mediation means in this kind of a system:

> Where the principle or the contract right is clear, the task of the chairman may be to persuade the losing party to accept that fact. But where the contract is unclear—as in the "just cause for discharge" concept—or where it simply does not cover a particular dispute, then the task of the impartial chairman is usually to develop a consensus which will clarify or supplement the parties' formal contract. The skillful chairman tells the parties that he can and will decide an issue himself if necessary, but that the solution is more likely to be mutually acceptable if they agree upon it themselves; he helps them to explore alternatives, and may greatly influence the outcome, but decisions on this kind of problem are basically the product of negotiation.[51]

Mr. Wallen successfully initiated a similar approach for Kaiser Aluminum and Chemical Company and the URCL&PWA in Bristol, Rhode Island, to alleviate a distressed grievance procedure. This kind of consensus approach to problem solving was one he used at the New York Urban Coalition. He saw "making little ones out of big ones" as one of the roles to be played by a mediator. He was particularly adept at "taking some overall, generalized issue, analyzing its origins and background, and breaking it down into its essentials in the hope that, thus reduced in scale, the problem becomes soluble."[52] He characterized a mediator as "a sparrow who got caught in a badminton game" and noted that if he "moves too boldly or too fast, he frequently gets a hell of a wack in the region of his tail feathers."[53]

RETURN TO NEW YORK

Saul Wallen was born and raised in New York City and graduated from New York University. He worked first as a labor adjuster for the United Association of Dress Manufacturers in New York City and then

---

[51] Charles C. Killingsworth and Saul Wallen, "Constraint and Variety in Arbitration Systems," *Labor Arbitration—Perspectives and Problems, Proceedings of the 17th Annual Meeting of the National Academy of Arbitrators, January 29-31, 1964*, Mark L. Kahn, ed. (Washington, D.C.: BNA, 1964), p. 59.

[52] Saul Wallen, "The Role of the Mediator in the Collective Bargaining Process," a speech delivered to the Air Line Pilots Association Negotiating Committee Seminar, Chicago, Illinois, December 13, 1967, p. 3.

[53] *Ibid.*, p. 2.

for the New York State Department of Labor, Division of Minimum Wage. After moving to Boston, he frequently traveled to New York City, but was no longer a New Yorker. His ties were in the Boston area where he worked and served the community through the Massachusetts State Employees Personnel Appeal Board, the Brookline Personnel Board, Massachusetts Blue Cross Blue Shield, and a Gay Head Community Council which worked to improve the relations between summer people and year-round residents, many of whom were Indians.

His return to New York City and its problems occurred, in part, several years before he became involved with the New York Urban Coalition. In 1965, Robert F. Wagner, then mayor, established a panel composed of representatives from his office, New York City union leaders, and impartial experts, including Saul Wallen, Peter Seitz, Reverend Philip A. Carey, and Vernon Countryman. This group, under the auspices of the Labor Management Institute of the American Arbitration Association conducted discussions on New York City's labor relations problems with various groups of city employees and with members of the committee which produced the Taylor Report and Act in New York State. These discussions on setting up a procedure for New York City continued after Mayor John V. Lindsay took office. In 1966, this tripartite committee issued a report which recommended machinery for collective bargaining and the resolution of disputes between the city and its employee organizations and laid the foundation for the New York City Office of Collective Bargaining. Mr. Wallen was instrumental in getting the city and union representatives to agree to a management rights provision which threatened to be a stumbling block. Impartial member of the committee and fellow arbitrator Peter Seitz said, "I never worked with anyone as good, cooperative, or persuasive as Saul. He was loved, admired and respected by his peers for his integrity, ability, dedication to his responsibilities, and his relentless pursuit of answers to questions."[54]

In 1967 the New York City Council passed a law amending the City Charter to create the OCB, and Mayor Lindsay issued an executive order implementing it. He then appointed Attorney Jesse Freidin and Deputy Mayor Timothy W. Costello as city members of the board and, on nomination from the Municipal Labor Committee, named Harry Van Arsdale, Jr., and Paul Hall as labor members. These four then unanimously elected three impartial members—Arvid Anderson, board chairman, Eric J. Schmertz, and Saul Wallen. Mr. Wallen served as an active member of the board from January 1968 until the time of his death.

---

[54]Personal interview, April 21, 1970.

In its 1969 annual report, the OCB noted that

> ... he brought to the Board more than 30 years of experience in labor relations plus a gift for human relations that years alone could not produce, and ... gave this agency his talents, energy, wise counsel, sense of fairness and ability to settle complex disputes in terms that were meaningful to all, and ... because of his presence, ... relations between the City of New York and its employees are more harmonious.

BEGINNING OF THE COALITION

It was after the riots in Detroit, Newark, and more than one hundred other cities that a group of about fifteen from the city, the business, labor, and minority communities, and the Ford Foundation met in the fall of 1967 to form the New York Urban Coalition, a branch of the National Urban Coalition. To head the organization they needed someone who could woo business for its money and other resources and labor for its resources and cooperation on jobs and who could bridge the gap between the various community organizations, hear what they had to say, and relate their problems to business and labor in a way that could be understood. Saul Wallen was known to many of them either personally or by reputation. His thirty years of experience as a mediator and arbitrator, his boundless energy, his ability to deal with people and issues, his credibility with labor and business, his sensitivity to minority problems, his new visibility in the city from the OCB, and his acceptability to Mayor Lindsay coalesced in his selection as executive director.

But this decision gambled on the possibility of a negative community reaction—a possibility which became a reality shortly thereafter. The Puerto Ricans and blacks were angered by the selection. Most did not know him. But many would have objected even if they had, simply because he was white.

The objections to his appointment were not wholly unlike those expressed in 1942 when he was named chairman of the New England Regional War Labor Board. As recently recalled by a fellow arbitrator, there were some at that time who thought "it was dangerous and unwise to send a young man to Boston, who was neither Irish or Italian, Catholic or Protestant, Lowell or Cabot, Saltonstall or Lodge, lawyer or graduate of Harvard, to be the guardian of peace in this major region of a nation at war."[55] Now some twenty-five years later, there were some who thought it dangerous and unwise to bring to New York a man well over

---

[55] Hill, *op. cit.*

thirty, who was neither black or Puerto Rican, business or labor, an administrator or a proven leader with a constituency, or an expert in manpower, economic development, housing or education affairs, to head an organization in this major region of a nation almost at civil war.

Under pressure from the black-Puerto Rican community caucus, in February 1968, the board of directors, which then numbered about twenty-five, voted to elect Mr. Wallen president of the NYUC with responsibility for policy formulation (subject to board of directors' approval) and overall administration and direction of the staff. As its first of many compromises it created two executive vice-president posts, one which would eventually be filled by a black and the other by a Puerto Rican. At that time the board regarded the consensual nature of the Coalition as a matter of highest importance. It sought to assemble a top staff with close ties to the community and to have executive responsibility involve close consultation with the staff and decision making by consensus.

Because of his charisma, Mr. Wallen was a good representative of the Coalition in its early stages. He spoke to many groups (social workers, textbook publishers, educators, labor, and management) spreading the word of the Coalition and urging them to "Give a Damn." What he said frequently revealed his deep understanding of the nature of the commitments of the various Coalition organizations and their potential points of conflict.[56] Speaking before a Family Service Association, he explained:

> The emergent pride and militance of the black communities impel them to reject the ministerial benevolence that tinges most white efforts to do something "for" the black poor. They want to do what has to be done for themselves. Hence the all-white board, or even the one with the token black with a white psychology, is not likely to be able to function in the militant black communities that today constitute most of the urban ghettoes. The cry today is for black participation, even black control, of staff and of board. As a result, the long-standing white benefactor and board member is often "turned off" by the insistence of minority community groups for a voice, sometimes a dominat voice, in the shaping of agency policy, in the expenditure of agency funds, in the selection of agency staff. What the community sees as a proper assertion of its newly developed spirit of independence and equality, the white board or

---

[56]For a detailed discussion of the problems that can be encountered when the world of work and industrial relations is merged with the world of the ghetto disadvantaged, see Saul Wallen, "Industrial Relations Problems of Employing the Disadvantaged," *Arbitration and Social Change, Proceedings of the 22nd Annual Meeting of the National Academy of Arbitrators, January 29-31, 1969*, Gerald G. Sommers, ed. (Washington: BNA, 1970), pp. 65-75; also "Employing the Disadvantaged," *Arbitration Journal* 24 (no. 3, 1969): 155-160.

staff member regards as an example of ingratitude and disdain of established prerogatives.[57]

As a realist Mr. Wallen was never overconfident about what could be done. He said, "We're not under the illusion that the private sector can turn the city around. But we can have an impact. One of the major accomplishments is maintaining a continuing dialogue between blacks and Puerto Ricans, business and labor. We don't have anything like that anywhere else in the city."[58] His appeal for help was not merely to humanitarian or guilt feelings but to self-interest. He said, "This is not an altruistic program. Readying people in jobs with upward mobility is the key to the city's manpower problem in the years to come."[59]

He also explained the commitment of major business corporations on this basis—"a sense of concern that springs from a healthy mixture of social responsibility and self-interest"[60] and more particularly:

> . . . a very human concern it shares with most of enlightened America about the appalling waste of human resources in ghetto life; . . . the deepening concern about the impact on business of the social instability expressed in the ghetto revolt; . . . the realization that the demographic changes that confront the nation for the next few decades are inexorable; that our cities will become increasingly populated by blacks and Puerto Ricans in the East and Middle West; by blacks and Mexican-Americans in the West; and that these will be the major source of our future labor supply in the cities; and that they will be the future market for industry's good and services.[61]

* * *

When Mr. Wallen came to the Coalition it was a four-man operation working out of a two-room office. He steered it from this modest beginning to a major private organization of more than 150 employees and 160 business, labor, and community leaders involved in the improvement of social and economic conditions for minority groups. During that time the Coalition attacked the problems through its task forces set up to cover four fronts—economic development, manpower, housing, and education and communications.

---

[57]"Society in Crisis," address delivered at the Board-Staff Conference of the Family Service Association's Middle and North Atlantic Regions, New York City, November 15, 1968, p. 1.

[58]*New York Times*, August 6, 1969, p. 39, col. 3.

[59]*Ibid.*

[60]"An Overview of Urban Needs from the Point of View of Management, Labor and the Public," a speech delivered at a Labor-Management Conference on Urban Problems, Boston, Mass., March 22, 1969.

[61]"Urban Problems and the Private Sector," an address to the Southern California Chapter of the Industrial Relations Research Association, May 1968, pp. 4-5.

JOBS, HOUSING, AND EDUCATION

One of its first projects was to devise a plan to aid and finance ghetto business. A task force of bankers, finance experts, and community people set up a management assistance corporation, a venture capital fund, and a small business investment corporation to furnish risk capital, soft loans, and technical assistance to minority businessmen whose proposals customary commercial funding sources might find too uncertain to finance with funds for which they had a fiduciary responsibility. The staff also developed connections between established companies seeking outlets for their goods and services and ghetto residents motivated to become distributors, franchisers, or subcontractors for their products.

The manpower problem in the ghetto was not simply one of jobs alone. It made no sense just to take a man leaning against a lamp post and lean him against a broom. The solution required the "promise of a job with a potential for upward mobility, the availability of motivational and attitudinal training, an input of remedial training for reading and arithmetic skills; and then skills training."[63]

In seeking such jobs the Coalition saw duplication of the effort of the National Alliance of Businessmen, whose national goal was to place 500,000 hard-core unemployed in jobs by 1971. This group had been working with the U.S. Department of Labor to supply training funds to employers who would hire and train such workers. One of Mr. Wallen's major contributions was achieving the merger of these two private organizations, MAB and NYUC, and in coordinating the efforts of the Manpower and Career Development Agency of the City's Human Resources Administration, the New York State Employment Service, and the various local community action programs.

The NAB's effort had a distinct business orientation evaluated in terms of number of jobs. The Coalition, on the other hand, was concerned with underemployment as well as unemployment, changing hiring practices, and creating as well as finding meaningful jobs. To merge the two, these organizational differences had to be reconciled. Mr. Wallen, and his executive assistant at the time, William Kaufman, who is now exective director of Coalition JOBS and metropolitan director of NAB, were able to blend NAB's organization and the Coalition's sensitivity by January 1969 into Coalition JOBS, which has since involved 900 companies in developing work for more than 14,000 people. The Manpower Task Force has also been engaged in developing a Cooperative Area Manpower Planning System (CAMPS) and a Puerto Rican Skills Bank for professionals.

---

[63]*Ibid.*, p. 8.

The housing problem, so vast and complicated, necessitated a more modest immediate goal—a bottleneck-unplugging service for nonprofit housing sponsors. A staff of expeditors was assembled to blast projects, which often languished awaiting necessary approval, out of each step and on to the next. It provided the necessary linkage between the sponsors and the housing departments of the city, state, and federal governments, acting as a broker to bring together sponsor, site, planner, funding sources, and architects. A similar approach was taken to convert 100 of the 500 parcels of vacant land owned by the city in ghetto areas to miniparks for neighborhood recreation. The parks department, which had funds for this purpose, was unable to free them because of delays encountered at each of the many stages from planning to approval to letting of the contracts. The Coalition persuaded business donors to contribute the money, got a neighborhood community organization to sponsor, help design, and maintain each project and private contractors to use the maximum degree of local labor in the conversion.

Such experiences no doubt led Mr. Wallen to say:

> The great impediment to the solution of the problems of urban decay by local government lies in just this encrustation of obsolete regulations, procedural roadblocks, special interest legislation, and bureaucratic timidity.[64]

The Coalition's relations with the city were generally good and the two cooperated on many projects. While decision making in the two bodies was separate and distinct, some tension developed over the amount of consultation on various programs and over fund raising. According to one source, the Coalition felt the city had not done an adequate job of fund raising and should be pleased that each year the Coalition turned $1.3 million over to the Mayor's Urban Action Task Force to provide jobs and recreation during the summer for disadvantaged youths; while the city was of the opinion that the Coalition could not really raise funds without the mayor's support.

The Coalition's Task Force on Education organized to help in the training of paraprofessionals to work with teachers in ghetto schools, to improve the communication between white middle-class teachers and Puerto Rican and black ghetto children, and to link the high schools and the business world in an effort to have the curricula of the former relate meaningfully to the requirements of the latter. The Coalition worked closely with the Urban League to spread the latter's "Street Academies"—tutoring programs outside the public school system to help dropouts go on to college. The Education Task Force became embroiled in the development of a school decentralization plan that would deal with the competing concerns of the communities, the

[64]*Ibid.*, p. 3.

Teachers' Union, and the City Board of Education. As will be seen below, the community control issue and the resultant teachers' strike almost killed the Coalition.

* * *

Saul Wallen, of course, helped to get these projects underway. While some at the Coalition took issue with his handling of these projects or questioned whether some should have been undertaken at all, the various segments agreed that his major contribution was holding the organization together in a most difficult time.

CONFLICT WITHIN

The sources of conflict were many. The Coalition is composed of a board of directors, representing business, labor, religious, and community organizations and of staff from these various groups. Many of these people had never come together before, except perhaps in confrontation. They joined the Coalition not merely as independent individuals but as leaders of constituencies. As such they had bases to protect.

From the beginning the Coalition was caught up in the dilemma of whether it was going to give and help raise funds for community organizations deemed worthy of such assistance or whether it was going to invest its money directly in problem-solving efforts. In the beginning it did some of both. Some of the community people would have preferred more financial help to their constituent organizations. "How can we retain credibility with our own organizations," they asked, "if we serve on the board and don't get any money?" Their supporters wanted to know what they had done for them lately. They also saw the Coalition as competing with existing community organizations for the same funds.

Budgeting was a bone of contention. In 1968 the Coalition operated on a funding of $4 million drawn from private and foundation contributions. In December 1968 the community representatives requested a $16 million budget for 1969. The business and labor representatives thought this totally unrealistic and pared it to $10 or $11 million, subject to raising the funds. However, even this was grossly overstated, for in the end the Coalition could raise only $6 million for 1969. In part this was because initial interest had waned somewhat, and because some corporations had set up their own urban affairs departments, which were siphoning money that probably would have gone to the Coalition.

As related above, Mr. Wallen's selection as head of the NYUC was immediately met by opposition from the community caucus of black and Puerto Rican leaders. They pegged him as labor and business's man and bemoaned the choice of someone who was not from the community. The two community representatives who came in May 1968 as executive vice presidents helped to give the Coalition credibility in the community. Lincoln Lynch, a black militant who had headed Long Island CORE, had great appeal to the black community. He was outspoken, a fact which sometimes embarrassed the labor people, and caused some difficulties for Mr. Wallen. Frank Espada came out of the civil rights movement, the antipoverty program, and more recently the city's Human Resources Administration. He had been active in community action organizations and was respected by the Puerto Rican community as an articulate, politically aware spokesman. Mr. Lynch was given charge of the Manpower and Education Task Forces, while Mr. Espada was vice president of the Task Forces on Housing and Economic Development. Both were great advocates for their respective constituencies. While their personal relations were cordial, there was a rivalry between them as there was between the black and Puerto Rican communities. The blacks saw the Puerto Ricans as riding on their coattails. The Puerto Ricans resented all the attention given to the blacks and felt that, while Puerto Ricans were willing to accept black leadership, the opposite was not the case. At the Coalition they hassled over the location and concentration of programs.

In the beginning, both also had generally good personal relations with Saul Wallen, but like other community people, neither felt particularly comfortable working for him. For one they felt he did not consult with them enough. The community people frequently took the position that whatever was done it was not enough and they had been "sold down the river." Mr. Wallen found it difficult to get them to recognize what he saw as the realities of the situation. He had limited room to maneuver and found himself in a position which left him open to charges of racism. Whereas when he had been an arbitrator and mediator he could reconcile differences or issue a decision and *leave* the parties to live with it, he now had to *implement* decisions reached through mediation.

The inability of the community people to accept Saul Wallen's role as a neutral was due in part to their need for clear unequivocal support. They had been sold out too many times in the past to accept representations. They needed overt actions and tangible results. Mr. Wallen was trying to get the community representatives to understand how business and labor operated so he could achieve consensus through mediation. Similarly he tried to get labor and business to understand the problems of the community people. Thus, he performed the mediator's education function, but at the risk of being charged with a "sell-out."

Many community groups were unfamiliar with collective bargaining and did not know how to formalize for negotiations. They came in with demands which they thought were the least they could accept. Thus, they had no fallback positions and no room for give and take. There also was a tendency toward rigid rhetoric. Mr. Wallen tried to sort out what was rhetoric and what was genuine (something he had frequently done as an arbitrator and mediator), find ways the community could be saved from itself (something he had also done often as a mediator), and allow it an out when its position became untenable. His job was further complicated by the reluctance of community groups to deal with subordinates. He had an open door policy and was always willing to listen to groups both inside and outside the Coalition. This gave rise to criticism by some who thought he got involved in too many situations. He had been a fire horse for years and this was in keeping.

It should be noted here that in characterizing these relationships, there were, of course, exceptions in every camp to the views generally held. While the author talked to many inside and outside of the Coalition, time and distance did not permit discussion with a representative of each of the factions within a camp.

Generally, the relations between the community and labor people can best be described as "armed truce," and nearer to "open conflict" during the school decentralization crisis. There were, of course, exceptions, but the union people, who for so many years had been trained not to see color, found themselves faced with having to recognize that there are black people. In general, labor saw the black and Puerto Rican requests for special treatment as "undemocratic demands." The community people saw labor as either "racist" or there simply to protect its own interests.

Relations between the two constituencies were further exacerbated by the need to protect their respective vested interests. For example, the union people objected to the Coalition's support of a nonunion "gypsy" cab company formed to alleviate the transportation problems of ghetto residents occasioned by white cab drivers who were reluctant to drive in ghetto areas. Also some industries dealt with racket unions, which exploited minority workers through phony contracts with unscrupulous employers. Neither the minority leadership nor the established employer organizations had joined with the Central Labor Council in its efforts to stop this evil.

Some of the community people viewed with suspicion the commitment of business. Was this just "the thing to do" at the time and would the business sector quickly lose interest or would it be caught up in an on-going commitment to the cause? Was it sitting down with the community to use it as an instrument of moral self-flagellation? At times the community people saw business in labor's camp, although during the school dispute, they had to agree business was in the community's camp. In general, they greatly admired Andrew Heiskell, then chairman of the NYUC and head of Time-Life.

Business and labor had been dealing with each other for some time, but on opposite sides of the bargaining table. While they understood each other's respective institutions, they were not a natural alliance. Their relations were sometimes strained by events outside the Coalition, as when the Transport Workers Union, whose president, Matthew Guinan, served on the Coalition's Board of Directors, struck Pan American World Airways, whose president, Najeeb Halaby was also a member of the Coalition's Board.

Mr. Wallen, however, kept everyone talking. His experience as a mediator enabled him to listen to all sides, reduce a lengthy session to the key issues, find the points of common ground, emphasize them, and guide to a consensus. He had a rough style combined with sensitivity. He would exhort people to "cut the crap" and get on with the job.

His role was viewed differently by the various groups and individuals in the various crises. Some thought he was too much of a mediator and should have taken a stronger stand on issues and provided more leadership. Others thought he was too much of an arbitrator and not enough of a mediator, presenting decisions as a fait accompli. Some also criticized his administrative ability or lack thereof. His administrative experience had been limited largely to his chairmanship of the New England War Labor Board in 1942 and a year as president of the National Academy of Arbitrators in 1954. As a self-employed professional he had been a loner and some at the Coalition felt he was a loner there too, caught in the crossfire. What some categorized as ineptitude, others conveniently called racism, and still others attributed to the nature of the problems and the structure of the Coalition. No one, however, doubted his interest or concern. All knew he was not using the Coalition as a stepping stone to higher office.

THE SCHOOL DISPUTE

It is difficult to pinpoint particular examples to show why the Coalition was always a tenuous proposition that could be splintered by almost any issue. The New York City school decentralization dispute, however, is a case in point.

A subcommittee of the Coalition Education Task Force undertook to develop a position paper based on the City Board of Education's proposed legislative bill for school decentralization. This subcommittee had only one labor member—a black from District 65 of the RWDSU, whom labor saw as a community representative rather than as an AFL-

CIO spokesman. This task force subcommittee came up with a paper which was unacceptable to labor and was rejected by the board of directors, although the board agreed to favor decentralization.

At the time, the tensions in the Coalition reflected those in the city. The United Federation of Teachers, headed by Albert Shanker, had struck to protest the actions of the community board of education in Ocean Hill-Brownsville. The strike had polarized various factions in the city and the atmosphere was charged with hatred, venom, and misunderstanding. The Central Labor Committee had voted to back Mr. Shanker. Saul Wallen was faced with keeping the Coalition from taking a public position that would antagonize labor and distrub what tranquility there was within. His role was a quiet, positive one. He served as a behind-the-scenes mediator, meeting with Albert Shanker, the City Board of Education, and Rhody McCoy from the Ocean Hill-Brownsville School District. He also set up a Coalition joint committee of two business representatives, two labor spokesmen, and two community leaders. This group met for six weeks in an attempt to develop an acceptable Coalition position on decentralization, to define the new issue of community control and to try, through the constituent representatives (who included Harry Van Arsdale of the CLC, Howard Samuel of the Amalgamated Clothing Workers for labor, Evelina Antonetty of United Bronx Parents and David Spencer of another independent school district, as community representatives), to resolve the dispute by returning to their respective constituencies (including Shanker and McCoy) to seek agreement. The attempt was not successful. For one, Harry Van Arsdale did not attend the meetings, and the effort went downhill as the UFT became confident that it could defeat a community control bill in the state legislature.

In the end, Mr. Wallen brought everyone together and they talked it through. He was faced with having to reconcile labor, who saw him as a party to the dispute and not as a neutral, with the community people, particularly Lincoln Lynch who, as administrative head of the Education Task Force, had taken a strong position for community control.

IN TRANSITION

By June 1969 Mr. Wallen was finding it more and more difficult to work with the administrative structure. The rift between Mr. Lynch and him had widened. The Coalition had survived the beginning but was having growing pains. A structural reorganization was being considered and Mr. Wallen was planning to leave to head a board of mediation for community dispute settlement. Despite his difficulties and frustrations, he liked being where the action was and saw it as doing his part to hold together the social fabric.

In mid-June he was called to the West Coast to settle a strike by the Air Line Pilots Association against Western Airlines, clients for whom he had been permanent arbitrator for a number of years. On his return trip he spoke to a labor law group in Colorado and then went directly to England to take part in a Ditchley Foundation conference on "Public Participation in Urban Planning." The pace was exhausting, even for a man of his energy. He died suddenly on August 5, 1969, at the age of 59.

His successor, Eugene Callender, is a politically sensitive black, who was a minister, head of the Urban League, and then deputy commissioner of the City Housing Administration. Under his strong leadership, the Coalition was restructured and its emphasis and method of operation changed. It no longer was to seek consensus among all factions but to take a more business-oriented approach, working with the existing community power structure. It reduced the number of programs, hired community consultants, and took a problem-solving approach to larger questions. For example, while in the past the Coalition had helped the Street Academies and Harlem Prep to send about one hundred dropouts on to college, it now aims at changing the public school system so there will no longer be a need for these programs. The community housing assistance program has been dropped in favor of a Rehabilitation Assistance Program (RAP). It is now "programmatic planning on a timetable."

While this approach appeals to the more moderate community people, who also represent the blacks and Puerto Ricans, it has "turned off" those who are more militant, and those who prefer the consensus approach to decision making, even if fraught with difficulty. Lynch and Espada found this change uncomfortable and left their administrative posts. The two executive vice president positions have been consolidated into a single administrative post filled by Manuel Diaz, a former executive director of the Puerto Rican Community Development Project and a first deputy commissioner of the NYC Manpower and Career Development Agency. Espada and Lynch are still listed as members of the board of directors. They and their supporters in the caucus feel that the Coalition should not be run like a business corporation but should be free swinging to allow ferment conducive to creativity and dynamism. At a recent retreat, some of these more militant community people met and reviewed the situation. In retrospect, they decided that Saul had played a far more constructive role than they thought at the time.

The essence of Saul Wallen's role at the Coalition and his contribution was caught best by the *Manhattan Tribune,* an inner-city newspaper aimed

As Perceived by Others

at providing a "common ground where the polarizing black and white communities can continue to talk to each other." In its August 16, 1969 editorial, "A Man Who Cared," the *Tribune* said:

> When Saul Wallen abandoned an exciting and lucrative career to become the New York Urban Coalition's Chief Executive, the city's labor, business and community leaders were conveniently isolated from each other by time, place, circumstance and interest. Few of those who formed the Urban Coalition had ever heard of each other, and most had never met for a quiet dinner. Wall Street is still a long way from Harlem, and the liberalism of the unions is not the liberalism which many community leaders now seek.
>
> Yet, within a year, Saul Wallen had helped to create a new community within the city, one which made neighbors of the bankers, the union presidents and the community militants. As a group, they almost always agreed on objectives, but as individuals they seldom agreed on pacing or methods.
>
> The discussions frequently turned into arguments. Many of the community leaders wore their frustrations on their sleeves. The business executive, coming into the open for the first time, was met by the torrent of history and frequently stood trial for crimes his ancestors were alleged to have committed.
>
> The unions were proud of what they had done for their workers, but the community leaders were intolerant of the delays in unionizing significant numbers of minority workers. The school strike polarized most of the community leaders and businessmen on one side of the fence and most of the labor leaders on the other.
>
> Yet, somehow, when the smoke cleared, the organization was still intact because Saul Wallen was the pivot, the target and the cement for much of what happened in the first modern community this city has ever seen.
>
> Saul Wallen, who died suddenly last week, left the security of his own community to enter the trubulent world of the inner city because he continued to "care." Early in life he had fought the battles of the New Deal and could have rested on those laurels. Instead, he chose to continue the fight, but on new grounds, with new rules and new leaders.
>
> The Urban Coalition, the city, and the people who never heard of him, will miss his leadership.

2. Saul Wallen—Generous, Creative, and Concerned:

How He Managed to Achieve So Much Is Suggested in This Affectionate Memoir*
by
Robert G. Spivack

In an era when some people see only the Ugly American, Saul Wallen personified the Beautiful American, a generous, creative, concerned citizen.

As all his friends on the Vineyard know he was a handsome man. Strong. Gentle. Even tempered. Wise. Well balanced.

The bare facts of his life, how he achieved a worldwide reputation as a labor conciliator (he wrote 5,000 decisions), were all set down in *The New York Times* obituary. What was not set down and what few people knew is how Saul Wallen managed to achieve so much, how he built the New York Urban Coalition of which he was president, from nothing to a major force in attempting to improve the status of the city's disadvantaged minorities.

His friends on the Island, in Boston, and in New York could probably fill the story out with more details and relate experiences that tell why it always was such a pleasure to be in his company. My own experiences are somewhat more limited. But they may shed some light on how solidly based was Saul Wallen's reputation as a working liberal.

Others moaned and groaned about the disintegration of the big cities. They were alienated by black power rhetoric and even more by the riots.

Saul Wallen was no less distressed. The difference was that, after analyzing the problem, he tried to do something about it. His native American optimism convinced him that something could be done, despite the surface hopelessness.

He felt that if you "give a damn" for this country or for your city you just did not sit and moan and groan and wring your hands. And you couldn't let yourself be thrown off the track by the excesses, verbal and physical, of black or white extremists.

---

*Vineyard Gazette (Edgartown, Mass.), August 8, 1969.

HE WAS DIFFERENT

There are many people, though, who share such feelings. Some are eloquent, others are glib. Not many get much done. Saul was different.

Let me interrupt this story briefly to give a partial list of what the New York Urban Coalition achieved in barely a year. He started out getting some 800 stores and private firms to promise to give jobs to those who otherwise might not be hired.

Under Saul Wallen's guidance the NYUC helped set up a Puerto Rican skills bank, a coalition venture corporation to lend money to small entrepreneurs who hoped to become black capitalists; NYUC lent $150,000 to the nonprofit Association of United Contractors of America so black and Puerto Rican contractors qualified to bid on city construction jobs. In cooperation with the Ford Foundation and innumerable corporate executives the NYUC helped purchase a clubhouse for the East Harlem Youth Federation Association, set up a small dress manufacturer, provided money for a record shop owner, got interest-free loans to help start four housing projects. The list of good Wallen works is long and impressive.

How, though, did Saul Wallen manage to achieve so much in so little time, despite the stresses (racial, ideological) under which the NYUC operated? Basically it was because he never took his eye off the goal, despite the diversions: the objective was to help New York avoid what happened in Watts, Newark, Detroit, and Washington, D.C., by finding jobs, creating jobs and helping the previously jobless learn enough to keep the jobs when they got them.

What I liked was the subtlety with which Saul Wallen worked.

Last year on a quiet evening I went to interview him at his home near Lobsterville to find out what the NYUC was all about and what it was doing. After the interview had gone on for a while the conversation turned to hiring practices in the news media, newspapers, magazines, etc. Saul told me of the splendid editorial cooperation he had been getting. But when it came to putting someone from a minority group on a metropolitan paper there was little progress.

Many Negroes were convinced it was white editors' bias that kept the doors closed. I told Saul that on most of the newspapers with which I had any acquaintance this was not the case. The trouble was that the job applicants usually did not know the first thing about putting out a paper. They did not know how to report, find facts, write. They didn't even know what kind of pencils were used to mark copy.

"What are you doing besides writing your column?" he asked. I told him I was starting Reporters' News Syndicate in Washington and, therefore, would soon be looking for talented writers and cartoonists.

"Would you consider training some of these youngsters?" he asked.

WAS HESITANT

The idea had never occurred to me and I was hesitant. Before the evening was over he had convinced me that if I really gave a damn, if I wanted to help bring black kids into this society under this system, I had a duty to do what I could do. He promised to help find foundation funds, if I would set the program up and bring the youngsters to Washington.

To make a long story short we are training ten young men and women in 1969; three have already proved apt students of newspaper techniques. The others show considerable promise. About a half dozen editors of large newspapers are waiting to see how the project works out and chances are they will give the youngsters a chance at employment.

In twenty-five years as a reporter, columnist, and editor I have interviewed dozens of public figures. But Saul Wallen was the first to persuade me that my duties were not done when the talking was over and the words had been written. He made me feel that I could do more to help get this country back on the track. We both knew it would not be easy, that some turbulence would be involved. But he had the same effect on other people. You just could not say "no" to Saul because you knew he was giving up so much more in a noble purpose and eventually he gave his life.

3. For Saul Wallen*
by
James C. Hill

Saul Wallen died suddenly of a heart attack on August 4, 1969, at the age of fifty-nine. He was a founder and a past president of the National Academy of Arbitrators. He was a man of great wisdom and compassion, boundless energy, and contagious love of life. Few men have been so widely known and respected, indeed beloved, by his colleagues and by leaders of management and labor throughout the nation.

For twenty-five years Saul Wallen's principal work was that of a neu-

---

*Arbitration and the Expanding Role of Neutrals, Proceedings of the 23rd National Academy of Arbitrators (Washington: BNA, 1970).

tral in the resolution of industrial labor disputes. He began this career as one of a handful of young men who were recruited in 1942 by the National War Labor Board as hearing officers and mediators and sent out to investigate and report, to persuade and cajole disputing employers and unions to resolve their differences without interruption of production in time of war. When the board established regional offices, Saul was named chairman of the Regional War Labor Board for the New England area. There were some who questioned this appointment. A principal officer of the board approached Chairman Will Davis and urged the view that this would be a mistake, that it was risky and unwise to send to Boston a young man who was neither Irish nor Italian, Catholic nor Protestant, lawyer nor Harvard graduate, Lowell, Cabot, nor Lodge to be the guardian of industrial peace in this major region of a nation at war.

Perhaps it was risky; it certainly was not unwise. Saul soon proved himself an ideal selection. One would be hard put to find anyone of New England labor or management who did not soon, surprisingly soon, come to admire and respect and genuinely like this newcomer. Mike Walsh, militant regional director of the Steelworkers Union and a labor member of the New England Regional Board, once remarked, "I never met a man who combined wisdom of mind and heart in such perfect balance."

After the war Saul entered private practice as a labor disputes arbitrator. He continued in this activity until January of [1968] when he accepted the presidency of the New York Urban Coalition. As an industrial peacemaker Saul played all the roles which neutrals are called on to perform—and more. He served with great skill and distinction as arbitrator, umpire, impartial chairman, mediator, factfinder, chairman of presidential boards of inquiry, and, throughout, as a trusted counselor and friend of the leaders of industry and labor, large and small. He probably served as permanent arbitrator under the agreements of more employers and unions, for a longer time, than anyone else in his profession ever has—General Motors and the auto workers, Raytheon and Sylvania Electric and the electrical workers, most of the major rubber companies and the rubber workers, five or six major steel companies and the steelworkers, seven major airlines in their contracts with the unions of pilots, flight engineers, stewardesses, and ground crews, and many others. At the same time he made himself available to thousands of smaller companies and unions all over the country who constantly sought his services.

Saul saw the labor agreement as a charter of a continuing relationship, to be construed and applied in terms of its inherent purposes and understandings, which sometimes means its silences as well as its written words. I think of one of his early decisions in 1947, which involved a Connecticut firm that had laid off certain workers and then assigned their work to others outside the bargaining unit represented by the union. The employer insisted that this was a reserved right of management, unrestricted by any clause in the agreement. Saul considered the implications of the agreement as a whole; he held that "job security is an inherent element of the labor contract, a part of its very being. If wages is the heart of the labor agreement, job security may be considered its soul. Those eligible to share in the degree of job security the contract affords are those to whom the contract applies." This, like some other landmark decisions he made, was attacked as heresy in some quarters. But it was heresy cut from the same cloth as some of the great dissenting opinions of Justice Holmes and Brandeis and Cardozo, which have since become cornerstones of accepted constitutional law.

As Bill Simkin said on a recent happier occasion, Saul was not only one of the five or six best arbitrators in the country but also an excellent mediator. The combination of these talents is rare; even more so is the sensitivity required to keep each role in its proper place. Saul had a basic understanding and respect for the separate needs and viewpoints of employers and unions, and an uncommon ability to find the points of common ground.

Saul was very much an innovator. I think of many examples. In his home community of Brookline, Mass., he organized an appeals board to consider the grievances of municipal employees long before we had come to establish procedures for collective bargaining with public employees. In Martha's Vineyard he was the founder and president of a community council to bring into open discussion, and so to resolve, some of the frictions that divided the summer visitors and the year-round residents.

As arbitrator and as mediator, or a combination of the two for which we seem to have no word, Saul often broke through the rigidities of formal litigation to counsel with the parties and to bring about concurrence, or to bring about what George Taylor has called the "consent to lose." I have known of situations where not only did Saul bring about the consent to lose, but somehow he seemed to make the losing party feel downright good about it. He did this through no magic or trickery—for he was completely without guile—but simply by the force of his open, honest, and friendly personality. He was a person people trusted; they liked him and felt comfortable in his presence.

One of the most significant testimonials to Saul's constructive mind and spirit is to be found in the Office of Collective Bargaining in New York City. Saul chaired the original mayor's committee which recommended machinery for collective bargaining and the resolution of disputes between the city and various organizations of its employees. He not only proposed a plan which is unique in this field, but then worked with the leaders of the unions and the municipal government to make this plan a success. He continued at their request as a public member of the Board of Collective Bargaining, and his influence is felt throughout the structure.

One can never forget Saul's prodigious energy. None of us could keep up with him. He carried an arbitration load two or three times as great as many full-time arbitrators. He relished work and he relished recreation. After full days of hearings he would work far into the evening, on airplanes and in hotel rooms, organizing his papers and his thoughts and writing draft decisions. And then, often around midnight, he was ready to go out on the town. He would join friends in pubs, in long walks, in long night bull sessions, fresh and eager as a college kid.

I don't know how he did it; I can suggest some reasons why. In part, of course, it was his way of unwinding after long hours of very taxing work. In part it was his sense of urgent need to clear the decks of today's affairs to meet his commitments the following day. And, perhaps most important, it was Saul's constant realization that the work he was doing, important and absorbing as it was, was only a segment of life, and so he crowded more of living into all his waking hours, which often ran to 18 or 20 a day.

Last year Saul gave up most of his arbitration work to give of himself, too unsparingly, as president of the New York Urban Coalition. In his brief tenure he built the Coalition from a name and a two-room office to a major organization with multiple programs for improvement of the economic and social life of minority groups in this city. This was a new chapter in his life, a tremendous burden and challenge. But for Saul it was also a continuing expression of his central character—active, optimistic, dedicated to the resolution of conflict, concerned that we do something about the social ills that beset us and not just bemoan our fate, insistent, in the words of the Coalition slogan, that we "give a damn."

What a world this might be if there were a thousand Saul Wallens, or even a hundred or a dozen. What a gap in our world it is not to have him with us. What a better world it has been for us to have known him.

August 4, 1969

Subject Index

	pages
Arbitrability, Role of the Courts	
"Recent Supreme Court Decisions on Arbitration: An Arbitrator's View"	8-20
Book Review, "Labor Arbitration: A Dissenting View" by Paul R. Hays	20-25
Arbitration, Grievances	
"A Formula For New England Prosperity"	2-5
Untitled Speech	5-8
"Recent Supreme Court Decisions on Arbitration: An Arbitrator's View"	8-20
"Arbitrators and Judges—Dispelling the Hays' Haze"	26-37
Decision of Factfinder in *Lowell School Committee (Lowell, Massachusetts) and Lowell Teachers Organization*	38-40
Arbitration, Grievances	
Role of the Courts	
"Arbitrators and Judges—Dispelling the Hays' Haze"	26-37
Arbitration, Interest Disputes	
Untitled Speech	5-8
Arbitration Clauses, Enforcement of	
"Recent Supreme Court Decisions on Arbitration: An Arbitrator's View"	8-20
Arbitration Clauses, Limitations on Arbitrator	
"Recent Supreme Court Decisions on Arbitration: An Arbitrator's View"	8-20
Business' Responsibility to the Community	
Report of Speech in *Providence Journal*	173

Subject Index

	pages
Collective Bargaining Agreements	
"Recent Supreme Court Decisions on Arbitration: An Arbitrator's View"	8-20
Contract Interpretation	
Clear and Unambiguous Language	
Arbitration decision in *Raytheon Manufacturing Company and International Brotherhood of Electrical Workers, AFL-CIO, Local 1505*	44
Contract Interpretation	
Custom and Practice	
Arbitration decision in *Draper Corporation and United Steelworkers of America*	72
Contract Interpretation	
Extracontractual Considerations	
Arbitration decision in *Witch City Tanning Company and International Fur and Leather Workers Union, Local 21*	110-111
Arbitration decision in *Sylvania Electric Products, Inc., and International Union of Electrical, Radio and Machine Workers, CIO, Local 608*	111-113
Arbitration decision in *H. K. Barnes Leather Company and International Fur and Leather Workers Union, Local 21, CIO*	113-114
Arbitration decision in *Firestone Tire and Rubber Company and United Rubber, Cork, Linoleum and Plastic Workers of America, CIO, Local 336*	115-116
Contract Interpretation	
Fairness and Equity	
Arbitration decisions in *Raytheon Manufacturing Company and International Brotherhood of Electrical Workers, AFL-CIO, Local 1505*	44
Arbitration decision in *Brown Company and United Mine Workers of America District 50, Local 12175*	44
Arbitration decision in *Coca Cola Bottling Company of Boston and Retail, Wholesale, and Department Store Union, Local 513*	70-72
Contract Interpretation	
Implicit Rights	
Arbitration decision in *Coca Cola Bottling Company of Boston and Retail, Wholesale, and Department Store Union, Local 513*	70-72
Contract Interpretation	
Integrity of the Agreement	
Arbitration decision in *Coca Cola Bottling Company of Boston and Retail, Wholesale, and Department Store Union, Local 513*	70-72

Subject Index

	pages
Contract Interpretation	
Intent	
Arbitration decision in *Merrow Machine Company and International Union of Electrical Workers, Local 249*	45-47
Arbitration decision in *Coca Cola Bottling Company of Boston and Retail, Wholesale, and Department Store Union, Local 513*	70-72
Contract Interpretation	
Past Practice	
Arbitration decision in *Brown Company and United Mine Workers of America District 50, Local 12175*	44
Arbitration decision in *Firestone Tire and Rubber Company and United Rubber, Cork, Linoleum and Plastic Workers of America, Local 336*	48
"The Silent Contract vs. Express Provisions: The Arbitration of Local Working Conditions"	61-64
Arbitration decision in *General Tire and Rubber Company and United Rubber, Cork, Linoleum and Plastic Workers of America, Local 9*	65-66
Arbitration decision in *Sylvania Electric Products, Inc. and International Union of Electrical, Radio, and Machine Workers and its Affiliated Local 352*	66-67
Arbitration decision in *The Fafnir Bearing Company and United Automobile Workers of America, Local 133*	67-68
Arbitration decision in *The Crescent Company, Inc., and United Steelworkers of America, AFL-CIO*	69
Arbitration decision in *Goodall-Sanford, Inc., and United Textile Workers of America, AFL-CIO, Local 1802*	69
Contract Interpretation	
Reasonableness	
Arbitration decision in *Raytheon Manufacturing Company and International Brotherhood of Electrical Workers, AFL-CIO, Local 1505*	44
Arbitration decision in *Brown Company and United Mine Workers of America District 50, Local 12175*	44
Arbitration decision in *Draper Corporation and United Steelworkers of America*	72
Discharge, Purpose of	
Arbitration decision in *Continental Airlines and The Flight Hostesses, Air Line Pilots Association, International*	87-88
Discharge vs. Lesser Penalties	
Arbitration decision in *Aluminum Company of America and Aluminum Workers International Union*	119-120

Discipline and Discharge, Just Cause
Arbitration decision in *Coca Cola Bottling Company of Boston and Retail, Wholesale, and Department Store Union, Local 513* — 70-72

Discipline and Discharge, Just Cause
Absenteeism
Arbitration decision in *Ford Motor Company and United Automobile Workers, Local 600* — 93-94
Arbitration decision in *The B. F. Goodrich Company and United Rubber, Cork, Linoleum and Plastic Workers of America, Local 43* — 127-128

Discipline and Discharge, Just Cause
Alcoholism
Arbitration decision in *American Airlines, Inc., and Transport Workers Union of America* — 122-123
Arbitration decision in *The Bassick Company and International Union of Electrical, Radio, and Machine Workers, Local 229* — 125-127
Arbitration decision in *The B. F. Goodrich Company and United Rubber, Cork, Linoleum and Plastic Workers of America, Local 43* — 127-128

Discipline and Discharge, Just Cause
Burden of Proof
Arbitration decision in *The Bridgeport Gas Company and United Mine Workers of America, Local 12298* — 90-92

Discipline and Discharge, Just Cause
Chronic Illness
Arbitration decision in *The B. F. Goodrich Company and United Rubber, Cork, Linoleum and Plastic Workers of America, Local 5* — 127

Discipline and Discharge, Just Cause
Conduct off the Job
Arbitration decision in *The Bridgeport Gas Company and United Mine Workers of America, Local 12298* — 90-92
Arbitration decision in *Southern Bell Telephone and Telegraph Company and Communications Workers of America, Local 3401* — 92-93
Arbitration decision in *Eastern Airlines, Inc. and Air Line Pilot Association, International* — 94-95
Arbitration decision in *Taft-Pierce Manufacturing Company and International Association of Machinists, District Lodge, 64* — 95

Discipline and Discharge, Just Cause
Conflict of Interest

Subject Index   207

pages

  Arbitration decision in *Taft-Pierce Manufacturing Company and International Association of Machinists, District Lodge, 64*   95
Discipline and Discharge, Just Cause
  A Fair Day's Work
    Arbitration decision in *Clarostat Manufacturing Company, Inc. and International Union of Electrical, Radio, and Machine Workers, CIO, Local 242*   72-73
    Arbitration decision in *Fabet Corporation and Gloucester Sea Food Workers Union, Series, 1572-1, International Longshoremen's Association*   73-74
    Arbitration decision in *Sylvania Electric Products, Inc., and International Union of Electrical, Radio, and Machine Worke of America, CIO, Local 608*   74-76
Discipline and Discharge, Just Cause
  Fighting
    Arbitration decision in *The B. F. Goodrich Company and United Rubber, Cork, Linoleum and Plastic Workers of America, CIO, Local 5*   101-102
    Arbitration decision in *Republic Steel Corporation and United Steelworkers of America, Local 1033*   116-117
    Arbitration decision in *J. Flynn and Sons, Inc., and Leather Workers International Union of America, Local 21*   117-118
Discipline and Discharge, Just Cause
  Inefficiency
    Arbitration decision in *Clarostat Manufacturing Company, Inc., and International Union of Electrical, Radio, and Machine Workers, CIO, Local 242*   72-73
    Arbitration decision in *Kennecott Wire and Cable Company and International Brotherhood of Electrical Workers, AFL, Local 1450*   100-101
Discipline and Discharge, Just Cause
  Length of Service (Consideration of)
    Arbitration decision in *Beggs and Cobb, Inc., and International Fur and Leather Workers Union, Local 22*   118-119
Discipline and Discharge, Just Cause
  Mental Illness
    Arbitration decision in *Aluminum Company of America and Aluminum Workers International Union, Local 110*   124-125
    Arbitration decision in *The B.F. Goodrich Company and United Rubber Workers of America, Local 318*   128-129
    Arbitration decision in *Warner Gear Division, Borg-Warner*

Subject Index

	pages
Corporation, and United Automobile Workers of America, Local 287	129-131

Discipline and Discharge, Just Cause
Past Practice (Consideration of)
Arbitration decision in *Premier Worsted Mills (Bridgeton Division) and Textile Workers of America, CIO, Local 423* — 120-122

Discipline and Discharge, Just Cause
Physical Requirements
Arbitration decision in *Connecticut Telephone and Electric Corporation and International Union of Electrical, Radio, and Machine Workers, CIO* — 102-104

Discipline and Discharge, Just Cause
Refusal of Assignment
Arbitration decision in *Aluminum Company of America and Aluminum Workers International Union, Local 104* — 54-55

Discipline and Discharge, Just Cause
Resistance to New Incentive System
Arbitration decision in *S.W. Card Manufacturing Company and United Steelworkers of America, AFL-CIO* — 88-89

Discipline and Discharge, Just Cause
Sleeping on the Job
Arbitration decision in *The General Tire and Rubber Company and United Rubber, Cork, Linoleum and Plastic Workers of America, Local 9* — 118

Discipline and Discharge, Just Cause
Theft
Arbitration decision in *The B.F. Goodrich Company and United Rubber, Cork, Linoleum and Plastic Workers of America, CIO, Local 318* — 102

Discipline and Discharge, Just Cause
Unsafe Employees
Arbitration decision in *American Textile Company, Inc., and Amalgamated Lace Operatives of America Branch A-6, Levers Auxiliary Section* — 89-90
Arbitration decision in *National Airlines and the Air Line Pilots Association, International* — 143-144
Arbitration decision in *Union Carbide Corporation, Linde Division and International Brotherhood of Teamsters* — 144-145

Discipline and Discharge, Just Cause
Unsuitable Employees
Arbitration decision in *Brown and Sharpe Manufacturing*

Subject Index

pages

Company and American Federation of Technical Engineers, Local 119	90
Discipline and Discharge, Parties' Responsibility	
Setting a Trap	
Arbitration decision in *N.H. Poore Company and International Fur and Leather Workers Union, CIO, Local 21*	48-49
Arbitration decision in *Woonsocket Rayon, Inc., and Industrial Trades Union of America*	49-50
Discipline and Discharge, Prerequisites	
Consistent Application	
Arbitration decision in *Beacon Tanning Company and Leather Workers International Union, Local 21*	99-100
Discipline and Discharge, Prerequisites	
Notice of Enforcement of Rules	
Arbitration decision in *The Crescent Company, Inc., and United Steelworkers of America, AFL-CIO*	69
Arbitration decision in *Goodall-Sanford, Inc., and United Textile Workers of America, AFL-CIO, Local 1802*	69
Discipline and Discharge, Prerequisites	
Progressive Discipline	
Arbitration decision in *Beacon Tanning Company and Leather Workers International Union, Local 21*	99-100
Discipline and Discharge, Prerequisites	
Timely Notice	
Arbitration decision in *Kennecott Wire and Cable Company and International Brotherhood of Electrical Workers, AFL, Local 1450*	100-101
Discrimination, Race	
Arbitration decision in *Texaco, Inc., and Oil, Chemical and Atomic Workers International Union*	105
Discrimination, Sex	
Arbitration decision in *Southern Airways, Inc., and Air Line Stewards and Stewardesses Association*	106
Emergency Disputes	
"National Emergency Disputes"	145-151
Employee Alcoholism, Employer Rights and Responsibilities	
Arbitration decision in *American Airlines, Inc., and Transport Workers Union of America*	122-123
Grievance Procedure, Purpose	
Arbitration decision in *Borden Chemical Company and International Chemical Workers Union, Local 553*	54

Subject Index

	pages
Arbitration decision in *Aluminum Company of America and Aluminum Workers International Union, Local 104*	54-55

Grievance Processing
Parties' Responsibilities
Arbitration decision in *William Whitman Company, Arlington Mills Division and United Textile Workers of America, Local 113, AFL* — 47-48

Grievance Processing
Right to Representation
Arbitration decision in *General Cable Corporation and International Association of Machinists, AFL-CIO, Lodge 2101* — 104
Arbitration decision in *The B.F. Goodrich Company and United Rubber, Cork, Linoleum and Plastic Workers of America, Local 281* — 104-105

Grievance Processing
Timeliness
Arbitration decision in *Firestone Tire and Rubber Company and United Rubber, Cork, Linoleum and Plastic Workers of America, Local 336* — 48

Handicapped Employees
Arbitration decision in *Curtiss-Wright Corporation and United Automobile Workers of America, Local 669* — 123
Arbitration decision in *Aluminum Company of America and Aluminum Workers International Union, Local 405* — 123-124

Illegal Work Stoppages
Arbitration decision in *Trailways of New England, Inc., and Division 1318, Amalgamated Transit Union, AFL-CIO* — 51-54
Arbitration decision in *Borden Chemical Company and International Chemical Workers Union, Local 553* — 54
Arbitration decision in *B.F. Goodrich Company and United Rubber, Cork, Linoleum and Plastic Workers of America, CIO* — 55-56

Illegal Work Stoppages, Union Officer
Responsibilities
Arbitration decision in *Trailways of New England, Inc., and Division 1318, Amalgamated Transit Union, AFL-CIO* — 51-54
Arbitration decision in *Aluminum Company of America and Aluminum Workers International Union, Local 104* — 55
Arbitration decision in *B.F. Goodrich Company and United Rubber, Cork, Linoleum and Plastic Workers of America, CIO* — 55-56

Subject Index

	pages
Individual vs. Concerted Conduct	
Arbitration decision in *Creese and Cook Leather Company and Leather Workers International Union of America, Local 21*	107
Arbitration decision in *Fitchburg Paper Company, Division of Litton Industries, and United Papermakers and Paperworkers, Local 12*	108-109
Inherent Rights	
Arbitration decision in *Novelty Shawl Company, Inc., and Textile Workers of America, CIO, Local 75*	77-78
Job Security	
Inherent Employee Rights	
Arbitration decision in *Coca Cola Bottling Company of Boston and Retail, Wholesale, and Department Store Union, Local 513*	70-72
Arbitration decision in *New Britain Machine Company and United Electrical, Radio, and Machine Workers of America, CIO, Local 207*	76-77
"How Issues of Subcontracting and Plant Removal Are Handled by Arbitrators"	78-81
Management Rights	
"How Issues of Subcontracting and Plant Removal Are Handled by Arbitrators"	78-81
Mediation	
"A Sparrow Who Got Caught in a Badminton Game—The Role of the Mediator in the Collective Bargaining Process"	133-138
Mediation	
Use of in a Permanent Umpire System	
"Constraint and Variety in Arbitration Systems"	140-141
Minorities	
Employment of	
"Industrial Relations Problems of Employing the Disadvantaged"	152-159
"Urban Problems and the Private Sector"	159-167
"Lessons from Arbitration in Dealing with Minority Problems"	167-172
Minorities	
Union Membership	
"Industrial Relations Problems of Employing the Disadvantaged"	152-159
"Urban Problems and the Private Sector"	159-167
"Lessons from Arbitration in Dealing with Minority Problems"	167-172

Subject Index

	pages
Minority Employees, Treatment of	
Arbitration decision in *Texaco, Inc., and Oil, Chemical and Atomic Workers International Union*	105
Arbitration decision in *Republic Steel Corporation and United Steelworkers of America, Local 1033*	116-117
New York Urban Coalition	
"Urban Problems and the Private Sector"	159-167
Unpublished letter dated 4/1/69	174-175
Physical Qualifications	
Arbitration decision in *Aluminum Company of America and Aluminum Workers International Union, Local 405*	123-124
Precedent, Use of in Arbitration	
Arbitration decision in *B.F. Goodrich Company and United Rubber, Cork, Linoleum and Plastic Workers of America, Local 43*	42
Railway Labor Act	
Emergency Board Procedures	
"Report to the President, Emergency Board No. 160"	138-140
Remedy Powers of Arbitrator	
Arbitration decision in *Firestone Tire and Rubber Company and United Rubber, Cork, Linoleum and Plastic Workers of America, CIO, Local 261*	42-43
Remedy Power of Arbitrator	
Retroactivity	
Arbitration decision in *William Whitman Company, Arlington Mills Division, and United Textile Workers of America, Local 113, AFL*	47-48
Safety, Employer Rights and Responsibilities	
Arbitration decision in *Aluminum Company of America and Aluminum Workers International Union, Local 405*	123-124
Seniority Rights, Foremen	
Arbitration decision in *Shahmoon Industries, Inc., and United Steelworkers of America, AFL-CIO*	114
Strikes	
"A Formula For New England Prosperity"	2-5
Subcontracting	
"How Issues of Subcontracting and Plant Removal Are Handled by Arbitrators"	78-81
Arbitration decision in *Anaconda American Brass Company and United Automobile Workers of America, Local 1078*	82-83
Arbitration decision in *Chase Brass and Copper Company and United Automobile Workers of America, Local 1565*	83-84

Subject Index

	pages
Arbitration decision in *Southwestern Bell Telephone Company and Communication Workers of America, District 6*	84-85
Umpire System, Role of	
Arbitration decision in *General Tire and Rubber Company, Waco Plant, and United Rubber, Cork, Linoleum and Plastic Workers of America, CIO, Local 312*	41-42
Union Discipline, Arbitration of	
Arbitration decision in *American Telephone and Telegraph Company, Long Lines Department, and American Union of Telephone Workers*	95-98
Union Officers, Job Rights	
Arbitration decision in *The Fafnir Bearing Company and United Automobile Workers of America, Local 133*	57-58
Arbitration decision in *Curtiss-Wright Corporation and United Automobile Workers of America, AFL-CIO, Local 669*	58-59
Union Security	
Arbitration decision in *American Telephone and Telegraph Company, Long Lines Department, and American Union of Telephone Workers*	95-98
Union Stewards' Rights	
Arbitration decision in *Boston Edison Company and Utility Workers Union of America, CIO, Local 369*	56-57
Urban Problems, Business' Responsibility	
"Urban Problems and the Private Sector"	159-167
Voluntary Quits, Intent	
Arbitration decision in *Firestone Tire and Rubber Company, Firestone Store and United Rubber, Cork, Linoleum and Plastic Workers of America, Local 7*	114-115
Women Employees	
Arbitration decision in *Premier Worsted Mills (Bridgeton Division) and Textile Workers Union of America, CIO, Local 423*	120-122